# Wrongdoing and the Moral Emotions

*Wrongdoing and the Moral Emotions* provides an account of how we might effectively address wrongdoing given challenges to the legitimacy of anger and retribution that arise from ethical considerations and from concerns about free will. The issue is introduced in Chapter 1. Chapter 2 asks how we might conceive of blame without retribution, and proposes an account of blame as moral protest, whose function is to secure forward-looking goals such as the moral reform of the wrongdoer and reconciliation in relationships. Chapter 3 considers whether it is possible to justify effectively dealing those who pose dangerous threats if they do not deserve to be harmed, and contends that wrongfully posing a threat is the core condition for the legitimacy of defensive harming. Chapter 4 provides an account of how to treat criminals without a retributive justification for punishment, and argues for an account in which the right of self-defense provides justification for measures such as preventative detention. Chapter 5 considers how we might forgive if wrongdoers do not basically deserve the pain of being resented, which forgiveness would then renounce, and proposes that forgiveness be conceived instead as renunciation of the stance of moral protest. Chapter 6 considers how personal relationships might function without retributive anger having a role in responding to wrongdoing, and contends that the stance of moral protest, supplemented with non-retributive emotions, is sufficient. Chapter 7 surveys the options for theistic and atheistic attitudes regarding the fate of humanity in a deterministic universe, and defends an impartial hope for humanity.

**Derk Pereboom** (Ph.D. UCLA) is the Susan Linn Sage Professor of Philosophy and Ethics in the Philosophy Department at Cornell University and Senior Associate Dean for Arts and Humanities in Cornell's College of Arts and Sciences. His areas of research include free will and moral responsibility, philosophy of mind, and early modern philosophy, especially Kant. He is the author of *Living without Free Will* (Cambridge 2001), *Consciousness and the Prospects of Physicalism* (Oxford 2011), and *Free Will, Agency, and Meaning in Life* (Oxford 2014). He has published articles on free will and moral responsibility, consciousness and physicalism, nonreductive materialism, and on Kant's metaphysics and epistemology.

# Wrongdoing and the Moral Emotions

DERK PEREBOOM

# OXFORD
UNIVERSITY PRESS

Great Clarendon Street, Oxford, OX2 6DP,
United Kingdom

Oxford University Press is a department of the University of Oxford.
It furthers the University's objective of excellence in research, scholarship,
and education by publishing worldwide. Oxford is a registered trade mark of
Oxford University Press in the UK and in certain other countries

© Derk Pereboom 2021

The moral rights of the author have been asserted

First published 2021
First published in paperback 2023

All rights reserved. No part of this publication may be reproduced, stored in
a retrieval system, or transmitted, in any form or by any means, without the
prior permission in writing of Oxford University Press, or as expressly permitted
by law, by licence or under terms agreed with the appropriate reprographics
rights organization. Enquiries concerning reproduction outside the scope of the
above should be sent to the Rights Department, Oxford University Press, at the
address above

You must not circulate this work in any other form
and you must impose this same condition on any acquirer

Published in the United States of America by Oxford University Press
198 Madison Avenue, New York, NY 10016, United States of America

British Library Cataloguing in Publication Data
Data available

Library of Congress Cataloging in Publication Data
Data available

ISBN 978-0-19-284600-6 (Hbk.)
ISBN 978-0-19-890378-9 (Pbk.)

DOI: 10.1093/oso/9780192846006.001.0001

Links to third party websites are provided by Oxford in good faith and
for information only. Oxford disclaims any responsibility for the materials
contained in any third party website referenced in this work.

# Contents

| | | |
|---|---|---|
| *Acknowledgments* | | vii |
| 1. | Introduction: Challenges to Anger | 1 |
| 2. | The Stance of Moral Protest | 27 |
| 3. | Defensive Harm and Measured Aggression | 54 |
| 4. | Crime, Protection, and Compassion | 78 |
| 5. | Forgiveness as Renunciation of Moral Protest | 103 |
| 6. | Love and Freedom | 123 |
| 7. | Religion and Hope | 149 |
| *Bibliography* | | 175 |
| *Index of Authors* | | 199 |
| *Index of Topics* | | 203 |

# Acknowledgments

Faculty colleagues, at Cornell and elsewhere, read and commented on the entire manuscript, and I am very grateful to them for these interactions, and for the ways in which they influenced my thinking about the issues addressed in the book. They are Rachana Kamtekar, Michael McKenna, Dana Nelkin, Shaun Nichols, Carolina Sartorio, David Shoemaker, and Robert Wallace. I would like to thank Grant Friedman for comments and discussion specifically on Chapters 1 and 2, John Doris on Chapters 2 and 3, Helen Frowe and Jonathan Quong on Chapter 3, Victor Tadros and Gregg Caruso on Chapter 4, Per-Erik Milam and Brandon Warmke on Chapter 5, and John Martin Fischer on Chapters 6 and 7.

The manuscript benefitted from seven seminars, one for each chapter, at the University of Arizona in November and December of 2020. The participants included faculty members Michael McKenna, Carolina Sartorio, and Robert Wallace, and graduate students Josh Cangelosi, Phoebe Chan, Andrew Lichter, Timothy Kearl, Max Kramer, Travis Quigley, Lucy Schwarz, Anna-Bella Sicilia, Sean Whitton, and Ke Zhang. All read the whole manuscript. These discussions shaped the final version, for which I am grateful.

Earlier versions of the material in the book were presented at a two-week seminar in the summer of 2017 in Riga, Latvia, hosted by the Moscow Center for Consciousness Studies and organized by Artem Besedin and Dmitry Volkov. This material was also discussed in a combination senior undergraduate and graduate seminar at Cornell University in the fall of 2018. The books benefitted from a two-day seminar at the Universidad de Los Andes in Bogota, Colombia in the summer of 2019, organized by Santiago Amaya and Manuel Vargas, and sponsored by the Templeton Foundation. I wish to thank all of the participants in these seminars for valuable discussion.

I am grateful to audiences at the following presentations, at which the discussion shaped the book in significant ways. Precursors to Chapter 2, "The Stance of Moral Protest," were presented at Ohio State University, Rice University, Florida State University, Davidson College, the University of Vermont, Rutgers University, the University of California-San Diego, the University of Rochester, Renmin University-Beijing, the University of Calgary, the University of Oslo, and the Pacific Division Meetings of the American

viii ACKNOWLEDGMENTS

Philosophical Association. A version of the first part of Chapter 3, "Defensive Harm and Measured Aggression," was presented at the *Conversations on War* workshop organized by Helen Frowe and Massimo Renzo on the Bay of Kotor in Montenegro, and co-hosted by the Stockholm Centre for the Ethics of War and Peace, Stockholm University and the Yeoh Tiong Lay Centre for Politics, Philosophy and Law, King's College, London. Chapter 4, "Crime, Protection, and Compassion," in varying stages, was presented at the University of Rome III, the University of Aberdeen, Cornell University, the University of Gothenburg, the University of Ghent, the University of Warwick, and at the Pacific Division Meetings of the American Philosophical Association in Seattle. Precursors of Chapter 6, "Love and Freedom," were presented at the University of California-San Diego and at the University of California-Riverside. Earlier versions of Chapter 7, "Religion and Hope," were presented at Yale University, Rutgers University, Georgetown University, and at a conference on analytic theology at the University of Innsbrück sponsored by the Templeton Foundation.

I also want to thank the following colleagues for interactions on these issues over the years: Marilyn Adams, Robert Adams, Gunnar Björnsson, Tad Brennan, Jennifer Chandler, Andrew Chignell, David Christensen, Randolph Clarke, Michael Corrado, Taylor Cyr, Eve Dietl, Keith DeRose, Louis DeRosset, Tyler Doggett, Austin Duggan, Laura Ekstrom, Augie Faller, Carl Ginet, Quitterie Gounot, Ish Haji, Shao-Pu Kang, Hilary Kornblith, Arthur Kuflik, Tim Kwiatek, John Lemos, Danielle Limbaugh, Don Loeb, Bill Mann, Al Mele, Mark Moyer, Matt Paskell, Ben Sales, George Sher, Angela Smith, Matt Talbert, Patrick Todd, Leigh Vicens, Ben Vilhauer, Bill Watson, Hannah Winckler-Olick, and Lyu Zhou.

Finally, I am very grateful to Peter Momtchiloff, the philosophy editor at Oxford University Press, for his ongoing support of this project, and to the three readers he recruited. Two were anonymous, and the other was Dana Nelkin.

# 1

# Introduction

## Challenges to Anger

In our practice of holding people morally responsible, emotions, together with their attendant justifications for action, feature prominently. These emotions include positive attitudes such as appreciation and gratitude for the good things others do, but also negative attitudes such as anger in response to the wrongdoing of others, and guilt in one's own case. Anger with wrongdoers is often accompanied by the supposition that its target deserves to be the recipient of an expression of this emotion, one that intentionally causes pain or harm. Insofar as anger is accompanied by a supposition of deserved pain or harm, it qualifies as a retributive emotion.

One of my aims in this book is to defend the thesis that we can do without retribution, whether it be in justifying our responses to wrongdoing, or in the emotions employed in those responses. We human beings have the capacity for a wide range of justifications and emotions in contending with wrongdoing, and we have alternatives to retributive anger, and to anger more generally, that are often practically and theoretically preferable. In the past I motivated this stance partly on the basis of skepticism about the control in action—the free will—required for retribution to be justified, and later in this chapter I will summarize that argument. But I believe that there are ethical considerations independent of the concern about control in action that serve to justify the antiretributivist stance. These ethical considerations arise in the context of treatment of criminals, as we shall see, but also in our personal and professional relationships.

Retribution is an element of our ordinary human practice of holding each other, and ourselves, morally responsible. Many authors are sanguine about our practice of holding morally responsible as it actually exists. Others contend that there are serious revisions to the practice that would better achieve its goals. Against such revisionists, P. F. Strawson wrote: "What is wrong is to forget that these practices, and their reception, the reactions to them, really are expressions of our moral attitudes and not

*Wrongdoing and the Moral Emotions.* Derk Pereboom, Oxford University Press. © Derk Pereboom 2021.
DOI: 10.1093/oso/9780192846006.003.0001

## 2 INTRODUCTION: CHALLENGES TO ANGER

merely devices we calculatingly employ for regulative purposes. Our practices do not merely exploit our natures, they express them" (Strawson 1962/2003, 93). In Strawson's conception, to have and express the attitudes that have a part in our actual practice of holding morally responsible is a significant feature of what it is to be human. We cannot conclude that some aspect of the practice should be altered or eliminated solely on the ground that it falls short in realizing anticipated good outcomes relative to available alternatives.

Strawson and those inspired by his view emphasize the role of certain types of anger in such relationships; specifically, resentment, directed toward someone due to a wrong done to oneself,[1] and indignation, the vicarious analogue of resentment, directed toward someone because of a wrong done to a third party (Watson 1987; Wallace 1994; McKenna 2012; Shabo 2012; Brink 2021). Resentment and indignation, in Strawson's terminology, qualify as *reactive attitudes*. In the past I've argued that for normal, adult human beings, resentment and indignation always presuppose that their targets deserve—more specifically, *basically* deserve (discussed below)—to be recipients of expressions of these reactive attitudes (Pereboom 2014, 128–9; McKenna 2021, 64–74).[2] I won't assume that view here, however. I don't reject out of hand the claim that one might direct anger toward a wrongdoer to forcefully communicate to him that he has done wrong, without presupposing that he deserves the pain or harm involved in being a recipient its expression. Still, here the resulting emotion seems like feigned anger to me. My sense is that genuine moral anger at least typically comes with a desert presupposition.

I contend that the basic desert presupposition of moral anger is false, and if I'm right, this raises a general challenge to anger in its retributive form. So far, this leaves non-retributive versions of moral anger in the clear. However,

---

[1] Resentment in this sense is not in common use in American English, where its usual meaning is close to envy. But even the sense tied to moral anger is not as broad as the definitions just provided. Jean Hampton writes: "resentment is a kind of anger which protests the demeaning treatment to one who could and should have known better, and this protest is frequently linked to verbal rebuke, reprimand or complaint direct at the insulter" (Murphy and Hampton 1988, 55). However, in the philosophical literature over the past decade or two the standard use has become the broader one, denoting any anger with someone due to a wrong he has done to oneself, and this is the sense I will assume throughout. There is controversy about what Strawson himself meant by "resentment," and I'm not relying on what he meant, specifically, by the term.

[2] As I argue in Chapter 2, the presupposition that a wrongdoer deserves to be targeted by an expression of resentment or indignation involves the belief that the pain or harm of being so targeted is appropriately *imposed* upon him because he has done wrong.

INTRODUCTION: CHALLENGES TO ANGER 3

I will argue that moral anger, whether or not it presupposes basic desert, has too prominent a place in our practice of holding morally responsible, and has too central a role in many normative accounts of that practice. That said, I maintain that resentment and indignation are sometimes practically rational, particularly in circumstances in which people are dominated or oppressed, and also that we have available a non-retributive measured aggressive stance that is in some respects similar to anger, and which facilitates legitimate defensive action.

It is widely held—and Strawson has been influential in this respect—that without reactive attitudes, and without resentment and indignation in particular, personal relationships would not retain the value that they in fact have for us. If these attitudes were excised from our practice, we would be left with a disengaged and clinical objective stance, incompatible with relationships that are genuinely personal in the way we value most deeply. I believe that this assessment underestimates the extent to which, due to the role of moral anger, the practice malfunctions in general and crucial respects. Consider first how it malfunctions in the context of personal relationships. This threat results from the alienating effect that expression of such anger has on others, and its propensity to occasion defensive or offensive reaction rather than contrition, reconciliation, and reform. Expression of anger tends to allow only either a humiliating or else a defiant response, and often those who wish to avoid humiliation are instead resistant, hindering reform and reconciliation.

As studies have confirmed, and as is true to our ordinary experience, when people are angry in these ways, they tend to misrepresent relevant features of the situation, and this tendency severely limits the potential for achieving reform and reconciliation.[3] Much current political interaction features accusation and blame not intended to reform and reconcile, but to disempower and defeat. Accuracy of accusation and moral appropriateness of blame are at best a secondary consideration. Anger has a significant role in this malfunction of the practice. As is readily evident, if one's attitudes toward others are angrily hostile, as they often are in politics, one will be predisposed to believe accusations about them, regardless of their evidential merit. This problem is manifestly not restricted to political discourse. In general, aims of the practice of holding morally responsible are frequently deflected by anger, often for the sake of personal or group advantage.

---

[3] Studies confirming these distortions, such as Alicke et al. (1994, 2012); Alicke (2000); Lerner et al. (1998); Goldberg et al. (1999); Litvak et al. (2010), are discussed in Chapter 2.

# 4    INTRODUCTION: CHALLENGES TO ANGER

This is not to say that controlling anger by itself will solve our current complex social and political problems. One component of this complexity is the striking degree to which human beings value relative status and relative dominance in possession of positional goods, both for themselves and the groups with which they identify.[4] This tendency occasions angrily hostile attitudes toward those who are perceived as seeking too high a relative status and too great a share of positional goods. Such anger facilitates misrepresentation that degrades, such as the fabricated or exaggerated accusation of members of groups seen as relative status threatening, which in turn diminishes the potential of these groups for achieving economic progress and maintaining well-functioning communities.[5] Reducing economic inequality and addressing exclusionary group identification are crucial for solving such problems. But attending to anger, and its place in these dynamics, also has a significant role to play.

A core reason why the practice of holding morally responsible malfunctions in personal and political relationships is that the angry emotions it invokes are in tension with other requirements for their value and stability. When wrongdoing is at issue, their preservation requires engagement that facilitates reform and reconciliation, not humiliation and defiance. In circumstances of conflict, maintaining good relationships requires that participants aim to believe the truth about the actions of others, and that the attitudes of the parties be compassionate and conciliatory. While angry emotions may supply an alternative to the clinical and the disengaged stance, they have destabilized countless personal relationships and weakened political institutions that have taken centuries to develop and mature. Because of its tendency to distort the truth and to distort it in different ways for different people, anger, in alliance with attitudes such as the overvaluing of relative status, issues in clashing representations of people, their actions, and their policies. Add to this the informational isolation of socio-political communities facilitated by the internet and social media, and the remarkable

---

[4] In a study on relative standing and positional goods, Sara Solnick and David Hemenway (1989) report that "respondents chose between a world where they have more of a good than others and one where everyone's endowment of the good is higher, but the respondent has less than others. Questions [were] asked about education, attractiveness and intelligence for one's child and oneself, income, vacation time, approval and disapproval from a supervisor, and papers to write. Half of the respondents preferred to have 50% less real income but high relative income. Concerns about position were strongest for attractiveness and supervisor's praise and weakest for vacation time." For a thorough account of the economic role of relative status and positional goods, see Frank (2011).

[5] For accounts of the role of groups and group identification in such dynamics, see, for instance, Herbert Blumer (1958), Lawrence Bobo (1999), and Kate Manne (2017).

imitative contagion of belief and behavior,[6] and the result is the fractured array of constructed alternative worlds we now see.

Many philosophical and religious traditions worldwide have emphasized the seriousness of the problems to which anger gives rise, but perhaps none so forcefully as Buddhism. A solution that this tradition emphasizes, in particular in the Mahāyāna form, is to replace it with compassion. Charles Goodman remarks that

> many modern analytic philosophers seem to think that philosophy must accept society's way of life as it is, and restrict itself to clarifying the conceptual presuppositions of that way of life. But in Buddhism, rational thought can be part of a process that leads people to turn against the way of life they know, and to seek spiritual values instead of worldly ones...for Mahāyāna Buddhists, it is possible to live as a layperson, in the midst of the demands and distractions of work and family life, while attaining the perfect wisdom that destroys hatred and leads to perfect compassion. From a Buddhist perspective, ordinary interpersonal relationships, though they may have some value, are pervaded with greed, anger, and delusion. To live the best kind of life, a Buddhist must transform the functions of his mind, as well as his relationships to others and to the world.
>
> (Goodman 2009, 163; cf., Caruso 2020a)

Compassion, in the Buddhist conception, aims at the well-being of others impartially. Directed toward those who have acted wrongly, compassion takes account of factors beyond their control that have contributed to their wrongdoing, and aims at their moral improvement and at reconciliation with them.

One might respond by contending that human nature is not malleable in the way the Buddhist conception presupposes. However, there are examples of changes in our practice of holding responsible over the past century that indicate that this is not so. It was once considered legitimate to blame people for being mentally ill, and in particular for behavior that manifests mental illness; to blame and punish people for being gay or lesbian and specifically for gay or lesbian behavior; for husbands to beat their spouses and for parents to beat their children; for teachers to express rage in the classroom and to beat their pupils; for criminals to be severely harmed,

---

[6] Robert Frank provides a thorough account of this phenomenon in his *Under the Influence: Putting Peer Pressure to Work* (2020).

## 6 INTRODUCTION: CHALLENGES TO ANGER

physically and mentally, in ways not subject to any remotely plausible moral justification. Humanity has made significant inroads against all of this, which indicates that the tendencies to negative emotions at work in the practice are malleable.

For anthropological evidence of malleability, we can turn to anthropologist Jean Briggs's (1970) in-depth study of the indigenous Utkuhiksalingmiut Inuit of Canada's Nunavut territory, who very rarely express anger. While the very young in this culture display familiar outbursts of angry emotion, children are educated by community role modeling and calm parental exhortation to avoid displays of anger. The process is generally successful, and the resulting dispositions persist and are ubiquitous in the community. This example illustrates how cultural regulation of emotion, understood as a process that results in the alignment of emotion with cultural values, objectives, and concerns (De Leersnyder et al. 2013), can make a significant difference for the expression and arguably for the occurrence of anger. On Briggs's proposal, closeness and harmony are the cultural goal that underlies this case of cultural regulation, occasioned by the potential destructive effects that divisiveness would have in the harsh Arctic climate. Perhaps our global situation is analogously harsh, and similar cultural regulation of anger would be to our advantage. At the same time, as Dana Nelkin counsels,[7] we would want to avoid unilateral emotional disarmament against injustice, and to cultivate confrontational emotions that facilitate the struggle against wrongdoing, an account of which I develop in Chapters 2 and 3.

Here are two themes on which I will elaborate. The first is emphasized by the Buddhist tradition, as well as by ancient Stoicism, and by strands in the great monotheisms, Judaism, Christianity, and Islam. A significant aspect of our actual practice is a sense of holding morally responsible that, by contrast with the model that foregrounds retributive anger, is instead largely forward looking. In this aspect of the practice, blame's predominant objectives include protection from dangers posed by wrongdoing, moral formation of the wrongdoer, and reconciliation with those who have been wronged. This aspect of blame does not essentially involve retributive anger. It features instead a stance of moral protest, whose aim and function is to achieve these forward-looking aims. This stance may be accompanied by emotions such as disappointment or sorrow or compassion for the wrongdoer, and, in heat of defensive confrontation, a stance of measured

---

[7] In correspondence.

aggression, none of which involve retribution. The stance of moral protest unaccompanied by retributive anger may communicate moral reasons to wrongdoers without occasioning only either humiliation or defiance, and without the truth-distorting effect of anger.

The second point is that even if, as is indeed plausible, retributive anger is inevitable for us in certain circumstances, we have the capacity to distance ourselves from this emotion. This capacity is also a distinctive feature of what it is to be human. We can distance ourselves from the retributive anger we acknowledge we feel by regarding this emotion as failing to license a response more severe than what moral protest would justify. The great twentieth-century leaders Mahatma Gandhi and Martin Luther King were champions of moral protest while disavowing its retributively angry forms. Their position impressively illustrates the proposal I will defend in this book. In the momentous political efforts in which they were engaged, the cost of expression of retributive anger beyond what the stance of moral protest would justify was high, and success mandated restraint.

Let me cite three concerns that have been raised for an ideal of the type we find in Mahāyāna Buddhism and in the other traditions I've cited. A first is that this ideal is not attainable for us, at least for those of us who live ordinary, non-monastic lives. A second is that those who believe that they have attained the ideal are often self-deceived. The recommendations of these traditions are difficult to secure, and the practitioner is apt to believe that success has been attained when it has not. What is attained may involve unacknowledged hostility and indirect expressions of retributive anger, which are apt to be destructive. A third concern is that even if the ideal is within reach, it would come at a great cost to relationships. Losing our susceptibility to retributive anger threatens to undermine the possibility of genuinely personal relationships with others. Personal connections would give way to the clinical attitude, or worse, indifference. The position I propose takes these concerns very seriously, as the ensuing discussion will show.

## Skepticism about Basic Desert

As I've specified, a further challenge to retributive justifications and emotions is that they are not appropriate given the kinds of beings we are, situated in a natural world of law-governed causes and effects. Our character and actions are conditioned by causes that we do not control—our genetic make-up, our upbringing, and our physical environment. Given that we are

# 8 INTRODUCTION: CHALLENGES TO ANGER

components of a natural world, does it make sense to be retributively angry when people act badly? The eighth-century Indian Buddhist philosopher Śāntideva thought not, as he indicated in his poem *Bodhicaryāvatara*:

> I feel no anger towards bile and the like, even though they cause intense suffering. Why am I angry with sentient beings? They too have causes for their anger. Whatever transgressions and evil deeds of various kinds there are, all arise through the power of conditioning factors, while there is nothing that arises independently. Therefore, even if one sees a friend or an enemy behaving badly, one can reflect that there are specific conditioning factors that determine this, and thereby remain happy. If it is their very nature to cause others distress, my anger towards these unwise ones is as inappropriate as it would be towards fire for its nature to burn.
>
> (Śāntideva 700/1995, 52–3)

Śāntideva is expressing skepticism about human free will, and counting this as a reason against being angry at all with people for the wrongs they have done.

The seventeenth-century philosopher Spinoza also advocates skepticism about free will, and a similar renunciation of anger. He contends that "in the mind there is no absolute, or free, will, but the mind is determined to will this or that by a cause which is also determined by another, and this again by another, and so to infinity" (1677/1985, *Ethics* II, Proposition 48, 483). The reason we don't have free will is that everything that happens is causally determined prior causes, resulting in chains of causes stretching to infinity. The ultimate deterministic cause of everything that happens is the divine nature; but even God does not have free will: "all things have been predetermined by God, not from freedom of the will or absolute good pleasure, but from God's absolute nature, or infinite power" (1677/1985, *Ethics* I, Appendix, 439). Like Śāntideva, Spinoza maintains that the doctrine that we lack free will has salutary consequences, for

> it teaches us...that we must expect and bear calmly both good fortune and bad. For everything that happens follows from God's eternal decree with the same necessity as it follows from the essence of a triangle that its three angles are equal to two right angles. This doctrine contributes to the social life by teaching us to hate no one, to disesteem no one, to mock no one, to be angry at no one, to envy no one.
>
> (1677/1985, *Ethics* II, Proposition 49, Discussion, 490)

Understanding that people lack free will counteracts hostile emotions we have toward others, and that anger is among them.

Still, most of us suppose that our actions are sometimes freely willed. When we choose from among offers of admission to colleges or for employment, we typically presume that we could have chosen differently from how we actually did choose. When we are angry with wrongdoers for their immoral actions, we assume that they could have avoided acting as they did. There are, however, reasons for believing that no one has free will, reasons that stem from various sources. One such source is invoked by Spinoza: that everything that happens, including human action, is causally determined by the divine nature.[8] Another is the non-theological, naturalistic view that the past in accord with the laws of nature determines a single unique future (van Inwagen 1983, 2). Given the prospect that some version of causal determinism is true, and that as a result all of our actions are causally determined by factors beyond our control and beyond our causal reach (Pereboom 1995, 2001, 2014; Sartorio 2014, 2016), is it reasonable to believe that some of our actions are freely willed nonetheless?

One concern to keep in mind in answering this question is that the term 'free will,' as it is used in philosophical debates, has a number of distinct senses, and the answer may depend on which sense is intended (e.g., Pereboom 2001, Latham 2004; cf. Chalmers 2011). Two of these senses have a prominent role in the historical and contemporary debate:

*free will AP* (for 'alternative possibilities'): Free will is an agent's ability, at a given time, either to act or to refrain: that is, if an agent acts with free will, then she could at that time have refrained from acting as she did.

*free will MR* (for 'moral responsibility'): Free will is an agent's ability to exercise the control in acting required for her to be morally responsible for her actions.

It was traditionally assumed that the ability to act and to refrain is required for moral responsibility, and for blameworthiness in particular. How can an agent be reasonably blamed for an action if he couldn't have refrained, if he didn't have refraining as an alternative possibility (e.g., Widerker 2000)? However, fifty years ago this assumption became controversial due to an

---

[8] For a current overview of theological determinism and its relation to divine foreknowledge and human free will, see Leigh Vicens and Simon Kittle (2019). Recently, Heath White (2019) has set out a comprehensive defense of this determinist perspective.

10  INTRODUCTION: CHALLENGES TO ANGER

argument advanced by Harry Frankfurt (1969), and the issue continues to be hotly disputed.[9] Because this book's discussion concerns moral responsibility, I will assume *free will MR*, as does much of the current debate.

However, the term 'morally responsible' also has multiple senses (e.g., Pereboom 2001, 2014; Latham 2004). As I pointed out earlier, our practice of holding morally responsible, and blaming in particular, has a number of objectives. One such aim is backward looking and involves the attribution of desert. Other objectives are forward looking, for example, moral reform and reconciliation in relationships. I contend that the specific sense of 'moral responsibility' that works best to distinguish the parties to the debate is one that involves desert, of the basic variety.

The parties to the free will debate are traditionally grouped into three camps. They first of all divide into *compatibilists* and *incompatibilists*:

*compatibilism*:  our having free will is compatible with determinism, with all of our actions being causally determined by factors beyond our control.

*incompatibilism*:  our having free will is not compatible with determinism, with all of our actions being causally determined by factors beyond our control.

Incompatibilists divide into those who hold that determinism is false and that we have free will—the libertarians—and those who hold that determinism is true and that we lack free will—the hard determinists (James 1884). Libertarians endorse:

*Indeterminism*:  not every event has causal antecedents that render it inevitable.

Two different ways in which the world might be indeterministic can be distinguished. The world might be indeterministic because at least some of the

---

[9] Here is Carolina Sartorio's (2016) version of Frankfurt's famous example: "A neuroscientist, Black, wants Jones to perform a certain action. Black is prepared to go to considerable lengths to get his way, but he prefers to avoid showing his hand unnecessarily. So he waits until Jones is about to make up his mind what to do, and he does nothing unless it is clear to him (Black is an excellent judge of such things) that Jones is going to decide to do something other than what he wants him to do. If it were to become clear that Jones is going to decide to do something else, Black would take effective steps to ensure that Jones decides to do what he wants him to do, by directly manipulating the relevant processes in Jones's brain. As it turns out, Black never has to show his hand because Jones, for reasons of his own, decides to perform the very action Black wants him to perform" (Sartorio 2016). One's intuition may well be that Jones is blameworthy for his action, despite his not being able to refrain. For further discussion, see Pereboom 2001, 1–37, 2014, 9–29.

SKEPTICISM ABOUT BASIC DESERT    11

fundamental laws are probabilistic, or it might be indeterministic because there are exceptions to deterministic laws (e.g., Vihvelin 2017).

Given our selection of *free will MR*, we can yet specify any of a number of senses of moral responsibility in the definitions of compatibilism, libertarianism, and hard determinism. Here is one principle for settling on definitions in contexts such as this one: select those that best distinguish contrasting positions that divide parties in the debate.[10] Now virtually everyone holds that causal determination by factors beyond our control is compatible with our having the control in action required for our being morally responsible in *some* sense, for example in a forward-looking sense. But participants in the debate do disagree about whether causal determination is compatible with our having the control in action required for being morally responsible for actions in a sense involving moral desert of pain and harm, pleasure and benefit. Noa Latham (2004), for example, argues that determinism rules out such desert: "What evaluative claims would be undermined by determinism? My answer is that it is all those entailing that the intrinsic goodness of a person's receiving pleasure or pain depends on the virtue or vice of the person. I shall call these desert principles" (Latham 2004, 154).[11] And as we shall see, many contemporary compatibilists maintain that determinism does not rule out such desert principles (e.g., Fischer 2007, 82; Nelkin 2011, 2019b; McKenna 2012, 2020; Sartorio 2016; Brink 2021). So here there is a genuine conflict, one that divides parties in the debate.

I contend that determinism rules out moral responsibility specifically in the *basic desert* sense:

> For an agent to be *morally responsible for an action in the basic desert sense* is for the action to be attributable to her in such a way that if she was sensitive to its being morally wrong, she would deserve to be blamed or punished in a way that she would experience as painful or harmful, and if she was sensitive to its being morally exemplary, she would deserve to be

---

[10] This isn't the only rule that's been proposed. Dennett (1984, 2003) favors: choose the sense of free will worth wanting. In Dennett's view, a kind of rational responsiveness that develops in evolution and in a person over time fits that definition. One issue is that almost everyone agrees that we have this sort of rational responsiveness, so on this definition, there is no controversy. Another problem is that many libertarians maintain that libertarian free will is worth wanting. Dennett thinks it isn't and so then the debate would be shifted to one about what sort of free will is worth wanting, and whether we have it, which is functionally equivalent to selecting the definition that divides the camps.

[11] It's clear from Latham's (2004) discussion that by "intrinsic goodness of a person's receiving pleasure or pain" he means what I mean when I say such pleasure or pain is basically deserved.

## 12 INTRODUCTION: CHALLENGES TO ANGER

praised or rewarded in a way that she would experience as pleasurable or beneficial. The desert at issue is basic in the sense that the agent, to be morally responsible, would deserve such blame or punishment, praise or reward, just by virtue of having performed the action with sensitivity to its moral status, and not, for example, by virtue of consequentialist or contractualist considerations.[12]

In many cases of wrongdoing, it's intuitive that the pain of guilt is basically deserved (Clarke 2013; Carlsson 2017; Duggan 2018), or the pain upon being targeted by overt resentment or indignation. In cases in which the wrongdoer, for instance an immoral political figure, is hardened and he won't feel guilty on account of his wrongdoing or pain upon being targeted by indignation (Nelkin 2019a), it may be intuitive that the pain resulting from public exposure of the wrongdoing is deserved. If he won't feel pain upon such public exposure, it may be intuitive that some type of harmful setback of his career is deserved, or if he's committed a crime, that some judicial punishment is deserved. Against the suggestion that only harm and not pain need be invoked, in certain cases only feeling guilty may be deserved, and it's not intuitive that the pain of guilt is a kind of harm (compare the pain of grief, which is also not intuitively a kind of harm). Parallelism recommends pleasure or benefit as what's basically deserved in the case of a morally exemplary action. In the case of wrongdoing, the claim that the agent deserves pain or harm is justified solely on the grounds of the agent's having done wrong with sensitivity to its being wrong, and not by virtue of further considerations, such as anticipated good consequences of imposing the pain or harm (Feinberg 1970; Pereboom 2001, xx; 2014, 2;

---

[12] This characterization can be extended to omissions. In earlier formulations (e.g., Pereboom 2001, xx, 2014, 2), included in what is specified as basically deserved is *to be blamed*. But on my own view of blame as moral protest (Chapter 2 and Pereboom 2017a) being blamed needn't involve any harmful or painful interaction with the person blamed, but at times only being confronted by reasons to act differently. Denying that being blamed in this sense is basically deserved doesn't adequately represent my concern for negative basic desert. This convinced me to specify the basically deserved negative outcome in the case of blame as pain or harm, and analogously, the basically deserved positive outcome in the case of praise as pleasure or benefit (Telech 2020). Thanks to an anonymous reviewer for raising this issue, and suggesting a more decisively retributivist characterization of negative basic desert. In addition, in earlier formulations I specified *understanding* of the wrongness of the action as a requirement of negative basic desert. Michael McKenna convinced me that this is too strong. On the supposition of basic desert, genuine understanding of the wrongness of an action isn't plausibly required for deserved pain or harm. McKenna suggested the example of an abusive partner who doesn't fully understand the wrongness of his abusive behavior, even representing it as justified, but who is nonetheless sensitive to its wrongness.

SKEPTICISM ABOUT BASIC DESERT     13

Scanlon 2013). Accordingly, the desert invoked here is basic. We'll consider the contrast between basic and non-basic desert in Chapter 2.

Given the selection of basic desert sense of moral responsibility in *free will MR*, here are the characterizations of the three traditional positions:

*hard determinism*:   because determinism is true, we cannot have the sort of free will required for moral responsibility in the basic desert sense.

*compatibilism*:   even if determinism is true, we can have the sort of free will required for moral responsibility in the basic desert sense, and we do in fact have it.[13]

*libertarianism*:   because determinism is false, we can have the sort of free will required for moral responsibility in the basic desert sense, and we do in fact have it.

Like the hard determinist, I side with a skeptical perspective on free will defined in this way.[14] But this is not because I'm convinced of the truth of determinism, and that all of our actions are causally determined by factors beyond our control. Rather, I argue that any sort of indeterminism that has a good chance of being true is also incompatible with free will in the sense just defined. We'll examine an argument for this conclusion in what follows. Critics have expressed a number of practical concerns about free will skepticism, that, for example, its rejection of basic desert moral responsibility is too costly, that it offers no viable policy for dealing with criminal behavior, and that it threatens emotional attitudes essential to personal relationships. I disagree, and this is one of the main concerns of this book.

---

[13] There is a broader sense of compatibilism on which one might be a compatibilist and deny that we have free will of the sort specified (Strawson 1986, 6). For example, one might believe that this sort of free will is compatible with determinism, but since our actions are never produced by conscious willing, we lack such free will (e.g., Wegner 2002).

[14] Historical advocates of skepticism about free will and/or basic desert include Spinoza (1677/1985), Paul d'Holbach (1770), Joseph Priestley (1788/1965), Arthur Schopenhauer (1818/1961), Friedrich Nietzsche (1888/1954); and in recent decades, C. D. Broad (1952), Galen Strawson (1986, 1994), Bruce Waller (1990, 2011, 2015), Michael Slote (1990), Derk Pereboom (1995, 2001, 2014), Saul Smilansky (2000), Daniel Wegner (2002), Gideon Rosen (2003, 2004), Joshua Greene and Jonathan Cohen (2004), Benjamin Vilhauer (2004, 2008, 2012); Shaun Nichols (2007, 2015), Tamler Sommers (2007, 2012), Brian Leiter (2007), Thomas Nadelhoffer (2011), Neil Levy (2011), Sam Harris (2012), Gregg Caruso (2012, 2016, 2021), 'Trick Slattery (2014), Per-Erik Milam (2016), Robert Sapolsky (2017), Stephen Morris (2018), Elizabeth Shaw (2019), and Farah Focquaert (2019). Arguments for skepticism about free will and basic desert vary considerably; for an overview, see Caruso (2018).

14 INTRODUCTION: CHALLENGES TO ANGER

Aspects of our practice of holding each other morally responsible that don't invoke basic desert have not been a focus of contention in the free will debate. For example, someone might be held morally responsible when his tendency to act badly stands to be modified or eliminated by blaming, and his dispositions to act well strengthened by praising (Schlick 1939; Nowell-Smith 1948; Smart 1961). Or for a variation on this idea, someone might be held morally responsible by asking her questions such as "Why did you decide to do that? Do you think it was the right thing to do?" so that she will appreciate the reasons for changing her dispositions, attitudes, and behavior, and undertake the requisite reform; what is invoked here might be classified as the *answerability* sense of moral responsibility (Bok 1998; Scanlon 1998; Smith 2008, 2013), by contrast with the *accountability* sense, which is essentially confrontational and is standardly conceived as licensing resentment and indignation (Watson 1996; Shoemaker 2011, 2015; Jeppsson 2022). Incompatibilists would not regard the control required for answerability to be incompatible with causal determination, and it is open to free will skeptics to endorse this notion of moral responsibility. Instead, it's the accountability sense, conceived specifically as invoking basically deserved pain or harm, that separates the parties in the debate.

Thus what I deny is that we have *free will MR*, the control in action required for moral responsibility, where the notion of moral responsibility specified is the one that involves basic desert. I'll now explain why.

## An Argument for Free Will Skepticism

I've defended my skeptical position about free will in *Living without Free Will* (2001) and *Free Will, Agency, and Meaning in Life* (2014). Here I present my argument for this position briefly in outline. The argument features challenges to the rival views, compatibilism and libertarianism, and if these challenges are sound, only the skeptical view remains standing.

One way to resist free will skepticism is to contend that even if all of our actions are causally determined by factors beyond our control, we can still be morally responsible in the basic desert sense for some of them. This is the compatibilist option. Compatibilists point out that many of the criteria we ordinarily use to judge whether people are blameworthy are compatible with such causal determination of immoral actions. For instance, in court cases we may want to make sure that the accused was rational and that he was not compelled by someone else to commit the crime. But rationality

AN ARGUMENT FOR FREE WILL SKEPTICISM    15

and absence of compulsion are conditions compatible with causal determination, and whether causal determinism itself is true is not debated in court cases. Compatibilists have proposed a range of such conditions for moral responsibility, and they hold that their satisfaction is sufficient for moral responsibility. Incompatibilists have objected that even if an agent satisfies the compatibilist conditions, causal determination by factors beyond her control rules out moral responsibility. Are we at a standoff?

I believe that the best way to argue against the compatibilist option begins with the intuition that if an agent is causally determined to act by, for example, neuroscientists who intentionally manipulate his brain, then he is not morally responsible for that action in the basic desert sense even if he satisfies the compatibilist conditions. The next step is to point out that there are no differences between such a deterministically manipulated agent and an ordinary causally determined counterpart that can justify the claim that the manipulated agent is not morally responsible while the ordinarily determined agent is responsible. The conclusion is that an agent is not morally responsible if he's causally determined to act by factors beyond his control even if he satisfies the compatibilist conditions.[15]

My multiple-case version of such a manipulation argument first of all develops examples of an action that results from intentional deterministic manipulation and in which the prominent compatibilist conditions on moral responsibility are satisfied. In the setup, in each of four cases an agent commits a crime, murder, for self-interested reasons. The cases are designed so that the action conforms to the compatibilist conditions. For instance, the action meets a condition advocated by David Hume (1739/1978; cf. Hobbes, 1654, Ayer 1954): the agent is not compelled to act by other agents or constrained by other factors such as drugs (cf., Paul Russell 2020). The action also satisfies the rationality condition proposed by John Fischer (1982, 1994): the agent's desires can be modified by, and some of them arise from, his rational consideration of his reasons, and if he understood that the bad consequences for himself that would result from the crime would be much more severe than they are actually likely to be, he would have refrained from the crime for that reason.

The individual manipulation cases serve to indicate that it's possible for an agent to be morally non-responsible in the basic desert sense even if the

---

[15] Manipulation arguments of this sort have been set out by Richard Taylor (1974), Robert Kane (1985, 1996), Carl Ginet (1990), Derk Pereboom (1995, 22–6; 2001, 110–20; 2014, 71–103), Noa Latham (2004), and Al Mele (2006, 2008).

16   INTRODUCTION: CHALLENGES TO ANGER

compatibilist conditions are satisfied, and that, as a result, these conditions are insufficient for such moral responsibility, contrary to what the compatibilist claims. The argument gains additional force by virtue of setting out three such manipulation cases, each of which is progressively more like a fourth, in which the action is causally determined in an ordinary and natural way; that is, by virtue of the past and the laws. The cases are set up so that there is no difference relevant to basic desert moral responsibility between any two adjacent cases. So if it's agreed that the agent isn't morally responsible in the first case, this feature of the argument will make it difficult to affirm that he is responsible in the final, ordinary case.

Here are the four cases:

Case 1:   A team of neuroscientists has the ability to manipulate Professor Plum's neural states at any time by radio technology. In this particular case, they do so by pressing a button just before he begins to reason about his situation, which they know will produce in him a neural state that realizes a strongly egoistic reasoning process, which they know will deterministically result in his decision to kill White. Plum would not have killed White had the neuroscientists not intervened, since his reasoning would then not have been sufficiently egoistic to produce this decision.

Case 2:   Plum is just like an ordinary human being, except that a team of neuroscientists programmed him at the beginning of his life so that his reasoning is often but not always egoistic (just as it is in Case 1), and at times strongly so, with the intended consequence that in his current circumstances he will be causally determined to engage in the process of deliberation that results in his decision to kill White for egoistic reasons.

Case 3:   Plum is an ordinary human being, except that the training practices of his community causally determined the nature of his deliberative reasoning processes so that they are frequently but not exclusively egoistic. The resulting deliberative process is exactly as it is in Cases 1 and 2: in his current circumstances he is causally determined to engage in the process of deliberation that results in his decision to kill White for egoistic reasons.

Case 4:   Everything that happens in the universe is causally determined by virtue of its past states together with the laws of nature. Plum is an ordinary human being, raised in normal circumstances, but his reasoning processes are frequently but not exclusively egoistic, and sometimes strongly so (as in Cases 1–3). In his current circumstances he is causally determined to engage in the process of deliberation that results in his decision to kill White, for egoistic reasons.

AN ARGUMENT FOR FREE WILL SKEPTICISM    17

Case 1 involves intentional manipulation that is local and causally determining, and is most likely of the cases to elicit a non-responsibility intuition. Case 2 is similar to Case 1, except that it restricts the deterministic manipulation to the beginning of the agent's life. Case 3 is distinctive in that the deterministic manipulation results from community upbringing. Case 4 is the ordinary deterministic case in which the causal determination of the action is not intentional, but results from the past and the laws. Case 4 is the kind of case about which compatibilists standardly claim that the agent is morally responsible despite being causally determined to act by factors beyond his control.

However, in Case 1, is Plum morally responsible in the basic desert sense for the crime? In this situation it seems clear that Plum is a causally determined victim of the conniving neuroscientists, and that he is not responsible. Are there responsibility-relevant differences between Cases 1 and 2 that would justify claiming that Plum is non-responsible in Case 1 but is responsible in Case 2? It was my aim to set out the cases so that it isn't possible to draw a difference relevant to the sort of responsibility at issue between any two adjacent cases. Given this absence of relevant differences, if Plum is not responsible in Case 1, he isn't in Cases 2, 3, and 4 either. I contend that the best explanation for Plum's non-responsibility (and for our intuitions of non-responsibility) in each case is that he is causally determined to act by factors beyond his control. This is the argument's anticompatibilist conclusion.

A number of objections to this argument have been raised, but one prominent concern claims that the difference between intentional manipulation by other agents and naturalistic determination is relevant to moral responsibility in the basic desert sense (e.g., Lycan 1987; Feltz 2013; Murray and Lombrozo 2015). Accordingly, a compatibilist might cite this as a justification for claiming that Plum is not responsible in this sense in Cases 1 and 2, but is in the ordinary Case 4. One might test this hypothesis by having subjects imagine further cases that are exactly the same as Case 1 or Case 2, except that the states at issue are instead produced nonintentionally. Gunnar Björnsson, for instance, constructs a scenario where all the prominent compatibilist conditions on moral responsibility are satisfied but in which a cause that isn't an agent—an infection—slowly renders the agent in the example increasingly egoistic without bypassing or undermining his agential capacities. Björnsson predicted that if subjects were prompted to view the agent's behavior as dependent on this non-agential cause, attributions of responsibility would be undermined to roughly the same extent as in cases of an intentional manipulator. This turned out to be true: in a study involving 416 subjects, the infection undermined attributions of free will

# 18 INTRODUCTION: CHALLENGES TO ANGER

and moral responsibility to the same degree as in cases of intentional manipulation (Björnsson and Pereboom 2016). Björnsson's study suggests that incompatibilists can employ the strategy used in manipulation arguments without introducing intentional manipulation.[16]

Making a case for free will skepticism also requires arguing against the rival incompatibilist position, libertarianism. On libertarian views generally considered, we do in fact have the capacity to freely will actions, and crucial to an action's being freely willed is that it not be causally determined by factors beyond the agent's control. We'll consider in turn the three sorts of libertarianism that have been proposed, *event-causal libertarianism*, *agent-causal libertarianism*, and *non-causal libertarianism*.

According to event-causal libertarianism, actions are caused solely by *events*, conceived as substances having properties at times, such as *Jane's wanting at noon today to give Mary her medicine*, and some type of indeterminacy in the production of actions by such agent-involving events is the key requirement for moral responsibility (Lucretius 50 BCE/1998; Machiavelli (DeCaro 2021); Kane 1996; Ekstrom 2000, 2019; Balaguer 2010; Franklin 2011). This view contrasts with a position according to which substances, such as people, particles, and planets, themselves can be causes. Those who claim that only events can be causes recognize that we may sometimes speak as if substances are causes, but argue that once we clarify such speech, we'll see that the event view is right. For example, suppose a car drives through a puddle of water and splashes you. You may say; "The car made me wet!" But speaking precisely, it's not the car, exactly, that made you wet, but an event, the car's driving through the puddle at 123 4th Street at 5 PM that had this effect (Davidson 1963). According to *agent-causal libertarianism*, by contrast, free will of the sort required for basic desert moral

---

[16] Challenges to manipulation arguments are issued by John Fischer (1994, 2004, 2016, 2021), William Lycan (1997), Ishtiyaque Haji (1998), Al Mele (2005, 2006), Lynne Baker (2006), Michael McKenna (2008, 2014), Kristin Demetriou (2010), Dana Nelkin (2011, 52–60), Stephen Kearns (2012), Gunnar Björnsson and Karl Persson (2012), Chandra Sripada (2012), Dan Haas (2013), Adam Feltz (2013), Justin Capes (2013), Matt King (2013), Hannah Tierney (2013, 2014), Adam Khoury (2014), Dylan Murray and Tania Lombrozo (2015), Carolina Sartorio (2016, 156–70), Kadri Vihvelin (2017, 148–55), Oisín Deery and Eddy Nahmias (2017), Maria Sekatskaya (2019), Sofia Jeppsson (2020), Marius Usher (2020), Daniel Dennett (Dennett and Caruso 2020), Taylor Cyr (2020), and David Brink (2021). Defenses of manipulation arguments are advanced by Derk Pereboom (2001, 117–20, 2007a, 2007b, 2008a, 2014, 71–103), Al Mele (2006, 2008), Patrick Todd (2011, 2013), Neal Tognazzini (2014), Ben Matheson (2016), Gunnar Björnsson and Derk Pereboom (2016), Hannah Tierney and David Glick (2020), Taylor Cyr (2020), Gregg Caruso in Dennett and Caruso (2020), and Derk Pereboom and Michael McKenna (2022).

AN ARGUMENT FOR FREE WILL SKEPTICISM    19

responsibility is accounted for by agents who, as substances, cause choices without being causally determined to do so. In this view, it is essential that the causation involved in an agent's making a free choice does not amount to causation among events involving the agent, but is instead fundamentally a case of the agent as a substance causing a choice.[17]

An influential objection to event-causal libertarianism is that if actions are undetermined in the way that this view requires for free will, agents won't have enough control in acting to secure moral responsibility; this concern is often referred to as the *luck objection* (e.g., Haji 2000; Latham 2004; Mele 2006; cf., van Inwagen 1983).[18] A classical presentation of this type of objection is found in Hume's *Treatise of Human Nature* (1739/1978, 411–12; cf., Hume 1748/2000), where he argues that if an action is not necessitated by factors involving the agent, the action will not have sufficient connection with the agent for her to be morally responsible for it. This idea might be developed as follows. For an agent to be morally responsible for an action (in the basic desert sense), she must have a certain kind of control in producing that action. But in an event-causal libertarian picture, preceding agent-involving events don't causally determine the action. So given the complete causal role of these preceding events, it remains open whether action occurs. What's more, the role of the agent in the production of the action is exhausted by these agent-involving events. Thus nothing about the agent *settles* whether the action occurs. For this reason the agent lacks the control required to be responsible for it. Since the agent 'disappears' at the crucial point in the production of the action—when its occurrence is to be settled—we can call this the *disappearing agent argument* (Pereboom 2004, 2014, 2017b; cf., O'Connor 2008).[19]

---

[17] The agent-causal libertarianism has in recent times been developed and defended by Roderick Chisholm (1964, 1976), Richard Taylor (1966), Randolph Clarke (1993, 1996, 2003), Timothy O'Connor (1995, 2000, 2008), Jonathan Lowe (2008), Meghan Griffith (2010), Richard Swinburne (2013), and Christopher Franklin (2018); see also Daniel Speak (2004). For historical precedents, see Immanuel Kant (1781/1787/1987), and Thomas Reid (1788/1983).

[18] For responses to the luck objection, see Robert Kane (2007), Mark Balaguer (2014), and Robert Hartman (2016).

[19] Here is the more exact statement of the disappearing agent objection to event-causal libertarianism (the Pereboom 2017c statement I currently prefer): "Suppose that a decision is made in a deliberative context in which the agent's moral motivations favor deciding to A, her prudential motivations favor her deciding to not-A, and the strengths of these motivations are in equipoise. A and not-A are the options she is considering. The potentially causally relevant events thus render the occurrence of each of these decisions equiprobable. But then the potentially causally relevant events do not settle which decision occurs, that is, whether the decision to A or the decision to not-A occurs. Since, given event-causal libertarianism, only events are causally relevant, nothing settles which decision occurs. Thus it can't be the agent or anything

20 INTRODUCTION: CHALLENGES TO ANGER

The agent-causal libertarian's solution to this problem is to specify a way in which the agent could in fact settle which of the options for action occurs. The proposal is to reintroduce the agent as a cause, this time not merely as involved in events, but instead fundamentally as a substance cause. The agent-causal libertarian maintains that we possess a distinctive causal power, a power for an agent, fundamentally as a substance, to cause a decision without being causally determined to do so, and thereby to settle which of several possible options for action actually occurs.

One important objection to the agent-causal libertarian picture is that it cannot be reconciled with our best scientific theories. Suppose we allow that agents are free in the way specified by agent-causal libertarianism, but that our best science tells us that the entire physical world is governed by deterministic laws. On the route to action that results from an undetermined agent-caused action, changes in the physical world, for example, in the agent's brain or some other part of her body, result. But at this point we would then expect to encounter divergences from the deterministic laws. This is because the alterations in the brain that result from the causally undetermined decision would themselves not be causally determined, and they would not be governed by deterministic laws. The agent-causal libertarian might propose that the physical alterations that result from every free decision just happen to dovetail with what can be predicted on the basis of the relevant past and the deterministic laws, and that nothing actually occurs that diverges from these laws. However, this proposal would seem to involve coincidences too wild to be credible. Thus it seems that agent-causal libertarianism is not reconcilable with the physical world's being governed by deterministic laws (Pereboom 1995, 2001, 79–81, 2014, 65–6).

A similar concern arises if the laws of physics are probabilistic and not deterministic. On the indeterministic interpretation of quantum mechanics, the physical laws are not deterministic, but probabilistic. Can agent-causal libertarianism be reconciled with this picture? Consider the class of possible actions each of which has a physical component whose antecedent probability of occurring is approximately 0.32. It would not violate the statistical laws in the sense of being logically incompatible with them if, for a large number of instances, the physical components in this class were not actually realized close to 32 percent of the time. Rather, the force of the law

about the agent that settles which decision occurs, and she therefore lacks the control required for moral responsibility for it." Objections to this argument are set out by Al Mele (2017) and Randolph Clarke (2019); for replies to these objections see Pereboom (2017c).

AN ARGUMENT FOR FREE WILL SKEPTICISM    21

is that for a large number of instances it is correct to *expect* physical components in this class to be realized close to 32 percent of the time. Are free choices on the agent-causal libertarian model compatible with what that law leads us to expect about them? If they were, then for a large enough number of instances the possible actions in our class would almost certainly be freely chosen close to 32 percent of the time. But if the occurrence of these physical components were settled by the choices of agent-causes, then their actually being chosen close to 32 percent of the time would amount to a wild coincidence. The proposal that agent-caused free choices do not diverge from what the laws would predict for the physical components of our actions would run so sharply counter to what we would expect as to make it incredible (Pereboom 1995, 2001, 81–3, 2014, 66–8).[20]

At this point, the agent-causal libertarian might propose that exercises of agent-causal libertarian freedom do result in divergences from what we would expect given our best theories of the physical laws. The idea is that divergences from the deterministic or probabilistic laws in fact occur whenever we act freely, and they are located at the interface between the agent-cause and the brain. The core objection to such proposals is that we currently have no evidence that such divergences actually occur. Thus agent-causal libertarianism is not reconcilable with the laws of nature, whether they are deterministic or probabilistic, and we have no evidence that the divergences from the laws that this view would therefore predict actually occur.

A third type of libertarianism is non-causal. The core provision of this view is that basic actions, such as decisions, for which agents are morally responsible are undetermined and uncaused events (Bergson 1889/1910; Ginet 1997, 2007; McCann 1998; Goetz 2008; Palmer 2021). Amy's decision at 9 AM this morning to give $500 to famine relief might be such a basic action. The event of Amy's so deciding is not probabilistically caused, by contrast with the event-causal libertarian view; it is not caused at all. She is also not the substance cause of the decision, as in agent-causal libertarianism; Amy is the subject of the decision and not its cause. On Carl Ginet's (1997, 2007) conception, besides the decision's being uncaused and the agent being its subject, the key condition for its being freely willed is that it has an actish phenomenological feel. In place of the actish phenomenological feel,

---

[20] Replies to this argument include those set out by Timothy O'Connor (2008); for defenses of the argument see Pereboom (2014, 68–9).

# 22 INTRODUCTION: CHALLENGES TO ANGER

Hugh McCann (1998) specifies that the action be intentional, and intrinsically and fundamentally so.

I argue that the non-causal view falls to a dilemma. About an action-event of the sort at issue Ginet writes: "It was up to me at time T whether that event would occur only if I *made it the case that it occurred*, and it was open to me at T *to keep it from occurring*" (Ginet 2007). Against this view it can first of all be objected that the making relation is just a causal relation. Causation, on the most prominent non-Humean conception, is fundamentally just *making something happen* or *producing something*. Ginet, just prior to the remark just quoted, writes: "To suppose it is possible for there to be indeterministic causation is to suppose that causation does not reduce, Humean fashion, to universal regularity but is rather a brute relation among particular events, a relation of *production*, a relation that may be impossible to specify in non-synonymous terms" (Ginet 2007, 244). But then, if the agent makes the event happen, then she causes it to happen.

Contemporary Humeans, on the other hand, tend to think of causation as difference making. David Lewis, for instance, proposes that "we think of a cause as something that makes a difference, and the difference it makes must be a difference from what would have happened without it" (Lewis 1986). Thus, on a 'difference making' account of causation, the agent's making a difference as to whether the event occurs amounts to the agent's causing it. But then, if the agent makes the difference as to whether an event happens, then she causes it to happen.

So here is the dilemma. Whether or not the non-causalist is a Humean about causation, if he agrees that in performing an action the agent makes the action-event happen or makes the difference as to whether it happens, he appears committed to the claim that the agent causes the event to happen. If, on the other hand, the non-causalist were to deny that the agent makes the event happen or makes the difference as to whether it happens, it would seem that performing the action is not an exercise of the agent's control, which it would need to be if the agent is to be morally responsible for the action. Furthermore, note that the problems for reconciliation with the laws of nature that arise for the agent-causal view also count against non-causal libertarianism. Uncaused events, like events caused by undetermined agent-causes, threaten not to conform to the natural laws, and if they indeed do not, we have no evidence that the divergences from the laws that the view would then predict actually occur.[21]

---

[21] For a recent response to this argument, see David Palmer (2021).

THE EFFICACY AND RATIONALITY OF DELIBERATION    23

Compatibilism falls to the argument from manipulation; event-causal libertarianism is subject to the disappearing agent argument; agent-causal and non-causal libertarianism are not reconcilable with the laws of nature; and non-causal libertarianism must commit to causation after all if it is to secure control. Free will skepticism is the view that remains standing. Many concerns raised for this view are practical: can we live with a conception of ourselves as lacking free will in the sense at issue? I address many of these practical concerns in this book. For the remainder of this chapter, let me answer several important questions about what effects our deliberation and choices can have given free will skepticism.

## The Efficacy and Rationality of Deliberation

On the supposition of determinism, how do we regard the efficacy of deliberation about what to do and the selection of one of the various options for action being considered? If all of our decisions and actions are causally determined by factors beyond our control, then which option an agent selects is made inevitable by causal factors beyond her control—the distant past and the laws of nature. The effects of that selection are also inevitable by virtue of such factors. In this respect how the agent chooses and the effects of those choices are beyond her control. At the same time, there is a sense in which how an agent deliberates and chooses makes a difference to the future. Suppose you were scheduled to lead a discussion yesterday, and you considered not preparing at all, and doing something else other than preparing instead. But after deliberating—thinking of and weighing reasons for each option—you decided to prepare. Imagine also that it was causally determined that you decided to prepare, and that as a result the discussion went well and the participants benefitted from it. It still may be true—and let's suppose it is – that if you hadn't prepared, the discussion would not have gone well, and the participants would not have benefitted. In this sense your deliberation made a difference to how the discussion went and to whether the participants benefitted. One might contrast this kind of difference-making control with what Eddy Nahmias calls *bypassing*— that "our rational, conscious mental activity is *bypassed* in the process of our making decisions and coming to act" (2011, 556). Causal determination does not entail bypassing, since causally determined conscious mental activity, and deliberation in particular, can make a difference in the way just specified.

24    INTRODUCTION: CHALLENGES TO ANGER

Still, given causal determination, there are factors beyond your control—the distant past and the laws of nature—that rendered inevitable how you deliberated, the choice that resulted, and the effects it had. This combination of views may initially seem paradoxical, but one must keep in mind that if determinism is true the difference one's deliberation can make is limited. Deliberation can indeed make a difference relative to other options one was considering, but given causal determination, the non-occurrence of the options that weren't selected was made inevitable by factors beyond one's control.

The foregoing is generally accepted. However, a further problem that concerns determinism and deliberation remains unsettled. If an agent believes determinism and its upshot, he will believe that he really has only one option for action. But deliberation presupposes the possibility of more than one option for action—deliberation just is deliberation among plural options for action. Deliberation requires, in a word, a future that's *open*. The resulting concern is that a determinist who deliberates will inevitably believe a contradiction: that he has more than one option for action and that he has only one option for action (van Inwagen 1983).

Determinists have responded by arguing that the openness that deliberation requires is not metaphysical but epistemic.[22] That is, deliberation does not require that there actually are plural options for action, but that there are plural options relative to what one knows or believes. This is a complex debate that features multiple counterexamples around which to navigate, but here is my version of an epistemic account (Pereboom 2008b, 2014). First of all, we should agree that if there is a specific option that one is certain one will take, then one can't deliberate about whether to select it. If there is a specific option that one is certain one will not take, one can't deliberate about whether to select it either. It may be that one is settled that one will take an option even if one isn't strictly speaking certain that one will take it, and we can agree that neither can we deliberate about whether to select such already settled options. So in order to deliberate, one's conception of one's future must feature plural options that one isn't certain one will take or not take, and which aren't already settled. Belief in determinism is consistent with this epistemically open conception of the future.

---

[22] Examples of deliberation compatibilists include Daniel Dennett (1984), Bruce Waller (1985, 49), Tomis Kapitan (1986, 235–41), Philip Pettit (1989), Randolph Clarke (1992), John Searle (2001), Dana Nelkin (2004a, 2004b, 2011), Neil Levy (2006), Derk Pereboom (2008b, 2014), and Gregg Caruso (forthcoming). Deliberation incompatibilists include Carl Ginet (1966), Richard Taylor (1966), Hector-Neri Castañeda (1975), Peter van Inwagen (1983), E. J. Coffman and Ted Warfield (2005), Ishtiyaque Haji (2012), Yishai Cohen (2018), and David Widerker (2019).

THE EFFICACY AND RATIONALITY OF DELIBERATION    25

However, van Inwagen (1983) has argued that this sort of specification is insufficient, using a nice example. The circumstances you're in if you believe that determinism is true but your future is still epistemically open is analogous to the following situation. You are faced with two doors either of which you can leave the room by, and you know that one is open but the other is locked, but you don't know which is which. Van Inwagen says that in this situation you can't deliberate about which door to open (by contrast, say, about which door to *try* to open), and this seems right. So similarly, if as a determinist you believe only one option is really open to you and all others are closed off by virtue of determinism, you can't deliberate about which option to take—at least so the argument goes.

Responding to this argument requires a further epistemic condition, which the determinist can also endorse without having inconsistent beliefs, and this condition specifies a belief about the efficacy of deliberation (Kapitan 1996; Pereboom 2008b, 2014). In order to rationally deliberate about whether to take option 1 or option 2, you must believe that if as a result of your deliberating you judge that it would be best to take option 1, then, you would also, on the basis of this deliberation, indeed take option 1, and similarly for option 2 (Pereboom 2008b, 2014). In the case of the two doors, you as deliberator do not satisfy this condition, because for one of the two options you do not believe that if as a result of deliberation you were to judge that it would be best to take it, you would indeed take it. About one of the two doors you believe that if you were to judge that it would be best to open it, you would not open it, since you believe you can't open one of the two doors due to its being locked. This contrasts with the discussion-preparation case given the supposition of determinism. There, for each of the two options you believe, and can rationally believe, that if you judged it best that you select it, you would, on the basis of that deliberation, indeed select it. True, you would believe about one of the two *judgments* that making it is ruled out by virtue of causal determination by factors beyond your control. But nonetheless, you rationally believe that *if* you were to make either judgment on the basis of your deliberation, you would actually select the option it specifies on the basis of that deliberation.

It's important for the position I set out in this book that we can make a difference to how the world turns out by our deliberation and choice, and that this view of ourselves as deliberators is in the clear. But as I will argue in Chapter 7, we must also address the prospect that how things turn out is made inevitable by factors beyond our control. What I propose is that a rational attitude for us to have is hope, specifically, the hope for the survival and flourishing of humanity in a thriving environment. Hope is rational

26  INTRODUCTION: CHALLENGES TO ANGER

and appropriate when our interest lies in an unknown outcome due to factors beyond our control. For an analogy, suppose that we are all participants in a grand lottery, and the numbers have already been drawn but we don't know what they are. Under these circumstances it's rational for you to hope that you've won. Similarly, supposing that the future of humanity has been set by factors beyond our control, it's still rational for us to hope for the survival and flourishing of humanity in a thriving environment, and more so to the degree that this outcome is supported by evidence available to us. I propose, inspired by John Dewey's *A Common Faith* (1934), that such a hope can unite all of us, no matter which religion or absence of religion one prefers.

## The Plan for This Book

In the rest of this book, we'll explore the implications of the view set out so far for a range of moral issues. Chapter 2 asks how we might conceive of blame without retribution, and proposes an account of blame as moral protest, whose function is to secure forward-looking goals such as the moral reform of the wrongdoer and reconciliation in relationships. Chapter 3 asks whether it's possible to justify effectively dealing with those who pose dangerous threats if they do not deserve to be harmed, and contends that wrongfully posing a threat, by contrast with deserving harm for posing the threat, is the core condition for the legitimacy of defensive harming, and that a non-retributive measured aggressive stance may appropriately facilitate taking such action. Chapter 4 provides an account of how to treat criminals without retributive justifications for punishment, and argues for an account in which the right of self-defense provides justification for incapacitation accompanied by rehabilitation. Chapter 5 considers how we might forgive if wrongdoers don't basically deserve the pain of being resented, which forgiveness would then renounce, and proposes that forgiveness be conceived as renunciation of the stance of moral protest instead. Chapter 6 considers how personal relationships might function without retributive anger having the central role in responding to wrongdoing, and contends that the stance of moral protest, supplemented with non-retributive emotions such as disappointment and sadness, is sufficient. Finally, Chapter 7 surveys the options for theistic and atheistic attitudes regarding the fate of humanity in a deterministic universe replete with wrongdoing, and the attitude defended is the hope for humanity I just described.

# 2

# The Stance of Moral Protest

A pressing concern for the Buddhist and Spinozist conceptions of the practice of holding morally responsible is that if we ceased treating wrongdoers as basically deserving of the pain or harm of blame and punishment, and if we refused to target them with retributive anger, we would be left with inadequate and unsatisfactory responses to their immoral behavior. In response, I propose a conception of blame as moral protest, a stance apt to engage and at times confront the wrongdoer with reasons to forbear, and conceived as forward looking, not as the backward-looking imposition of pain or harm a wrongdoer basically deserves. I'll argue that this conception is not only practically satisfactory, but preferable from the moral point of view.

## Different Aspects of the Practice of Holding Morally Responsible

Our actual practice of holding morally responsible involves a number of different aims, and a range of responses justified by those aims. Some have argued that this complexity can be regimented, and that there is ultimately a single sense of moral responsibility that serves to unify the practice (e.g., Wallace 1994; Sher 2006; Scanlon 2009; Smith 2012). I claim that such unitary views misrepresent the practice, and here my potential allies include Gary Watson (1996), John Martin Fischer and Neal Tognazzini (2011), Dana Nelkin (2011), and David Shoemaker (2011, 2015). With them I believe that there are multiple senses of moral responsibility corresponding to different aims and attendant justifications, each of which is an aspect of our practice of holding morally responsible. While these senses are related as components of the practice, there is no simple, non-disjunctive characterization that captures them all.

Consider specifically the blaming part of the practice. One might argue that blaming essentially involves a supposition that wrongdoers deserve to feel guilt, which blame has the role of occasioning (e.g., Clarke 2013;

*Wrongdoing and the Moral Emotions.* Derk Pereboom, Oxford University Press. © Derk Pereboom 2021.
DOI: 10.1093/oso/9780192846006.003.0002

## 28  THE STANCE OF MORAL PROTEST

Carlsson 2017; Duggan 2018). Often blame is in fact intended to induce a feeling of guilt conceived as deserved due to a wrong knowingly done. However, this purpose does not exhaust the role of blaming. Political protestors might justifiably blame a leader just to motivate him to end a discriminatory policy, while not having an intention of inducing a feeling of guilt in him. There may be no significant chance of him ever feeling guilty about supporting the policy, and this may be evident to the protestors. Parents may blame their teenage children for ignoring assigned household chores just to see to their moral formation, specifically by calling them to account and presenting them with reasons to do their part. They may well not do so with an intention of inducing a feeling of guilt.

In response, the advocate of a unitary sense has several options. One is to contend that what might seem to be different senses really have a common essence. For example, one might argue that each sense of blameworthiness features, at its core, a belief that the wrongdoer is an appropriate target of resentment or indignation (Strawson 1962; Wallace 1994, 2022; Smith 2012). A second option is to eliminate all but one sense on the substantive ground that the others are not genuinely senses of moral responsibility, or for the reason that simplicity in theory is preferable. I resist these strategies, partly because I think that they don't withstand scrutiny in their own right. But I also believe that some of the senses are best eliminated from the practice while others are legitimate and remain in place. This proposal presupposes that there be distinct senses of moral responsibility in the actual practice, some to be eliminated, others retained. Reasons for maintaining that some are best eliminated are twofold. The first is that they can successfully be criticized on moral grounds, and the second is that they can be challenged because they require a sort of control in acting we do not have.

One aspect of the practice of holding morally responsible features the notion of basic desert, discussed in Chapter 1. Here again is its characterization:

> For an agent to be *morally responsible for an action in the basic desert sense* is for the action to be attributable to her in such a way that if she was sensitive to its being morally wrong, she would deserve to be blamed or punished in a way that she would experience as painful or harmful, and if she was sensitive to its being morally exemplary, she would deserve to be praised or rewarded in a way that she would experience as pleasurable or beneficial. The desert at issue is basic in the sense that the agent, to be morally responsible, would deserve such blame or punishment, praise or

reward, just by virtue of having performed the action with sensitivity to its moral status, and not, for example, by virtue of consequentialist or contractualist considerations.

We can add that the imposition of such basically deserved pain or harm, pleasure or benefit, is non-instrumentally good, in accord with Noa Latham's (2004) and Michael McKenna's (2012, 2020) specifications.[1] By contrast, the imposition of non-basically deserved painful or harmful blame, or the provision of pleasurable or beneficial praise, when justified on grounds that are ultimately forward looking (discussed below), would be merely instrumentally good, that is, only by virtue of a distinct good.

There are proposed senses of moral responsibility that feature non-basic desert. James Lenman (2006) and Ben Vilhauer (2009a) articulate views on which deserved harms, that is, deserved punishments, are justified not by consequentialist but by contractualist considerations. On Vilhauer's conception, legitimate punishments are those agreed upon by parties in a hypothetical contracting situation, whose objective is to set up a just society (Rawls 1971). While at the level of judicial decision the justification for such impositions is backward looking, the overarching practice itself is justified by contractualist reasoning aimed at justice, and not by backward-looking, desert-involving considerations.

Another notion of non-basic desert invokes good consequences to justify desert claims (or does so more directly than the contractualist position just canvassed). John Rawls (1955) presents a two-tiered theory in which legal justifications for punishment are entirely backward looking, in that lawyers, judges, and juries appeal only to backward-looking reasons for punishment, while the practice itself is justified on forward-looking, consequentialist grounds. In a similar vein, Daniel Dennett (1984, 2003; Dennett and Caruso 2020) and Manuel Vargas (2013, 2015, 2022) advocate views according to which the practice-level justifications for blame and punishment invoke backward-looking considerations of desert, while that desert is not basic because at a higher level the practice is justified by the anticipated consequences, such as fostering and refining the ability to recognize and respond to moral considerations, and protecting people from the dangers

---

[1] Latham (2004) uses the term "intrinsically good" for what McKenna (2012, 2020) calls "non-instrumentally good." For McKenna, X is intrinsically good just in case X's being good is independent of its relations to anything wholly distinct from X, and this definition fits naturally with the meaning of "intrinsic" as "non-relational."

# 30 THE STANCE OF MORAL PROTEST

wrongdoers pose.[2] On the two-tier accounts developed by Dennett and Vargas, our practice of holding agents morally responsible in a desert sense should be retained because doing so would have the best overall consequences relative to alternative practices.[3]

One might object that penalties and rewards justified by anticipated consequences on the two-tier model do not really qualify as genuinely *deserved*, since on such a view they are ultimately just incentives (Doris 2015). In reply, to cite the sports analogy endorsed by Vargas (2013, 2015) and Dennett (Dennett and Caruso 2020), it seems legitimate to say that someone who commits a foul in a sport deserves the penalty for that foul. But such sports desert isn't basic—it's instead founded in considerations about how the particular sport works best. As Vargas puts it, "foul calls in a sport can have an explicitly teleological justification and this need not preclude our fully inhabiting our righteous anger at the execution of some foul internal to the game" (Vargas 2015, 2667). Similarly, suppose penalties for criminal behavior are justified on consequentialist, say deterrence grounds, by the anticipated effect of safety. Imagine that, as on Rawls's proposal, lawyers and judges consider only backward-looking reasons to punish, while their practice is justified on forward-looking grounds that lawyers and judges never consider or invoke. It then arguably makes sense for the lawyers and judges to regard the penalties as deserved (in Rawls's (1971) theory, such desert is conceived as "post-institutional"). The crucial point for the present purpose, however, is that on the accounts proposed by Dennett and Vargas, the ultimate justifications are forward looking, and they do not endorse justifications that appeal to basic desert, and in this respect they are amenable to the free will skeptic. Whether expressions of resentment and indignation can sometimes be justified on

---

[2] Although Vargas did not explicitly invoke a two-tier view in his book *Building Better Beings* (2013), he did endorse this position two years later in a response to John Doris's (2015) symposium comment: "I am happy to adopt the two-tiered view about desert that [John Doris] extracts, with some charity, from my discussion in [*Building Better Beings*]. What his discussion has helped me to appreciate is that I can allow that first-order desert claims are justified retrospectively while maintaining that, at the level of the practice, these kinds of desert claims are prospectively justified" (Vargas 2015, 2666). Victoria McGeer (2014) and Dale Miller (2014) argue that a careful reading of P. F. Strawson (1962) indicates that he held such a view, despite how it is typically characterized.

[3] In my terminology, desert on a two-tiered conception, where the ultimate justificatory tier is consequentialist and/or contractualist, counts as non-basic desert. Vargas (2022) suggests a definition of basic desert on which desert can count as basic on such a two-tiered conception.

practical and forward-looking grounds is an important issue we'll consider in due course.

For many the intuition that wrongdoers deserve to be punished concerns basic desert in particular, by contrast with its non-basic counterpart. This diagnosis can be supported by a type of thought experiment about punishment that derives from Kant (1797/2017), in which there is no instrumental good to which punishing a wrongdoer would contribute. Imagine that someone on an isolated island brutally murders everyone else on the island, and that he is not capable of moral reform due to consuming hatred and rage. Add that there is no longer a society on the island whose rules might be determined contractually. It's not difficult to summon the intuition that this murderer still deserves to be punished severely. But this desert would be basic, since the example eliminates the options for non-basic desert. Similar examples can be constructed to test whether a case of moral anger with wrongdoers has a basic desert presupposition. Often one's attitude toward a wrongdoer has both a forward-looking and a backward-looking desert component. But set up an example in which the forward-looking component is subtracted. Would one still think the attitude, and targeting the wrongdoer with its expression, is legitimate? Very often the reflexive answer will be affirmative.

However, there are reasons to be skeptical of the sense of moral responsibility that involves basic desert. As discussed in Chapter 1, a major concern is that for an agent to basically deserve pain or harm she must have a kind of control in action, a type of free will, that is unavailable to us, and the free will skeptic argues that this concern can't be successfully countered (Strawson 1986; Waller 1990, 2011; Pereboom 1995, 2001, 2014; Levy 2011; Caruso 2012, 2021). A further issue is that for a number of contending general normative ethical theories, the notion of basic desert would seem to have the role of an awkward supplement. For instance, despite Kant's (1797/2017) apparent invocation of basic desert in justifying the death penalty, that appeal would seem not to be justified by any formulation of the Categorical Imperative, which he held to be the supreme and comprehensive moral principle. An additional objection is that the conception of basically deserved harm amounts to the idea of harm as a non-instrumental good (McKenna 2012, 2019), and whether a harm can be a non-instrumental good might be doubted. Motivated by these concerns, the conception of moral responsibility I endorse rejects basically deserved pain and harm, pleasure and benefit, altogether.

32  THE STANCE OF MORAL PROTEST

## Moral Anger and Basic Desert

A free will skeptic calls into question the role of moral anger in our practice of holding morally responsible insofar as that anger presupposes basically deserved pain or harm. Cognitivists about the emotions hold that emotions have a component that is cognitive—a judgment, a thought, an appraisal, or perhaps a belief held with some degree of confidence, that is, a credence (e.g., Lazarus 1991; Nussbaum 1997). These components count as cognitive because they can be true or false, by contrast, say, with sensations of taste on typical accounts. Martha Nussbaum argues that "emotions are evaluative appraisals that ascribe high importance to things and people that lie outside the agent's own sphere of control." In her view, these appraisals are cognitive and also *eudaimonistic*, that is, made from the perspective of its subject's aims (Nussbaum 2004, 443; see also 2001). An instance of fear tends to involve a cognitive appraisal regarding the presence of danger, conceived as a threat to the subject's goals. Some cognitivists, for example Robert Solomon (1988), hold that emotions just are such cognitive elements, and nothing more. A criticism of that view is that two subjects might each make cognitive appraisals regarding the presence of danger, conceived as a threat to their goals, while one has fear and the other not. This criticism suggests the cognitivist position on which an emotion consists of a cognitive and a distinct affective component.[4] I've been attracted to such a view in the past, at least for higher-level emotions such as resentment and indignation.[5] With regard to resentment and indignation, I endorsed the view that they involve as a cognitive component the supposition that the offender basically

---

[4] This is compatible with Nussbaum's view that no specific feeling or bodily state should be included as a necessary element in the definition of a type of emotion, because of the variety with which a single emotion is realized in different people (Nussbaum 2004, 443; see also 2001). In favor of her demotion of a feeling component Nussbaum cites the fact that emotions can be non-conscious; but, plausibly, feelings—consider anger with a parent—can be non-conscious. Against this, Nussbaum (2004, 475) writes: "Michael Stocker tries to get round the problem non-conscious emotions pose for a feeling-based view problem by speaking of 'unconscious affect,' but I just don't know what he is talking about (see p. 61 n. 62). Whatever 'affect' is in his account (and I really am not sure), surely the idea of an 'unconscious feeling' would be a contradiction in terms." On Nussbaum's view, animals have emotions, and for this reason cognitive components need not be linguistically formulated, and instead they may require only "the general ability to see X as Y, where Y involves a notion of salience or importance for the creature's own well-being" (2004, 444; see also 2001).

[5] On Paul Griffiths's (1997) view, there are basic emotions, had by non-human animals, for example, which he calls "affect program emotions," of which a type of anger is a species. Perhaps no anger had by non-human animals has a basic desert presupposition, and this may also be the case for very young children (Pereboom 2014, 128–9).

MORAL ANGER AND BASIC DESERT    33

deserves to be the recipient of their expression (Pereboom 2014, 128–9; cf., Pereboom 2007a, 119; Wallace 1994; Nussbaum 2016, 93). However, as I indicated in Chapter 1, while I believe that resentment and indignation often and typically involve that supposition, I do not defend the more inclusive claim. But insofar as his resentment and indignation do feature that supposition, the skeptic about basic desert would stand to be doxastically irrational, since he would then have conflicting cognitive attitudes.

Alternatively, one might opt for non-cognitivism about the emotions, and for the reactive attitudes specifically. Ted Honderich, for example, denies that having a reactive attitude constitutively involves having any belief. He maintains, however, that having a reactive attitude is nevertheless nomologically connected with a belief about desert-involving moral responsibility. If one loses the belief that an agent is morally responsible in this sense, it's psychologically impossible to persist in having the associated reactive attitude (Honderich 1996, 856–9). Given this conception, a free will skeptic's having a reactive attitude would result in doxastic irrationality for the reason that it conflicts with a belief she has that is nomologically connected with the attitude.

Justin D'Arms and Daniel Jacobson maintain that while emotions are not to be individuated by any cognitive content, they nevertheless propose that emotions can be *cognitively sharpened* by such content. In their example, a faculty member is furious upon being denied tenure, and such "tenure rage is what we will call a cognitive sharpening of anger." More generally, cognitive sharpenings of an emotion are "types constructed by specifying a subclass of instances of an emotion, or other affective state, in terms of some thought that they happen to share" (D'Arms and Jacobson 2003, 137). Given such a view, moral anger might be cognitively sharpened by a belief that its target basically deserves to be blamed and perhaps punished in a way that she would experience as painful or harmful. A skeptic about free will who had such cognitively sharpened moral anger would be doxastically irrational by virtue of having conflicting beliefs, one theoretical, the other serving to sharpen her emotion.

A further view, which I now find very attractive, is devised to address the problem of recalcitrant emotions. One may fear flying, despite judging and believing that it's safe. Patricia Greenspan (1988, 1992), noting this problem, responded by contending that "instead of claiming that emotions entail evaluative beliefs I take it that they sometimes just involve evaluative thoughts held in mind by intentional states of comfort or discomfort" (Greenspan 1992, 293). Such thoughts are held in the mind but not

## 34 THE STANCE OF MORAL PROTEST

endorsed by the subject. On the version of this view set out and defended by Robert Roberts (1988, 2003, 2013), the cognitive component of an emotion is a *concerned construal*, a kind of response-relevant perceptual take that need not include a belief or judgment as a component. Emotions represent an agent as being a certain way that calls for a response, but the subject who has the emotion can avoid affirming that the agent is correctly represented that way.[6] In Roberts's phrasing, the emotion features an analogue to a judgment that the subject of the emotion does not necessarily share, even if the subject does share it in typical cases. In his example, someone raised in a strict religious household but who has since become more worldly may feel guilty for going to the theatre, but not affirm that he has done something wrong, which is nonetheless a component of his emotion of guilt:

> The subject's judgment often coincides with the emotion's "judgment," but often it does not. In this way our emotions are like other perceptions: Usually we believe our eyes and ears, but not always. Our perception tells us that the stick in the water is bent (this is how we perceive it), but we judge otherwise, disagreeing with our eyes. Similarly, I may know that my anger is unjustified—not a correct perception of my situation. In that sort of case, it is wrong to say that my anger is my judgment. We might say that it "has a mind of its own." (Roberts 2003, 89)

From my point of view a valuable feature of Roberts's account is that it can explain how one can be retributively angry with someone while at the same time denying that she basically deserves to be the recipient of an expression of that anger. Retributive anger is a perspectival take that has a basic desert presupposition, but its subject might not affirm or endorse this presupposition, or have significant credence in it.

My critique of our practice of holding morally responsible is compatible with each of the proposals on the nature of emotion considered so far, and so my project does not require arguing for one view to the exclusion of the others. Here is an ecumenical compromise among the proposals canvassed that is sufficient for my purposes. When a mature human subject targets another with an expression resentment or indignation, her moral anger will typically be associated with the cognitive content that he basically deserves

---

[6] R. Jay Wallace (1994, 45–6) also affirms that a subject of an emotion may not accept its content.

MORAL ANGER AND BASIC DESERT    35

to be blamed and perhaps punished in a way that he would experience as painful or harmful. However, it is possible that the subject of the emotion at the same time reject that content about basic desert, for instance if she is convinced by free will skepticism. On a view in which the subject of the emotion must actually have a belief with the content associated with an emotion, she would have contradictory beliefs if she retained the moral anger. On a view in which the emotion features the content as a construal but the subject of the emotion need not endorse it, she need not then have contradictory beliefs. On either type of account, rejecting the basic desert belief, as the free will skeptic recommends, would destabilize the emotion, which would, barring countervailing considerations, tend to result in its fading away.

Critics sometimes suggest that the claim that our ordinary attitudes have a basic desert presupposition or associated belief implausibly overintellectualizes them, in particular given the complexity of the characterization of basic desert. However, as Frank Jackson (1998) argues, many of our ordinary ethical concepts turn out to have philosophical characterizations that are quite complex, and this complexity can be drawn out by philosophical reflection that uses examples to test and refine proposals for such characterizations. Accordingly, our ordinary ethical notions may often have complex characterizations which are never or hardly ever explicitly represented. The concept 'lying' is a famous case. Virtually everyone in our moral community has this concept, and uses it in thought and speech, but arguably almost no one explicitly represents its complex accurate characterization, since almost no one has thought about it carefully, and even those who have are likely to get it wrong. That this is so is illustrated by the complexity of James Mahon's recent proposal, a contender for the best characterization of lying currently available:

> To lie $=_{df}$ to make a believed-false statement (to another person), either with the intention that that statement be believed to be true (by the other person), or with the intention that it be believed (by the other person) that that statement is believed to be true (by the person making the statement), or with both intentions.
>
> (Mahon 2008, 227–8; for a thorough discussion see Mahon 2016)

Similarly, ordinary moral anger might well have a complex basic desert presupposition, one which is seldom if ever explicitly represented.

## 36 THE STANCE OF MORAL PROTEST

### Moral Responsibility without Basic Desert

The sense of moral responsibility, and blame in particular, that I endorse is largely forward looking with regard to how blaming and punishing, praising and rewarding are morally justified (Pereboom 2013a, 2014, 131–8; 2015, 2017a). Blaming in this sense does not involve the intentional infliction of pain or harm conceived as basically deserved, or as a non-instrumental good. Rather blaming is morally justified insofar as it can be anticipated to secure good consequences, such as protection from harmful immoral behavior, reconciliation with those who have done one wrong, moral formation of those disposed to do wrong, and retention of integrity of victims of wrongdoing.[7] Immoral actions are often harmful, and we have a right to protect ourselves and others from those who are disposed to behave harmfully. Immoral actions stand to impair relationships, and we have a moral interest in undoing such impairment through reconciliation. Because we value morally good character and actions that accord with it, we have a stake in the moral formation of character when it is beset by dispositions to misconduct. We also have an interest in restoring the sense of integrity of victims when it has been undermined by wrongdoing. On some conceptions such restoration of integrity is secured by the wrongdoer being punished on the ground of basic desert, but it need not be. It might be secured instead by apology and compensation upon recognition of wrongdoing and sincere contrition.

Michael McKenna (2012) has proposed a communicative conception of moral responsibility that, with just a few revisions, is amenable to the view I endorse.[8] In his *conversational* theory, actions of a morally responsible agent are potential bearers of a type of meaning by indicating the quality of will the action manifests (McKenna 2012, 92–4; see also Arpaly 2006). Blaming an agent who manifests an immoral quality of will in action is an expression of an attitude such as resentment or indignation, and its goal is to communicate to him a moral response to the quality of will the action

---

[7] Forward-looking accounts of blame have recently been set out by Manuel Vargas (2013, 2015), Victoria McGeer (2014, 2015), McGeer and Philip Pettit (2015), Coleen Macnamara (2015a, 2015b), Daphne Brandenburg (2019), and Anneli Jefferson (2019). Note that one might hold such a forward-looking view of the justification of blame while also affirming that basic desert claims place limitations on who can legitimately be blamed and in which ways.

[8] Communicative theories of blame, broadly speaking, are endorsed by Manuel Vargas (2013, 2015, 2022); Victoria McGeer (2013, 2015); McGeer and Philip Pettit (2015); Coleen Macnamara (2015a, 2015b); Miranda Fricker (2016); Daphne Brandenburg (2019); Elinor Mason (2019); Anneli Jefferson (2019); and Santiago Amaya (2019).

indicates. Morally responsible agents understand that other members of the moral community are apt to attribute this type of meaning to their actions. When their actions are morally charged, they understand themselves to be introducing such a meaningful contribution to a conversational exchange. McKenna labels this initial stage of the conversation *moral contribution*. In the case of apparent wrongdoing, in the second stage the agent is blamed by a respondent; McKenna calls this stage *moral address*. In the third stage, *moral account*, the blamed agent may offer an excuse, a justification, or an apology. The respondent might at this point continue the conversation by forgiving or punishing the wrongdoer. In a subsequent stage the blamed agent may be restored to full status in the moral community. McKenna points out that not all blaming conforms to this model; blaming the dead, for instance, does not. Here he invokes a paradigm-similarity model for the meaning and extension of a concept (Rosch 1972, 1973). The blame conversation as he describes it is a paradigm case of blaming, and examples of other sorts, such as blaming the dead, qualify as instances of blaming because they are sufficiently similar to such paradigm cases.[9]

I endorse a conversational model of blame, with the provision that the objectives of blaming are forward-looking goals such as protection, reconciliation, moral formation, retention of integrity, and that intentional infliction of pain or harm conceived as basically deserved is excised (Pereboom 2013a, 2014, 2017a). In addition, by contrast with Dennett's and Vargas's accounts, those who blame represent forward-looking considerations such as reconciliation and moral formation as their explicit objectives, and they do not endorse blame as featuring intentional infliction of pain or harm conceived as deserved. Being called out for having done wrong may be painful, and one may experience the pain of regret (to be discussed) as a result. However, those who blame do not conceive of the pain of blaming as a non-instrumental good imposed in blaming, but rather as an instrumental good in service of the forward-looking goals to be secured. The rejection of the pain of blaming as non-instrumental good is

---

[9] As an attractive alternative to McKenna's Rosch-inspired view on such cases, Elinor Mason (2019) distinguishes *detached* blame from *communicative* blame. Communicative blame involves an expectation on the part of the blamer that the wrongdoer recognizes the wrong and feels remorse. Detached blame, by contrast, does not aim for recognition from the agent. Unlike communicative blame, the detached sense is not essentially concerned with the wrongdoer's quality of will. Blaming the dead and blaming political figures with which one has no connection may qualify as detached and not communicative blame.

38 THE STANCE OF MORAL PROTEST

significant, and lies at the core of what motivates the forward-looking account.

Similarly, one who rejects basically deserved pleasure and benefit might also adopt a conversational account of praise. Daniel Telech (2021) sets out a conversational view of praise, on which emotional attitudes, such as approbation and gratitude, that are connected with praise, have the role of directing moral invitations to their targets, specifically, "invitations to jointly value the meaning of the addressee's action for the praiser" (Telech 2021, 165). The praiser initiates this interaction by inviting the praiseworthy agent to emotionally engage with the praiser's recognition of the action. The aim of this invitation is to occasion in that agent a self-reactive attitude that mirrors the content of the praiser's attitude. That attitude is a type of pride, "directed pride," a reflexive emotion whose evaluative focus is "the meaning for another of one's manifestation of good will" (Telech 2021, 164). When praise is accepted in this way, praiser and praiseworthy agent mutually recognize one another as standing for a common value. Telech points out that such an account of praise may accommodate the notion of basically deserved benefit, it need not, and I agree. On the forward-looking version, we may praise an agent for morally exemplary actions in order to strengthen the dispositions by which they are motivated. Doing so can also have a protective goal, because strengthening such dispositions has the effect of reducing the incidence of dangerous behavior. Corresponding to reconciliation is the notion of celebrating successes in relationships. Praising an action, on Telech's account, may have this celebratory function as well (Pereboom 2001, 2014; Telech 2021).

On the conversational model I envision, as in McKenna's, the agent's responsiveness to reasons is engaged in the envisioned process for both blame and praise. Focusing on blaming, it qualifies as a mode of communication whose objective, in the first instance, is having a wrongdoer acknowledge that the reasons for which he acted are morally inadequate. At the stage of moral address, we may ask the wrongdoer for the reasons why he acted, with the intent of having him acknowledge the wrongness of his action. If in the moral conversation it becomes clear that he acted without moral excuse or justification, we may intend for him to come to see that the disposition issuing in the action is best eliminated. If the conversation proceeds as it should, this change is produced by way of the wrongdoer's recognition of moral reasons to make it. More generally, it is an agent's responsiveness to reasons together with the forward-looking aims that explains why he is appropriately blamed in this conversational and largely forward-looking sense.

Note that responsiveness to reasons is sometimes conceived as a kind of free will, in particular by contemporary compatibilists. But since no one denies that human beings are reasons-responsive, no one denies that we have free will in this sense. Reasons-responsiveness enters the arena of controversy only because compatibilists propose it as a substantive necessary condition for basic desert responsibility (e.g., John Fischer (2007, 82); Michael McKenna (2012, 2020); and Carolina Sartorio (2016)). The largely forward-looking conception of moral responsibility I advocate is also compatible with agents' being causally determined in their actions by factors beyond their control, but this is uncontroversial and hasn't been challenged. It's noteworthy that there is a transparent connection between reasons-responsiveness and the forward-looking notion of responsibility, and that a similar tie is lacking for basic desert moral responsibility. Responsiveness to reasons is clearly required for an agent to be subject to moral formation on the basis of presentation of reasons, while the link between reasons-sensitivity and an assumption of basic desert and the attendant reactive attitudes is not similarly transparent or direct. Even if we are so constructed as to assume basic desert or have basic desert-linked reactive attitudes when and only when reasons-responsive agents act wrongly, the transparent connection that we see with the forward-looking notion of moral responsibility is absent.

## The Stance of Moral Protest

Pamela Hieronymi (2001), Matthew Talbert (2012), and Angela Smith (2013) have proposed that blame be understood as moral protest. I follow their lead, not for characterizing blame generally, which I believe has multiple senses, but for the sense of blame I endorse. For Hieronymi, Talbert, and Smith, the negative reactive attitudes have an essential role in blaming as moral protest, while in my view they do not. Blame has the function of engaging with the wrongdoer, but that engagement need not be facilitated by the reactive attitudes, but instead by the stance of moral protest. As I see it, moral protest is a psychological stance, a posture of mind that has certain functions, which are manifest as dispositions to act (Schwitzgebel 2013). It is a stance of opposition to an agent for having performed (or apparently having performed) a specific immoral action or a number of immoral

40   THE STANCE OF MORAL PROTEST

actions, or for having (or apparently having) a disposition to act immorally (and similarly, *mutatis mutandis*, for immoral omissions). Its function in our moral practice is primarily to engage wrongdoers by communicating opposition to wrongdoing of a general type, together with moral reasons for the agent to refrain from it. This communication might be confrontational to varying degrees, depending on the circumstances.[10]

As just noted, Hieronymi (2001) connects moral protest to the negative reactive attitudes, as do the others just mentioned. For Hieronymi moral protest in fact is a reactive attitude such as resentment, which Strawsonians understand as a second-person attitude I have toward an agent who has wronged me (cf., Darwall 2006).[11] By extension, Strawsonians may include indignation as a kind of moral protest, which they understand as a vicarious attitude one has toward an agent who has wronged someone else. By contrast, the notion of moral protest I want to single out lacks any essential connection to these negative reactive attitudes or to their expression. Like resentment and indignation, the stance of moral protest motivates engagement with the wrongdoer, which may be confrontational. But unlike the reactive attitudes, it is distinguished by its forward-looking objectives, typically aiming to change, for the better, an agent's dispositions to act. The ultimate goal of many instances of moral protest is to transform states of affairs beyond an agent's dispositions, for example improve a relationship or the life of a family, or to enhance economic and social justice.

David Brink and Dana Nelkin (2013) view blame as having a core-and-syndrome structure, and I agree that this is so for the moral protest sense of blame. They argue that there is a core present in all cases of blame, an aversive attitude toward the wrongdoer that is predicated on the belief or judgment that he is blameworthy. The syndrome features the disposition to manifest this aversive attitude in various ways. For the sense I blame I endorse that core is the stance of moral protest, which does not essentially involve anger, whether it be retributive of any other sort, but rather constructive, forward-looking engagement with wrongdoers.

David Shoemaker (2017) argues that anger is essential to blame—that is, blame in the accountability sense (more on this later). Accordingly, one might hold that an agent is blameworthy just in case he merits anger for his wrongdoing. As Shoemaker points out, there are two versions of this view,

---

[10] This moral protest account responds to George Sher's (2006, 1–6) and Shaun Nichols's (2007) criticisms of my earlier view (Pereboom 1995, 2001), insofar as their concern was that the blaming stance that I then endorsed was insufficiently engaged and confrontational.

[11] Hieronymi, however, does not affirm that resentment typically involves a presupposition of desert, and neither does Strawson, while I contend that it in fact does.

one response-dependent, the other response-independent. He himself develops and defends a Strawsonian response-dependence account of blame, in which the designated response is anger:

*Fitting Response-Dependence about the Blameworthy*: The blameworthy (in the realm of accountability) just is whatever merits anger (the angerworthy); that is, someone is blameworthy (and so accountable) for X if and only if, and in virtue of the fact that, she merits anger for X.

Shoemaker argues that what unifies all of the properties that make anger an appropriate response to wrongdoing is just that it merits anger, and this is what makes the account truly a response-dependent one. I don't wish to focus on the response-dependence feature of the account, but rather on the choice of anger as the designated response. One should note that Shoemaker individuates emotions by what they motivate, and he understands anger as the emotion that motivates confrontation. I contend that one can confront a wrongdoer for the wrong he has done without in any natural sense being angry with him (more on this below).[12]

The response-*in*dependent account also features anger as a response, but not as a response in which blameworthiness *consists*:

*Response-Independence about the Blameworthy*: The blameworthy consists in a property (or properties) of agents that makes anger at them appropriate, a property (or properties) whose value making is ultimately independent of our angry responses. Anger at someone for X is appropriate if and only if, and in virtue of the fact that, she is antecedently blameworthy (and so accountable) for X. What makes her blameworthy is thus ultimately response-independent.

On such an account, blameworthiness is not essentially dependent on the response of anger. As I'll understand this view, anger, in the form of reactive attitudes such as resentment and indignation, is instead the property that fixes the referent of the term 'blameworthy'. The blameworthy consists in properties that in fact actually merit such anger, even if blameworthiness doesn't just consist in whatever merits anger.

Here I raise two concerns about the choice of anger in each of these accounts. First, there are cases of blameworthiness that are plausibly not

---

[12] Shoemaker's specific understanding of 'anger' raises a question about whether my concerns about anger as a general response to wrongdoing joins the issue with Shoemaker's position, a question I won't aim to answer here.

42   THE STANCE OF MORAL PROTEST

cases of angerworthiness. Athena is a parent, and her teenage children misbehave in minor, common, predictable ways; they squabble, fail to clean their rooms, text their friends when they should be sleeping. Some parents would respond with anger, but Athena doesn't, and instead responds from the sense of a duty to morally educate, combined with care, but not with anger. The angry response is at best optional, in many such cases inappropriate. This is also the case for Basil, a high school teacher, whose students often misbehave in common ways. They come unprepared not having done the assigned reading, distract their classmates by talk not related to class material, and surf the internet instead of participating and paying attention. Basil responds with protest, engaging his students constructively, but not with anger. For both Athena and Basil, the angry response stands to be counterproductive and to undermine forward-looking effectiveness and respect, occasioning counterproductive reaction without moral improvement. Evidence for the inappropriateness of anger in these kinds of cases is that parents and teachers who express anger in such situations are routinely criticized for responding inappropriately (Pereboom 2019, 2020).

One possible fix is to claim that the misbehavior in these cases is nevertheless *pro tanto* angerworthy, and that's enough to make it blameworthy. In reply, extending a point Victor Tadros (2016, 119) makes against Michael Moore's (1998) view about alleged *pro tanto* duties to criminalize, it's a strike against a response being *pro tanto* justified if it is almost never appropriate, which in these kinds of cases the angry response would seem to be (Pereboom 2019).

A second concern is that anger has a strong tendency to distort judgments of blameworthiness, and that it's *prima facie* questionable that to be blameworthy is to be worthy of a reactive attitude that systematically distorts precisely those judgments. Surveys conducted by psychologist Mark Alicke and his associates indicate that subjects who spontaneously evaluate agents' behavior unfavorably are apt to exaggerate their causal control and any evidence that might favor it while deemphasizing counterevidence, thus distorting blameworthiness judgments (Alicke et al. 1994, 2012; Alicke 2000). Alicke calls this tendency *blame validation*. In the last several decades, impressive experimental evidence that blaming behavior is widely subject to problems of these kinds has been mounting (Nadelhoffer 2006). As Austin Duggan (2020) contends, there is reason to believe that it's the anger that accompanies blame that leads to these problems. Anger increases tendencies to overlook mitigating features of the relevant circumstances, to discount the role of uncontrollable factors, and to rely on stereotypes, for example, about ethnicity, in assessing blameworthiness (Lerner et al. 1998;

Goldberg et al. 1999; Litvak et al. 2010). Psychologist Julie Goldberg and her associates found in one of their studies that when the retributive desire to harm is not satisfied, anger "activate[s] an indiscriminate tendency to punish others in unrelated situations without regard for whether their actions were intentional" (Goldberg et al. 1999, 783).

One might object that even if anger has these blame-distorting propensities, it might still be the best candidate for a general emotional attitude associated with blame. But I contend that moral protest, as a psychological stance, is in general a better fit. As the examples of Athena and Basil illustrate, in relationships between children and parents, teachers and students, anger is frequently non-optimal in realizing moral improvement, and is often regarded as inappropriate, while the moral protest is not similarly defective. The stance of moral protest avoids anger's propensity to allow only a humiliating or else a defiant response. Protest without anger that communicates moral reasons to forbear allows for acknowledgment and acceptance of those reasons without humiliation, preserving self-respect.

By contrast with relationships between parents and their children and teachers and their students, Strawson (1962) draws our attention to the emotional attitudes that serve as responses to serious wrongdoing in intimate relationships and close friendships. My sense is that the influence of Strawson's account has had the effect of participants in the debate about moral responsibility focusing intensely on those attitudes, and thus on resentment in particular, and much less so on attitudes appropriate for typical wrongdoing in other kinds of human relationships and interactions. Negative reactive attitudes may be particularly salient for serious wrongdoing in the context of intimate relationships and close friendships (although not only in such contexts). However, much wrongdoing takes place in relationships in which such attitudes and their expression are generally questionable and often inappropriate, such as those between parents and children and teachers and students.

One might object that in this context these relationships are not paradigm cases, since they are not relationships of mutual regard but in which there is a relevant discrepancy in maturity. But consider relationships among college faculty members and administrators. Wrongdoing in such professional relationships is to be expected from time to time. For example, faculty are partial to their close colleagues and political allies when it comes to hiring and perks, and often the resulting advocacy is wrong. Suppose Chloe is a professor who at times faces these sorts of issues with her colleagues. Imagine she responds not with anger, but calmly with arguments

## 44 THE STANCE OF MORAL PROTEST

that invoke the wider moral considerations. In such cases, angry responses often reduce one's effectiveness, and tend to cause false judgments which in turn motivate defective solutions (cf., Nussbaum 2016). Here again, anger is typically suboptimal as a response to wrongdoing, and often inappropriate and out of place.

### Blame as Moral Protest

These observations call for a sense of blame that does not invoke anger as an essential component. It's moral blame that I'm concerned with, not, for instance, sports blame or aesthetic blame. I'm proposing blame as involving the stance of moral protest, where moral protest is not essentially tied to anger of any sort. When Athena, Basil, and Chloe protest the wrongdoing at issue, they are morally concerned, but not resentful or indignant, and particularly intent on engaging the wrongdoer with reasons to forbear. Blame as moral protest, in which the notion of anger has no role, can be normatively characterized as follows:

*Moral Protest Account of Blame*: For A to appropriately blame B is for A to adopt a stance of moral protest against B for immoral conduct B has performed and that A is epistemically justified in attributing to B, and A's adopting this stance is morally justified.

The immoral conduct will typically be an immoral action or omission. There are cases in which an action considered separately from the reasons for which it's performed is not wrong, but the reasons for which the agent acted make the overall conduct wrong, and worthy of moral protest (Haji 1998; Hanser 2005; Markovits 2010; Nelkin 2011, 104–5). Sometimes blame is misplaced, since no immoral conduct has been performed, and then moral protest would still count as blame but not as appropriate blame. For example, A may adopt a stance of moral protest against B but believe falsely and without adequate justification that B acted wrongly, for instance when A's belief is defectively motivated by anger or envy. It's possible that A believe truly and with epistemic justification that B acted wrongly and not be morally justified in adopting the stance of moral protest, if, for example, B is known by A to be mentally ill in a way that precludes the moral justifiability of blame. Often blame has the objective, as in Hieronymi's (2001) proposal, of moral protest against an agent for a past immoral action that indicates a continuing threat due to the agent's persisting disposition to behave in that immoral way. Moral protest might in fact be directed at an agent specifically for having the disposition to act wrongly, without singling out a particular instance of wrongdoing. But not all appropriate moral protest need be focused on reforming dispositions. For instance, blame as moral protest may have a role for a victim of wrongdoing in the process of reasserting and retaining her integrity even when the wrongdoer has already undergone reform.

An objection to this moral protest conception of blame is that while unexpressed blame is possible, the idea of unexpressed protest is not even coherent, and hence blame cannot be moral protest. The concern is that protest is essentially communicative, and unexpressed protest is not communicative. Eugene Chislenko (2019) has recently provided a reply to this objection, citing the distinction Coleen Macnamara draws between the activity of communicating—of which mental states kept private are not instances—and the idea of a communicative entity (Macnamara 2015b, 217). An unsent email, even though it does not actually perform the function of communicating, nevertheless has the function of evoking uptake of representational content in a recipient (Macnamara 2015a, 548). An unsent email is thus communicative in nature. Similarly, unexpressed protest is communicative in nature. For a case in point, an unsent email might be an unexpressed message of protest. Chislenko writes: "We can even say, as [Angela] Smith does of blame, that the email 'expresses protest, and...seeks some kind of moral reply' (Smith 2013, 39), even when the email is unsent" (Chislenko 2019, 169). To this we might add that the email can express moral protest even if its author never intends to send it. Similarly, someone who privately blames may never intend to communicate it.

On my proposal, moral protest is fundamentally a psychological stance one takes in opposition to wrongdoing, one that is apt for being communicated, and which has the general function of being communicated to the wrongdoer, a function that may not be implemented in specific instances. Having a function that is not actually implemented in certain instances is familiar from biology—for example, a heart that fails to pump blood and yet has the function of pumping blood—and should not be regarded as unusual.

In accord with the protest account of blame, we can specify the following amended version of Shoemaker's response-dependent view about the blameworthy in the specific sense I want to endorse:

*Fitting Response-Dependence about the Blameworthy*: The blameworthy just is whatever merits moral protest (the protestworthy); that is, someone is

## 46 THE STANCE OF MORAL PROTEST

blameworthy for X if and only if, and in virtue of the fact that, she merits moral protest for X.

This sense has a response-independent variant, which also invokes moral protestworthiness but features properties that make wrongdoing protest-worthy but are independent of our protest responses. Appropriate moral protest can nonetheless serve to fix the properties that the term 'blamewor-thiness' picks out:

*Fitting Protest-Response-Independence about the Blameworthy*:   The blame-worthy consists in a property (or properties) of agents that makes morally protesting their wrongdoing appropriate, a property (or properties) whose value making is ultimately independent of our response of moral protest.

I won't choose between these two positions.

To each of them one might object that the sense of blameworthiness characterized cannot qualify as accountability, as in Shoemaker's specifica-tion, for the reason that accountability (as a kind of blameworthiness) essentially involves the supposition of the appropriateness of resentment or indignation, types of anger. However, Shoemaker proposes the following characterization of accountability:

> To be accountable for something is to be liable to being appropriately *held* to account for it, which is to be eligible for a range of fitting responsibility responses with a built-in confrontational element.   (2015, 87)

Moral protest, in my conception, may indeed be confrontational. But being confrontational is compatible with absence of any sort of anger or any expression of it. One might be firm in one's engagement with the wrongdoer without being angry. Note also that it's possible to be confrontational and feign anger, and not to be genuinely angry. Parents sometimes feign anger with their children when they believe it best for effective communication of wrongdoing. If, alternatively, accountability is specified as presupposing that the wrongdoer basically deserves to be the recipient of a painful or harmful confrontational response, I would want to frame the discussion in terms of a different sense of blameworthiness.

In the proposed sense of blame, blaming does not essentially involve retributive anger, or anger of any sort, while it does essentially involve tak-ing on the stance of moral protest. But despite retributive anger involving a presupposition of basic desert, which according to the desert skeptic is a false presupposition, retributively angry blame on the part of the skeptic may still sometimes be practically rational, where practical rationality encompasses the prudential and the moral. It may be, for instance, that in certain cases opposition to abuse is especially effective if it is motivated by retributive anger. Then retributively angry protest may be practically rational for the desert skeptic, and the putative epistemic irrationality of a false presupposition might be accepted for practical reasons.

More generally, moral anger can be epistemically and motivationally valuable in discerning cases of immorality in which the wrongdoer has the capacity for reform, by contrast with cases in which reform is ruled out. When it's ruled out, for example, when the wrong is done by someone who has an incurable mental illness that impairs moral functioning, we tend not to be angry and instead take the objective attitude. If it's possible to affirm moral anger insofar as it has this epistemic and motivational function while rejecting its role in justifying deserved pain or harm, then such anger may qualify as practically rational even for the basic desert skeptic,[13] although it may be that the epistemic and motivational role can be played by other attitudes we've discussed. In addition, as we shall see in Chapter 3, there is an attitude that is plausibly classified as a form of moral anger that does not involve a supposition of desert: the measured aggressive stance that, for instance, soldiers may adopt in battle, which may be fully epistemically and practically rational for the skeptic about basic desert. This stance may be decisively confrontational, and I would thus agree with Shoemaker that there is a type of angry confrontation with wrongdoers that is entirely in the clear.

The forward-looking view of moral responsibility I've set out is in broad agreement with Martha Nussbaum's (2016) account. Civil rights leader Martin Luther King is one of her main illustrations of how retributive anger might ideally be transformed into forward-looking attitudes and responses, a transformation that she calls "the Transition." About King's "I have a dream" speech, she writes:

> There is indeed anger in the speech, initially, and the anger summons up a vision of rectification, which naturally takes, initially, a retributive form. But King gets busy right away transforming retributivism into work and hope. For how, sanely really, could injustice be made good by retributive payback. The oppressor's pain and lowering do not make the afflicted free.

[13] Thanks to Michael McKenna for this point.

48 THE STANCE OF MORAL PROTEST

Only an intelligent and imaginative effort toward justice can do that. This is what I mean by "the Transition." (Nussbaum 2016, 32–3)

King's speech includes, for example, "I have a dream that one day even the state of Mississippi, a state sweltering with the heat of injustice, sweltering with the heat of oppression, will be transformed into an oasis of freedom and justice," which in Nussbaum's view expresses both the initial anger and the transition to a forward-looking perspective. She tends to think of this transition as featuring a forward-looking kind of anger, transition anger, which in a strong form qualifies as outrage, and is focused on unjust circumstances, for example. Nussbaum (2016, 36) discusses the objection that this state isn't really a species of anger, and responds that she doesn't care much how we answer that question. What I propose in its place is the stance of moral protest, which can be firm and resolute, and in these respects can be similar to outrage—but not always. For Athena, Basil, and Chloe the protest stance is appropriate, but outrage is not. My sense is that the protest stance was common for King in his fight for civil rights. In addition, although he was angry, it's not evident that his anger was typically retributive, by contrast with being defensive and protective of a community and a people. There is an important difference, in that defensive anger, as I'm conceiving it, needn't presuppose basically deserved targeting, as we will discuss in Chapter 3.

## Self-Blame and Regret

Just as one might adopt a stance of moral protest against another for his having performed an immoral action, one might also take on such a stance in response to one's own immoral actions (Pereboom 2021b). One might view an action one has performed as wrong, and the disposition that issues in it as morally defective, and as a result take on a stance of opposition against oneself for having performed the action, a stance that includes opposition to one's acting wrongly in this general way based on moral reasons to refrain from it. In adopting this stance, one may aim at one's own moral formation or at reconciliation with someone one has wronged. If, for example, one has verbally abused a friend, and the relationship with him has been impaired as a result, one might assume a stance of protest against that past action with the aims of eliminating one's disposition to act wrongly in this way and of reconciliation with the friend.

SELF-BLAME AND REGRET   49

In accord with Randolph Clarke's (2013) suggestion, in this context we might consider whether a wrongdoer deserves or basically deserves to feel guilty and the pain that it features (cf., Carlsson 2017; Duggan 2018). Clarke proposes, first, that there is value in the recognition by an agent who is blameworthy that he is blameworthy, and a further response, the feeling of guilt, provides a morally valuable and intuitively fitting addition to this acknowledgment. This response would have value insofar as it expresses moral concern for having done wrong and for those one has wronged.

To facilitate this discussion, let's adopt the convention—which is not intended to reflect natural language—to have 'guilt' refer to an attitude that presupposes basic desert, that is, one's basically deserving to feel pain accompanying the recognition that one has done wrong, and 'regret' refer to a similar attitude, which also involves feeling pain that accompanies the recognition that one has done wrong, but does not presuppose that this pain is basically deserved. Given these definitions, I contend that regret can be a morally fitting additional reaction to one's own wrongdoing, which can adequately play the moral role that guilt often has. Two of my allies on this point, Bruce Waller (1990) and Hilary Bok (1998), argue that the fittingness of a pained feeling can be accounted for by a recognition that one has not lived up to one's standards for morality and self-control without the need to invoke desert at all. Bok sets out an example in which one has done something wrong on account of which one suffers a painful response, a response that she compares to heartbreak (1998, 168–9). Bok calls this response 'guilt,' but I'm substituting 'regret' for her 'guilt,' given the specified convention of reserving 'guilt' for a desert-involving feeling:

The relation between the recognition that one has done something wrong and the guilt one suffers as a result...is like the relation between the recognition that one's relationship with someone one truly loves has collapsed and the pain of heartbreak. Heartbreak is not a pain one inflicts on oneself as a punishment for loss of love; it is not something we undergo because we deserve it...Similarly, the recognition that one has done something wrong causes pain. But this pain is not a form of suffering that we inflict on ourselves as a punishment but an entirely appropriate response to the recognition of what we have done, for two reasons. First, our standards define the kind of life we think we should lead and what we regard as valuable in the world, in our lives, and in the lives of others. They articulate what matters to us and living by them is therefore by definition of concern to us. If we have indeed violated them, we have slighted what we take to be of value, disregarded principles we sincerely think we should live by, and failed to be the sorts of people we think we should be. The knowledge that we have done these things must be painful to us.

I think Bok is right to contend that feeling pain on account of a recognition that one has not lived up to one's moral standards or standards for self-control need not involve a presupposition of desert.

Here are several additional analogies. One might appropriately feel pained that one failed to meet one's standards for playing chess when one understands that one's substandard performance is due to factors beyond one's control, while this pain is not deserved, let alone basically deserved (Pereboom 2017a). A similar example is due to Shoemaker (2021), one in which a baseball player feels pain upon making a mistake while he doesn't deserve to feel this pain. A different kind of example is due to McKenna: it would appropriate, and basically so, to feel the pain of grief upon the death of a loved one, while this pain is not deserved (McKenna 2012, 2019). Each of these examples features the appropriateness of feeling pain without its being deserved.

By analogy, I contend that it's appropriate that wrongdoers feel regret for what they've done without the pain of regret being basically deserved, or deserved at all. But how might the feeling of pain upon recognition of wrongdoing be appropriate—and basically so—but not be basically deserved? What's required is an indicator for distinguishing basically deserved pain from merely basically appropriate pain. Both Andreas Carlsson (2017) and I (Pereboom 2017a, 2021b) have suggested that the pain of guilt, due to its presupposition of desert, would be prima facie appropriately *imposed*, while the pain of grief would never be. Let me now try to make this suggestion more precise.

If pain were basically deserved on account of wrongdoing, this would give rise to a prima facie moral permission for suitably situated agents to intentionally impose it on the wrongdoer for a non-instrumental reason. If a wrongdoer basically deserves to be punished, then there is a prima facie presumption that the right sorts of authority, perhaps parents or state officials, are prima facie permitted to intentionally impose it on him for a non-instrumental reason. Guilt, given that it presupposes basic desert, would then involve pain that one regards as appropriately intentionally imposed on oneself by oneself or by suitably situated others. The pain of grief lacks this feature. Despite grief and the pain that it involves being basically appropriate for those who have experienced loss of a loved one, no one is permitted to intentionally impose the pain of grief on someone in such circumstances for a non-instrumental reason. One may inform the bereaved that she has undergone the loss of a loved one, and it may be evident that she will feel the pain of grief as a result, but this does not amount to intentionally imposing the pain of grief for a non-instrumental reason. The pain of grief is never basically deserved despite at times being basically appropriate. Accordingly, the permissibility of imposition for a non-instrumental reason serves as a criterion for distinguishing basically deserved from non-basically deserved but appropriate pain.

In the passage from Bok that we just examined, she makes two claims regarding her analogy of the pain of regret to the pain of heartbreak. The first is that the pain of regret is not a pain that one inflicts on oneself as a punishment. The second is that it is not a pain that we undergo because we deserve it. Her phrasing suggests that she conceives of the two claims as linked: the pain of heartbreak's not being appropriately imposed is connected with its not being deserved. My related proposal is that it is impermissible to intentionally impose the pain of regret for a non-instrumental reason, and this is what distinguishes it from the putative basically deserved pain of guilt (cf., McKenna 2012, 2019). This allows that one may issue a moral protest against a wrongdoer for the reason that it stands to result in moral formation, foreseeing that it will result in the pain of regret. Here it is not the case that pain is imposed on a wrongdoer for a non-instrumental reason. Perhaps it is intuitive that in certain circumstances it is permissible to intentionally impose the pain connected with recognition of wrongdoing on others and on oneself for a non-instrumental reason, but the retraction of basic desert has its costs, and this is one of them.

Dana Nelkin provides a thought experiment that in her view supports the stronger conclusion that the pain of any attitude in the vicinity of guilt and regret is never appropriately imposed for a non-instrumental reason. This allows that it be appropriately imposed for instrumental reasons, for the sake of some further good:

> Imagine that you have a special power (call it "The Look"). By looking at another person in the right way, you can bring about feelings of guilt. The other person culpably wrongs another—it is not a trivial offense, but neither is it the worst possible. Imagine that she betrays the confidence of a friend and as a result the friend has a bad day. You now have the chance, by looking at the offender in that way you have mastered so well, to bring about guilt feelings in her. It would be the easiest thing, requiring nothing

52 THE STANCE OF MORAL PROTEST

in the way of effort or sacrifice. But now also imagine that there is no further good to come from your exercising this power you have. The offender
has already resolved not to do the same sort of thing again, no one else is
around to experience the results, the relationship is either already irrepa-
rably damaged no matter what, or all has been forgiven, so that there is no
benefit to the relationship to be had, and so on. Would you be making a
mistake, or leaving a reason on the table, so to speak, by taking a pass on
inducing this painful feeling? Would there be a (non-instrumental) moral
good that would have been costless to achieve that you failed to promote?
I do not have the intuition here that you would be making this kind of
mistake. That suggests to me that there is not a pro tanto reason to induce
guilt that stems from blameworthy action alone.   (Nelkin 2019c, 186)

Focusing on the case in which the wrongdoer has resolved not to betray
again and has been forgiven, the thought experiment provides intuitive reason to deny that the pain of recognition of wrongdoing is ever basically
deserved and thus appropriately imposed for a non-instrumental reason.
However, it does not yield a challenge to regret, since the pain of regret may
never be appropriately imposed for a non-instrumental reason, because it is
never, by its nature, basically deserved (Pereboom 2021b).

There are in addition forward-looking justifications for regret. Ben
Vilhauer (2008) advocates an account of a pained response upon wrongdoing that grounds it in sympathy with those one has wronged, and on which
such regret is fitting because that sympathy is morally appropriate. It's credible that such sympathy-based regret can motivate repentance and moral
reform and reconciliation with those one has wronged. Vilhauer argues that
because such sympathy-based remorse is also other-directed rather than
merely self-directed, it is morally preferable to guilt grounded in basic
desert. Guilt so conceived has no essentially forward-looking moral objective. By contrast, sympathy-based remorse involves taking on the perspective
of the agent one has wronged, which has morally beneficial consequences.

## Summary

I've set out and endorsed a conception of blame on which to blame another
does not essentially involve a supposition of basically deserved pain or
harm, or anger of any sort. To blame is rather to take on a stance of moral
protest in virtue of an action one regards as morally wrong, which need not

involve anger. The reasons for taking on this stance are forward looking: moral formation or reconciliation in a relationship that has been impaired as a result of the wrongdoing, protection from wrongdoing, and restoration of the integrity of victims of wrongdoing. Regret, a painful response to one's own wrongdoing which (by stipulation) does not involve the supposition that the pain it involves is basically deserved, may appropriately accompany self-blame. The pain of guilt, an attitude distinct from regret, conceptually involves basic desert since it involves the supposition that it would be prima facie permissible for those who are suitably situated to intentionally impose it on a wrongdoer for a non-instrumental reason. The pain of regret, by contrast, does not involve this supposition.

# 3

# Defensive Harm and Measured Aggression

## Introduction

It's generally agreed that we have the right to harm in self-defense and defense of others. But under what conditions do we have this right? A controversial issue concerns the role of moral responsibility in the account of this right to harm. Does this right require that the agent who is liable to such harm be morally responsible, let alone morally responsible in the basic desert-involving sense, for posing a threat? I will argue that moral responsibility does not have this crucial role, and that instead the crucial criterion is weaker, that of wrongly posing a threat. This requires that it's possible for an agent to wrongly pose a threat without being morally responsible in any sense for doing so. This result is highly relevant to my views on dealing with criminal behavior, since I argue that the right to detain criminals is grounded in the right to self-defense and defense of others, and that this right to detain a criminal does not depend on his moral responsibility.

In addition, we are emotional beings, and we are apt to confront injustice emotionally. If defensive action against wrongdoing is justified and involves risk, an appropriate emotional attitude is arguably required for it to succeed. Given that the right to defensive harm does not depend on its target's moral responsibility, that attitude should not require an assumption of deserved infliction of pain or harm. I shall argue that we have available to us in such contexts a measured aggressive stance that may presuppose that its target wrongly poses a threat, while it does not depend on the assumption that its target deserves infliction of pain or harm.

A number of philosophers have proposed that moral responsibility, and culpability or blameworthiness in particular, for posing a threat indeed has this crucial role in account of defensive liability. (In this context, 'blameworthy' and 'culpable' are treated as synonymous.) Kimberly Ferzan, for instance, has developed a detailed account on which culpability is necessary

*Wrongdoing and the Moral Emotions.* Derk Pereboom, Oxford University Press. © Derk Pereboom 2021.
DOI: 10.1093/oso/9780192846006.003.0003

INTRODUCTION 55

for liability to defensive force (Ferzan 2012; cf., Alexander and Ferzan 2009). The term 'moral responsibility' as used in this particular philosophical discussion has a number of distinct senses, some of which, as we shall see, have no essential connection with blameworthiness or culpability. The sense of moral responsibility invoked by the accounts at issue is essentially tied to culpability and thus to blameworthiness, so that necessarily, if an agent is morally responsible in this sense for knowingly having done wrong, she is culpable and blameworthy for the wrongdoing. This philosophical discussion focuses on the role of moral responsibility in the justification of defensive killing in particular, and here I follow suit.

Seth Lazar (2009) raises a practical concern for culpability having this proposed grounding role. He cites the context of war, but the concern arises in other situations in which the permissibility of defensive killing is at issue:

> What culpability [i.e., moral blameworthiness] gains in theory, however, it loses in application: many unjustified combatants are morally innocent of the threats that they pose, excused either by duress or because they reasonably believe their cause to be justified, in conditions of uncertainty and high risk. Moreover, in the radically information-poor context of war, there is no way for justified combatants to discriminate between innocent enemies and those who are indeed culpable for fighting. (Lazar 2009, 701)

I agree with Lazar that in practice the culpability criterion often isn't feasible. If one holds that ethics is essentially practical in the sense that its principles and recommendations must be feasible in the actual situations to which they apply, this will be an especially pressing concern.

But furthermore, I contend that the culpability criterion does not withstand scrutiny based on moral intuitions about specific cases together with their systemization. Lieutenant Colonel Peter Kilner, who has taught military ethics at the United States West Point Military academy for many years, cites the type of case my argument invokes:

> Consider this: You are a military police officer on post. You know and genuinely like a friendly, mentally disabled teenage boy who lives in a housing area. One day, you respond to a report of a man carrying a gun outdoors. As you approach the scene, you realize that the man with the gun is the disabled teen, and he is approaching a group of children in a fenced-in park. As you exit your vehicle—separated from the boy by 10 yards and a chain-link fence—he begins firing on the children. Should you immediately

shoot the boy? Yes. Will it feel good? No, because you recognize the tragedy of the situation. You know that he is not entirely morally responsible for the harm he is doing. You don't blame the boy. You blame whoever left the gun unsecured, whoever permitted him to play first-person-shooter video games, etc., but you also recognize that it is your moral duty to protect the innocent people who will be killed if you don't act. Likewise, soldiers should be taught that they inflict lethal violence on enemy combatants in war not because they hate the enemy—and not because the enemy soldiers are evil—but because they love those they are sworn to protect and defend. It is appropriate for combat veterans to feel sadness for the enemy they killed. It is also appropriate and good for them to feel an enormous sense of pride and satisfaction for the civilians and fellow soldiers they protected.

(Kilner 2017)

This example casts doubt on the culpability condition, and is also, as Kilner's reflection suggests, relevant to the kinds of emotional attitudes that appropriately accompany defensive killing.

In the view I propose, whether an agent is a threat by virtue of what he wrongly does or omits to do is the core explanatory consideration, and the main necessary condition, for whether he is liable to be defensively killed. In this context, to act wrongly is to perform an action that is itself morally prohibited, and to do so for bad moral reasons. So in this context to administer an antidote when one thinks one is administering a poison, and to do so because one wants to kill the victim for immoral reasons, doesn't count as wrong because the action is itself not morally prohibited. An animal who cannot consider and act on moral reasons cannot wrongly pose a lethal threat, even though that animal can pose a lethal threat which is unjust in the sense that the person who is lethally threatened isn't liable to it. Whether an agent is in addition culpable is not such a core explanatory consideration or necessary condition, although it may be relevant to determining who, of a number of competing threats, are permissibly killed (Arneson 2018). I shall argue that while an agent who is culpable for posing a lethal threat is a prototypical example of liability to defensive killing, paradigm cases also include non-culpable mentally ill and clinical psychopaths who wrongly pose lethal threats.[1] Emotions other than retributive anger are appropriate to defensive killing. Kilner mentions sadness in the case he cites, but in the

---

[1] This view is in important ways similar to the one suggested by Elizabeth Anscombe (1956/1981).

PERMISSIBILITY OF DEFENSIVE KILLING 57

heat of confrontation, an occurrent, temporary, measured aggression would be fitting, or so I will argue.[2]

## Permissibility of Defensive Killing

The following is an example of defensive killing that would be accepted as morally permissible by virtually anyone who agrees that we have a right to defensively kill:

*Rational Threat*: Al attempts to extort money from Beth by threatening to kill her unless she pays. Beth, who is innocent in all relevant respects, refuses to pay. One night soon afterward, Beth sees Al, gun in hand, stealthily entering her bedroom. The only way Beth can reliably defend herself against being shot is to shoot to kill Al first. Beth knows that Al is rational and suffers from no mental illness and was not coerced or manipulated.

If defensive killing is ever permissible, it is for Beth in this case. Why is this so? First, Al would seem to be a prototypical example of an agent who is *defensively liable*. Jonathan Quong characterizes this notion as follows:

*Defensive Liability*: A is liable to have some harm, H, imposed on him by B when he forfeits at least one of the claim rights he possesses against B's imposition of H, and where the imposition of H is part of defending some person from a wrongful threat. (Quong 2020, 21)

Al poses a wrongful lethal threat to Beth, and in Quong's view he thereby forfeits a claim right he has not to be killed. Claim rights are rights that are matched by corresponding duties (Hohfeld 1919). On one conception, if Al has a claim right not to be killed, all others have at least a *pro tanto* duty not to kill him. On Quong's account, Al forfeits this claim right and is thus

---

[2] Ishtiyaque Haji (1998, 2002) has argued that actions cannot be wrong if the agent is causally determined to act by factors beyond her control. If an action was wrong for an agent, then she ought not to have performed it. But 'ought' implies 'can,' and so if she could not have avoided performing it, it's false that she ought not to have performed it, and then it's false that it was wrong for her to have performed it. Immanuel Kant (1781/1787/1987) invokes such a consideration in his claim that determinism and morality are incompatible (Pereboom 2006b). I address this argument in Pereboom (2001, 141–8, 2014, 138–46), and in this book in Chapter 6, pp. 148–49.

58   DEFENSIVE HARM AND MEASURED AGGRESSION

liable to defensive killing.[3] In defining liability one might forgo invoking rights forfeiture in favor of duties, as Victor Tadros (2011, 2016) and Helen Frowe (2014) propose. One might contend, for example, that due to violating a duty not to lethally threaten, Al has no legitimate complaint against Beth eliminating the threat by killing him, and argue that by contrast with rights forfeiture, this is what grounds his liability to defensive killing.

Quong specifies that for an agent to be defensively liable she must pose a wrongful threat. As he points out (Quong 2020, 20), Derek Parfit (1984) distinguishes distinct notions of wrongness relevant to this characterization. An act is wrong in the *fact-relative* sense when it would be wrong if the agent knew all of the relevant facts. An act is wrong in the *belief-relevant* sense if it would be wrong if the wrongdoer's relevant non-moral beliefs were true. An act is wrong in the *evidence-relevant* sense when the act would be wrong if the relevant facts are what the available evidence provides reason to believe they are.

The fact-relevant sense as applied to actions is fairly remote from any sense of 'wrong' invoked in our ordinary moral practice. If an action is merely fact-relevantly wrong, but not belief- or evidence-relevantly wrong, it's dubious that it's true to say it's wrong. Consider Judith Thomson's example of an action that is merely fact-relatively wrong:

> *Day's End*: B always comes home at 9:00 p.m., and the first thing he does is to flip the light switch in his hallway. He did so this evening. B's flipping the switch caused a circuit to close. By virtue of an extraordinary series of coincidences, unpredictable in advance by anybody, the circuit's closing caused a release of electricity (a small lightning flash) in A's house next door. Unluckily, A was in its path and was therefore badly burned. (Thomson 1990, 229)

If someone who understood these facts were to say to B "what you did was wrong!" what's said would widely be regarded as false. Wrongness in the ordinary sense is instead a matter of the reasons on which one acts or omits to act, or of those one negligently omits to access or act on (Haji 1998; Hanser 2005; Markovits 2010; Nelkin 2011, 104–5); or else of the quality of will with which one acts or omits to act (Arpaly 2006; McKenna 2012). Is this ordinary sense the belief-relevant one? A parent who gives a child

---

[3] Even if rights forfeiture is not deeply explanatory, use of the term is arguably in the clear (Renzo 2017).

medicine that makes her ill but which the parent believes to be safe is nonetheless acting wrongly in the ordinary sense if the parent would have believed that the medicine was unsafe had she read the warning on the container. Here evidence-relevance comes into play. However, if evidence of the medicine's being unsafe would turn up only in a not-yet conducted scientific study, the parent would not be acting wrongly in the ordinary sense. Here Quong (2020, 30) appeals to reasonable expectations for responsiveness to evidence, and I think this resolution is plausible. I prefer an account on which the evidence-relative wrongness of posing a threat is relevant to defensive liability while the fact-relative sense is not, although such an account faces countervailing pressure.[4]

As I see it, the way to formulate the most pressing moral issue for liability to defensive killing is by asking: which features of agents and their threat-posing actions and omissions ground the *prima facie* moral permissibility of third-person intentional killing of one such agent to save just one innocent potential victim? First, it is generally wrong to intentionally kill one innocent person to save one innocent person. Perhaps it is generally permissible to intentionally kill one innocent person to save ten, but not to save just one. However, in paradigmatic cases of defensive killing in which the right to harm in self-defense is invoked, it is permissible to intentionally kill one person to save one innocent person. Second, as Ferzan (2012) and Quong (2012, 2020) argue, if an agent A is liable to defensive killing by virtue of wrongly posing a lethal threat to B, then, in general, not only B but also a third party is *prima facie* morally permitted to intentionally kill A.[5] Quong (2020, 59–67) differentiates such cases from those in which one has only an agent-relative permission, that is, a permission that doesn't generalize to other agents (Nagel 1986), to kill a lethal threat.[6] He contends that only such agent-relative permissibility holds for person C who due to no

---

[4] I address Quong's (2020) concession to fact-relativity briefly below, without providing a detailed defense of my preference for avoiding it.

[5] The permissibility is *prima facie*; as Doggett (2018) and Quong (2020, 6) argue, actual permissibility requires that provisions other than liability be met.

[6] Larry Alexander and Michael Moore (2016) characterize agent-relativity as follows: "An agent-relative reason is so-called because it is a reason relative to the agent whose reason it is; it need not (although it may) constitute a reason for anyone else. Thus, an agent-relative *obligation* is an obligation for a particular agent to take or refrain from taking some action; and because it is agent-relative, the obligation does not necessarily give anyone else a reason to support that action. Each parent, for example, is commonly thought to have such special obligations to his/her child, obligations not shared by anyone else. Likewise, an agent-relative *permission* is a permission for some agent to do some act even though others may not be permitted to aid that agent in the doing of his permitted action. Each parent, to revert to the same example, is commonly thought to be permitted (at the least) to save his own child even at the cost of not saving two other children to whom he has no special relation."

## 60 DEFENSIVE HARM AND MEASURED AGGRESSION

fault of her own is falling towards another person D, thereby posing a lethal threat to D (Nozick 1974, 24–5; Otsuka 1994; see Frowe 2020 for objections to agent-relative accounts). In such innocent-threat cases, Quong maintains that D may kill C in self-defense, but no third party may kill C to defend D. (I don't think that it is clear that D may kill C, and discuss this issue below.)

In accord with these provisions, here is a notion of liability to defensive killing salient to the discussion. Where A and B are individual human persons,

A is *robustly liable to defensive killing* just in case A poses a threat to B as a result of which B and third parties are *prima facie* morally permitted to intentionally kill A to defend B from that threat.

As Tyler Doggett (2018) points out, 'liable' has multiple senses in legal and philosophical discussions, and I do not claim that this is the only viable or philosophically interesting sense. Rather, this definition singles out a sense of defensive killing which is salient in that justification for liability in this sense would be distinct from and must be stronger than other proposed justifications. Specifically, agent-relative justifications do not license killing by third parties, and lesser-evil justifications do not generally license killing one to save one. Lesser-evil justifications of defensive killing appeal to the greater good that can thereby be attained. One might argue, for instance, that it is permissible to intentionally kill one innocent person to save ten innocent people because killing the one is the lesser evil. Lesser evil justifications need not be consequentialist, since they may be sensitive to outcomes and to deontological considerations (e.g., Tadros 2011; Frowe 2014, 2020). One might be justified on lesser evil grounds in foreseeably but unintentionally killing one innocent person for the sake of five, but not in intentionally killing one for the sake of five.

## Against Culpability

Quong characterizes culpability as follows, and subsequently argues that it is not a necessary condition for defensive liability. I agree with his conclusion, but the case I make differs from his:

*Culpability*:
1. The agent acts in a way that results in a threat of impermissible harm to an innocent person or persons.

AGAINST CULPABILITY    61

2. The agent intends or foresees this harm, or else is acting recklessly or negligently.
3. There are no relevant excusing conditions (e.g. blameless ignorance, duress, or diminished mental capacity). (Quong 2020, 23; cf. Ferzan 2012)

Condition 3 collapses P. F. Strawson's (1962) distinction between excuses and exemptions (cf., Watson 1987). Excuses appeal to temporally specific circumstances of action or omission to mitigate blameworthiness, while exemptions invoke long-lasting or permanent conditions such as mental illness to indicate general absence of moral responsibility. Ferzan in effect invokes both excuses and exemptions: "an intention to kill that is the product of duress, insanity, or mistake, is also not a culpable attack" Ferzan (2012, 684). Quong's criterion is incomplete, as the widely endorsed requirement of adequate responsiveness to reasons—and to moral reasons in particular—is absent (e.g., Wolf 1990; Fischer 1994; Wallace 1994; Nelkin 2011; McKenna 2012; Sartorio 2016).

The following is an example, similar to the one cited by Kilner, of an agent who is intuitively robustly liable to defensive killing for wrongly posing a threat, but not culpable for posing the threat due to exemption from moral responsibility:

*Mentally Ill Threat*:   Chris has abducted a child, has a knife at her throat, and threatens to kill her. He is mentally ill, as a result of which he is insufficiently responsive to reasons to count as morally responsible. But he understands what it is for an action to be morally wrong and can reliably distinguish acts that are morally wrong from those that are not. Chris is threatening to kill the child because he wants to extort a ransom from her parents. Deb is on the scene, is an excellent shot, and can easily kill Chris without harming the child. Deb's shooting Chris is the sole means available to save the child. Deb knows that Chris suffers from the mental illness and is generally exempt from moral responsibility and is thus not culpable for posing a threat to the child.

Despite Chris's not being culpable, this an intuitively clear case of permissibility of third-person defensive intentional killing of one to save one. Suppose the scenario were real, and Deb refrained from shooting Chris citing the reason that Chris is exempt from moral responsibility due to mental illness and thus not culpable. Imagine that Chris then killed the child. Most people would be morally outraged. The proposal that culpability is a necessary condition of the permissibility to

## 62 DEFENSIVE HARM AND MEASURED AGGRESSION

intentionally kill one to save one conflicts with widespread intuitions about *Mentally Ill Threat*.

Consider also a lethal threat posed by a clinical psychopath, that is, someone who scores over 30, that is, very high, on Hare's Psychopathy Checklist, an interview and case history-based measure, the current diagnostic standard (Hare 2003):[7]

*Psychopathic Threat*: Ed has abducted a child, has a knife at her throat, and threatens to kill her. He is a clinical psychopath, as a result of which he is insufficiently responsive to reasons to count as morally responsible, although he understands what it is for an action to be morally wrong and can reliably distinguish acts that are morally wrong from those that are not.[8] Ed is threatening to kill the child because he wants to extort a ransom from her parents. Frank is on the scene, is an excellent shot, and can easily kill Ed without harming the child. Frank's shooting Ed is the sole means available to save the child. Frank knows that Ed is a clinical psychopath and is hence generally exempt from moral responsibility, and is thus not morally responsible for posing a threat to the child.

Despite Ed's not being culpable for posing the threat, this is also an intuitively clear case of moral permissibility of intentional killing of one to save one.[9] These examples suggest that the core necessary and explanatory condition for the permissibility of defensive killing is wrongly posing a sufficiently serious threat, by contrast with culpably doing so.[10]

It is indeed possible for an agent to act wrongly, that is, for bad reasons or with bad quality of will, while being exempt from moral responsibility—in any sense essentially connected with culpability or blameworthiness—due

---

[7] For commentary, see Forth et al. (2013). North American non-incarcerated males score a rate at a mean of 4 on the Psychopathy Checklist, while inmates score a mean of 22 (Kiehl 2014, 10). Those scoring 30 or higher are in a sense extreme cases (Doris and Murphy 2022).

[8] See Shoemaker (2015, 146–57) for an argument that psychopaths have this cognitive ability. In his view, discussed below, what's missing is certain forms of empathy (157–62).

[9] Another possible case of wrongly but not culpably posing a threat involves brain manipulation. If the manipulation is suitably set up, the agent would wrongly pose the threat without being culpable for doing so. Doggett (2018) uses a manipulation case to argue against the culpability condition, and his case might be embellished so that it's intuitive that the manipulated agent nevertheless wrongly poses the threat.

[10] One might resist this conclusion by stipulating moral responsibility, and culpability in particular, as a necessary condition of defensive liability. A problem for this move is that the moral phenomenon at issue may generalize beyond the boundary of this stipulation, and it would then be only the stipulation that would preclude a more expansive purview for defensive liability.

AGAINST CULPABILITY    63

to being insufficiently sensitive or responsive to reasons. John Fischer (1994; cf., Fischer and Ravizza 1998) divides responsiveness to reasons into two factors: *receptivity*, that is, the ability to recognize reasons for acting, and *reactivity*, the ability to act on reasons that one recognizes to be good reasons. On the most plausible view, agency must exhibit certain *significant patterns* of receptivity and reactivity to reasons to count as morally responsible (McKenna 2005; Pereboom 2006a). This allows for the possibility that an agent generally fails to exhibit the right sorts of patterns of reasons-responsiveness while still acting on reasons, and in fact on morally bad ones.

A clinical psychopath might commit a crime for a morally bad reason while impaired in his capacity for empathy, thus being insufficiently responsive to moral reasons to count as a morally responsible agent (Watson 2011; Nelkin 2015). David Shoemaker (2015) argues that psychopaths are not blameworthy due to a defect in empathy of specific kinds. On his account, there are several varieties of empathy, including cognitive empathy, the ability to cognitively discern the mental states of others without a connection to motivation, which psychopaths typically do have. But absent in central cases of psychopathy are evaluational and emotional empathy. The capacity for evaluative empathy is the ability to see the projects of another as worthwhile from her perspective. The capacity for emotional empathy is the ability to engage with another's perspective so that one feels what she feels, "not as a matter of mere emotional contagion, but as a function of genuine engagement with your affective stance" (Shoemaker 2015, 159). Due to lacking capacities for evaluational and emotional empathy, psychopaths are impaired in their responsiveness to moral reasons, and as a result not blameworthy in either the accountability and answerability sense (Chapter 1, and discussed below). John Doris and Dominic Murphy defend a similar position: clinical psychopaths are not morally responsible because they suffer from *moral blindness*, "an inability to genuinely appreciate the reasons, like avoiding causing suffering to others, for refraining from wrongdoing." In their view, "this inability does not...prevent psychopaths from identifying conduct regarded as illegal, or, we're inclined to think, immoral. But what this impairment does involve...is an inability to *care* about moral considerations, except in so far as it has implications for the psychopaths' perceived self-interest" (Doris and Murphy 2022). Like Shoemaker, Doris and Murphy contend that normal moral cognition when situated in actual social interaction is emotional (for similar views, see Nichols 2004; Prinz and Nichols 2010; Greene 2014; D'Arms and Jacobson 2021). They argue that due to their emotional deficits, psychopaths are largely incapable of

64 DEFENSIVE HARM AND MEASURED AGGRESSION

such engaged moral cognition, and are therefore entitled to exemption from culpability.[11]

My claim is that *Mentally Ill Threat* and *Psychopathic Threat* are cases in which agents are permissibly defensively killed due to wrongly but not culpably posing lethal threats. An alternative is to contend that the justification for defensive killing in these examples is the same as in the case of a lethally dangerous grizzly bear (Otsuka 1994). The bear neither culpably nor wrongly poses a threat to the hiker, yet it would be generally agreed that a ranger may intentionally kill the bear to prevent the hiker being killed. So perhaps Chris and Ed are permissibly defensively killed not because they wrongly pose threats, but because they are relevantly similar to a dangerous grizzly bear, whose posing a lethal threat is neither culpable nor wrong. Michael Otsuka (1994) suggests that some mentally ill lethal threats, such as those who suffer from incurable acute forms of psychosis, are relevantly similar to grizzly bears in moral standing, and are permissibly killed for that reason. But in *Mentally Ill Threat* and *Psychopathic Threat* Chris and Ed understand what it is for an action to be morally wrong, they can reliably distinguish actions that are morally wrong from those that are not, and they can act on moral reasons. These characteristics relevantly distinguish them from grizzly bears. They are not culpable for posing threats only because they are not sufficiently responsive to moral reasons. We treat mentally ill people like Chris and psychopaths like Ed very differently from non-human animals, and the characteristics of Chris and Ed just discussed explain why we do. Given these considerations, it's implausible to assimilate the permissibility for defensive killing in the case of Chris and Ed to the case of the dangerous grizzly bear.

As mentioned earlier, culpability, supposing it involves basic desert, may still, if we were ever culpable in this sense, be relevant to who is permissibly intentionally killed to save an innocent person. Faced with the choice of

---

[11] Doris and Murphy (2022) point out that "different individuals fall on different points on the PCL-R, and an individual scoring 20, while still quite different from the norm, might present differently than someone meeting the conventional cutoff of 30, who in turn might be distinguishable from a high-scorer with of 34 or better—individuals who impress researchers as possessed of 'something qualitatively very different' compared with individuals scoring only a few points less at 30 (Borg & Sinnott-Armstrong 2013, 108). Different individuals with psychopathic tendencies, even those who score similarly, might present with differing endowments of capacities relevant to the attribution of moral responsibly, and it is possible that high-function 'successful psychopaths' are sometimes morally responsible—at least to a greater extent than the low functioning, high-scoring recidivist." They also speculate that there may well be multiple types or subtypes of psychopathy (Mokros et al. 2015), or alternatively, that psychopathy should not be thought of as a single disorder (Maibom 2018, 72).

preventing the death of an innocent person by killing an agent who culpably poses a lethal threat or one who wrongly but non-culpably poses a lethal threat, it might be that only the culpable threat is permissibly killed (e.g., Arneson 2018). But that issue is distinct from what accounts for the permissibility of intentional killing of one to save one.

One might argue that Chris and Ed are permissibly killed not because they wrongly pose lethal threats, but just because they pose lethal threats, and would be permissibly killed even if they were innocent. So, in general, are innocent lethal threats, those that pose a lethal threat but neither culpably nor wrongly, robustly liable to defensive killing, that is, are they subject to the *prima facie* permissibility of third-person intentional killing of one to save one? Some think so (e.g., Thomson 1991; Tadros 2011; Frowe 2014; Doggett 2018), and this results in a potential objection to my proposal, since my view features wrongly posing a threat as a necessary condition on robust liability to defensive killing. Consider agents who pose lethal threats who do not do so wrongly, such as:

> *Falling Person*: Falling Person is blown by the wind down a well at the bottom of which Victim is trapped. Falling Person will crush Victim to death unless Victim vaporizes her with his ray gun. If he does not vaporize her, Victim will cushion Falling Person's landing, saving her life.
> (Nozick 1974, 24–5; Otsuka 1994; this is Frowe's 2014, 22 version)

Ferzan (2012) and Quong (2016, 2020) contend that it's intuitively impermissible for a third party to vaporize Falling Person, and for this reason she is not robustly liable to defensive killing. I agree. (Quong argues instead that Victim has an agent-relative permission to kill Falling Person. Frowe (2020) argues against Quong's view.)

Frances Kamm (1993, 47) suggests that Falling Person is permissibly defensively killed at least partly due to obligations or duties she has with which she does not comply. Kamm remarks that the position of the falling person "is different from that of a natural object—for example, a stone that the wind hurls at a person—because she is not a stone but, rather, a person who should not be in an inappropriate position relative to others." Tadros (2011, 248–56) endorses this idea, arguing that together with lesser-evil considerations, it yields a justification for the permissibility of defensively killing Falling Person. He contends that "it is the fact that I am responsible for what my body does, even when that is not a product of my agency, that gives rise to the permission to harm innocent attackers and innocent

66 DEFENSIVE HARM AND MEASURED AGGRESSION

threats. And I bear that responsibility because that body is me" (Tadros 2011, 254). Frowe (2014, 67–70), citing Kamm and Tadros, also endorses this general strategy, and in her view the resulting permissibility is not agent-relative.

Against this idea, first, a person's body considered apart from her psychological states is not a person—it's not, contra Tadros, me—it's only an aspect or part of me as a person. Second, given the circumstances of the case, it's implausible that Falling Person is in any sense responsible for what her body does. The case is aptly devised to rule this out. Third, it's dubious that Falling Person ought not to be falling toward Victim. Very plausibly, 'ought' implies 'can,' and typical purported counterexamples to that principle are cases in which the agent could at some time have made it the case that she does what she ought to do, even if she now cannot do what she ought. But the scenario is set up so that Falling Person could not have made it the case that she was not falling toward Victim. I conclude that permissibility of defensive killing in this case cannot be grounded in the way that Kamm, Tadros, and Frowe suggest.[12]

Thus I think that it's difficult to justify the claim that Victim is robustly liable to defensive killing, and in particular to third-party permissibility. By contrast, in *Mentally Ill Threat* and *Psychopathic Threat*, a third party is clearly permitted to intentionally kill in defense of the innocent, and thus these cases are clear instances of robust liability to defensive killing. If the wrongness of Chris and Ed's posing a threat were irrelevant, and it would make no difference if they were innocent, then we'd lack an explanation of why they are permissibly killed by third parties such as Deb and Frank.

## Fact-Relatively Wrongful Threats

I've now presented my argument for my position on the conditions for robust liability to defensive killing. There are, however, a number of contrasting positions for which their proponents have provided impressive arguments. Let me briefly outline the reasons I have for not endorsing these alternatives.[13]

Jeff McMahan (2009, 162–7) in effect rejects culpability as a necessary condition on robust liability to defensive killing. But he also denies that

---

[12] I also agree with Doggett's (2018) and Quong's (2020, 62–4) criticisms of this strategy.

[13] Doing full justice to these positions requires a longer and deeper discussion, of a sort that has been provided by many authors, but this is not my intention here.

FACT-RELATIVELY WRONGFUL THREATS    67

wrongly posing a threat is such a necessary condition. He contends that if an agent can foresee that an action of hers has some chance of posing a lethal risk to someone, no matter how small the risk, and the threat becomes actual, she is thereby permissibly killed, even if the action was morally permissible. While McMahan does classify such an action as one for which the agent is morally responsible, the sense of moral responsibility he invokes is not essentially tied to culpability or blameworthiness.

Here is an example of his in which an agent is responsible in his sense for posing a lethal threat, but not blameworthy for it, since doing so is only fact-relevantly wrong:

> *Ambulance Driver*: An emergency medical technician (EMT) is driving an ambulance to the site of an accident to take one of the victims to the hospital. She is driving conscientiously and alertly but a freak event occurs that causes the ambulance to veer uncontrollably towards a pedestrian. The out-of-control ambulance will now kill the pedestrian unless the pedestrian destroys it with a grenade, thereby killing the EMT (the victim whom the EMT was going to pick up will be fine).
>
> (McMahan 2009, 165, with Quong's (2020, 27) revisions)

Is the EMT robustly liable to defensive killing? On McMahan's view the EMT would be, since she can foresee that driving the ambulance carries the risk actualized in the example. But according to Ferzan (2012) and Quong (2016, 2020, 27–8) the EMT is not liable to defensive killing in that sense, since it would not be morally permissible for a third party to kill her. That this would be impermissible seems clear to me, and so I agree with them. If it would be permissible for the pedestrian to kill the EMT (about which I'm far from sure), it would have to be on some basis other than robust liability; Quong argues for agent-relative permission in this case. Accordingly, I concur with Ferzan and Quong (and others, e.g. Lazar 2009; Tadros 2011) that McMahan's proposal is not a plausible criterion for robust liability. His notion of responsibility, in the absence of wrongdoing, does not suffice for such liability.[14]

Judith Thomson in effect also rejects culpability as a necessary condition for robust liability. She defends a fact-relative view of when agents' rights are violated, denying that an agent must be at fault to violate right. What is

---

[14] But see Gordon-Solmon (2018) for a development and defense of McMahan's position.

68    DEFENSIVE HARM AND MEASURED AGGRESSION

required for B to violate A's right is just that A has a right not to be harmed, and B harms A. For example, in the *Day's End* case, by flipping the light switch B violates A's right not to be harmed. For Thomson, such merely fact-relative rights violations issue in robust liability to defensive harming. Quong (2020, 26–57) argues that wrongly posing a threat in a merely fact-relative way, for which the agent is not culpable, may under certain types of circumstance issue in robust defensive liability. In support, he cites an example of McMahan's:

> *Mistaken Attacker*: The identical twin brother of a notorious serial killer is driving during a stormy night in a remote area where his car breaks down. Unaware that his brother has recently escaped from prison and is known to be hiding in the same area, he knocks on the door of the nearest house, seeking to phone for help. On opening the door, Resident justifiably believes the harmless twin is the killer. Resident has been warned by the authorities that the killer will certainly attack anyone he meets on sight, and so Resident lunges at him with a knife.
>
> (Quong's 2020, 23–4 revision of McMahan 2009, 164)

Resident's defensive act is morally permissible in the evidence-relative sense, and he is thus not culpable. However, Quong finds it intuitive that Resident is permissibly harmed: "After all, the identical twin is the victim of an unprovoked and intentional attack by Resident. Surely the person who intentionally initiates the fact-relative wrongful attack—Resident—is liable to defensive harm" (Quong 2020, 24).

As an indication that this isn't merely a case of agent-relative permissibility of harming, but of robust liability to defensive harm, which issues in third-person permissibility, Quong embellishes *Mistaken Attacker* as follows:

> *Police Intervention*: Just at that moment, a police officer arrives on the scene who *knows* the person being attacked by Resident is the killer's innocent twin. The police officer realizes the mistake that Resident has made, and now sees that the only way to save the twin from being killed is to shoot and kill Resident first. Alternatively, the police officer could let Resident kill twin.    (Quong 2020, 33)

Quong believes that "it is clear that the police officer is morally permitted to shoot Resident in order to save the twin."

## FACT-RELATIVELY WRONGFUL THREATS    69

On Quong's (2020, 34–57) account, Resident is robustly liable to defensive harming because the evidence-relative permissibility of the lethal threat he poses involves the assumption that the twin does not have a right that he in fact does have. Even though Resident does not act wrongly in posing a lethal threat to the twin, his justification for lunging at him with a knife does involve the mistaken assumption that the twin has forfeited the right not to be killed. For this reason Resident is robustly defensively liable. Quong's view represents a compromise with a fact-relative account, without accepting a thoroughgoing version such as Thomson's. In Quong's view, when posing a threat is not evidence-relatively wrong but does not involve a false assumption about a right the potential victim has, the threating agent is not robustly liable to defensive harm. In Thomson's *Day's End*, Quong's criterion does not rule that A is robustly liable to defensive harm, since A's evidence-relative permissibility of flipping the light switch does not involve the assumption that B lacks the right not to be harmed.

I am not sure that Quong is right about *Mistaken Attacker*. I think that it is unclear that the police officer may kill Resident. It does seem that the officer may inflict fairly serious non-lethal harm on Resident, but this might be justifiable on lesser-evil grounds. *Mistaken Attacker* would then be reconcilable with the evidence-relative account of robust liability I prefer. At the same time, I am open to Quong's compromise with fact-relativity, especially since there are other cases (such as *Duped Soldiers* (Quong 2020, 33)) that may be more difficult to reconcile with an evidence-relative view (Frowe 2015; Quong 2020, 34).[15]

At the outset of this discussion I cited Seth Lazar's (2009) practical concern for the view that culpability for posing a sufficiently serious threat is a necessary condition for liability to defensive killing. He points out that many unjustified combatants are not culpable for threats they pose, that they often are "excused either by duress or because they reasonably believe their cause to be justified, in conditions of uncertainty and high risk." He also contends that "in the radically information-poor context of war, there is no way for justified combatants to discriminate between innocent enemies and those who are indeed culpable for fighting" (Lazar 2009, 701). In

---

[15] In *Duped Soldiers*, soldiers are deceived by a regime into believing that innocent people are terrorists, and intuitively, the innocent people have the right to defensively kill the soldiers when they attack. But this case is not one that features the simple structure of threats to innocent lives posed by evidence-relatively innocent agents. It also features complexities such as the soldiers functioning as a tool of the non-duped regime, members of which are not evidence-relevantly innocent, and a threat to independence and liberties as well as innocent lives.

70   DEFENSIVE HARM AND MEASURED AGGRESSION

favor of the alternative condition I've proposed, wrongly posing a threat, justified combatants can more easily identify enemies who wrongly threaten. Non-culpable mentally ill or psychopathic enemies can typically be ascertained as wrongly posing a threat, even if their non-culpability cannot be determined. Whether a threat is evidence-relatively wrong may be more difficult to discern than whether it is merely fact-relevantly wrong. However, as is indicated by the critical discussion of Thomson's resolutely fact-relative account, such a view, although arguably more practically feasible, is challenged by considerations of intuitive plausibility.

## Defensive Harm and Senses of Moral Responsibility

What might moral responsibility be such that it can potentially have the role in the justification of defensive killing, and defensive harming more generally, that some propose? I've argued (in Chapter 1) that in the debate about free will, the sense of moral responsibility that has the pivotal role is the one that invokes basic desert. It's generally agreed that adequate reasons-responsiveness is one necessary condition of responsibility in this sense (e.g., Fischer 2007; Nelkin 2011; McKenna 2012; Sartorio 2016), often called accountability (Watson 1996; Shoemaker 2011, 2015). *Mentally Ill Threat* and *Psychopathic Threat* indicate that basic desert-invoking accountability for posing a wrongful threat is not a necessary condition of liability to defensive killing, that is, for the *prima facie* moral permissibility of third-person intentional killing of one to save one, since Chris and Ed do not satisfy the reasons-responsiveness requirement.

As discussed in Chapter 2, another sense of moral responsibility involves desert but in a non-basic sense—for example, blameworthiness that invokes desert grounded in consequentialist (Dennett 1984, 2020; Vargas 2013) or contractualist (Lenman 2006, Vilhauer 2013) considerations. On one such account, our practice of holding agents morally responsible in a desert sense should be retained because doing so would have the best consequences relative to alternative practices. Daniel Dennett (1984; Dennett and Caruso 2020) endorses this position, as does Manuel Vargas (2013). Vargas agrees that adequate reasons-responsiveness is necessary for being morally responsible in this sense, and Dennett would concur. *Mentally Ill Threat* and *Psychopathic Threat* thus indicate that this sense of moral responsibility is also not a necessary condition of liability to defensive killing, since, again, Chris and Ed are not sufficiently reasons-responsive.

THE MEASURED AGGRESSIVE STANCE    71

A further sense of moral responsibility is forward looking. In the version of this conception I set out (Pereboom 2014, 2017a, and in Chapter 2), blaming is this sort of calling to account and can be justified by forward-looking elements such as the good of reconciliation with the wrongdoer, the good of the moral formation of the wrongdoer, the right of those wronged or threatened by wrongdoing to protect themselves and to be protected from immoral behavior and its consequences, and the retention of the integrity of victims. In accord with Angela Smith's (2008) and Michael McKenna's (2012) models, in this view it's again the agent's responsiveness to reasons that's engaged in central cases of blaming. On this answerability sense of responsibility, we request an explanation with the intent of having the agent acknowledge a disposition to act badly, and then, if he has in fact so acted without excuse, we aim for him to come to see that the disposition issuing in the action is best modified or eliminated. This change is produced by his recognition of moral reasons to make it. Thus it's an agent's responsiveness to reasons, together with our interest in, for example, his moral formation and our reconciliation with him that explains why he is an appropriate recipient of blame. Given that reasons-responsiveness is required for this forward-looking notion, *Mentally Ill Threat* and *Psychopathic Threat* also indicate that this sense of moral responsibility is not a necessary condition of robust liability to defensive killing.

For an agent to be morally responsible, and culpable or blameworthy in particular, in all of these senses requires that she meet certain epistemic and control conditions. For each sense, adequate responsiveness to reasons in particular is required. But there are cases of mentally ill or psychopathic lethal threats in which the agent does not meet the relevant reasons-responsiveness standard and is yet permissibly killed by a third party to defend one innocent person. Since the three notions of moral responsibility canvassed span the range from the most to the least demanding on offer, I think it's safe to conclude that culpability or blameworthiness is not a necessary condition for robust liability to defensive killing.

## The Measured Aggressive Stance

The considerations raised so far and the criterion I propose align with an account of which emotional attitudes appropriately accompany defensive killing. In the typical case of legitimate defensive killing, those in a position to exercise the right are not in a position to determine whether those who

72   DEFENSIVE HARM AND MEASURED AGGRESSION

pose lethal threats are blameworthy or deserve to be targets of retributive anger. In the passage quoted at the beginning of this chapter, Kilner (2017) cites sadness as an emotion that sometimes appropriately follows defensive killing, in particular when the agent is known to be mentally ill. One might ask: which aggressive emotions appropriately accompany defensive killing if retributive anger is ruled out? When a mother bear protects her cubs against a lethal threat, she displays a strong aggressive emotion, which intuitively counts as anger. In Paul Griffiths's (1997) view, there are basic emotions, had by non-human animals, which he calls "affect program emotions," of which this type of anger is a species. This emotion is not retributive anger, since the presupposition that the threat deserves to be harmed does not plausibly have a role in the bear's emotional stance. In Griffiths's view, these affect program emotions can be overlain or invested with cognitive content, but for one type of anger we can have, in some respects similar to the anger of the mother bear, the cognitive content does not feature desert. It is an emotion invoked in battle, for example, and in (Pereboom 2014) I classified such anger as "fury." In personal correspondence with Kilner, I described fury as I just did here, and he reports the following on the basis of conversations with combatants:

> When it comes to emotions in battle, I'd label them as fear (prior to the fight), fury (during the fight), and a combination of relief, satisfaction, and sadness after the fight and/or deployment. When soldiers are out to get payback after a casualty, the list would be anger, fury, satisfaction. The fury is controlled. It's not raging; it's focused determination and energy. It's a "them or us" competition where nothing else matters for the time being. "Measured aggression" is a term I've heard used.

Such a stance is normatively measured in the sense that the degree of aggressive emotion should be proportional to the defensive task at hand, and thus its intensity should not exceed what is appropriate to that task. While this stance does not presuppose that the target of aggression deserves or basically deserves to be harmed, it may, as I'm envisioning it, presuppose that the aggressor is wrongly posing a threat, and it would then plausibly qualify as a kind of moral anger. This, I propose, is the morally preferable emotional stance to take when defensive harming is required. In some cases, in particular those involving intense and dangerous conflict, the stance may be like that of the mother bear, with neither the desert or the wrongness presupposition. The aggressive emotional stance typically

THE MEASURED AGGRESSIVE STANCE    73

invoked in combat sports has neither the desert nor the wrongness presupposition, and that same stance might be recruited, for example, in intense combat in war. In any case, we have available to us a measured aggressive stance for legitimate defensive killing, and legitimate defensive harming more generally, which isn't retributive.

Accordingly, several emotional attitudes appropriately accompany defensive killing and defensive harming more generally that do not presuppose basically deserved pain or harm. They include sadness and sorrow, and a measured aggressive emotional stance that may presuppose that the aggressor wrongly poses a threat, but not that he deserves to be harmed. The availability of these specific attitudes is fortunate given that defensive harming is frequently justified in situations in which blameworthiness cannot be determined, and in situations in which it's clear that the threat is not blameworthy.

In her book on Theodore Roosevelt and William Howard Taft, twenty-sixth and twenty-seventh presidents of the United States, Doris Kearns Goodwin recounts a story of Roosevelt as a young New York state assemblyman being bullied at a roadhouse near Albany, the state capital:

Late one winter afternoon Roosevelt entered Hurst's and was greeted by three jeering bullies, who raucously mocked his appearance and lack of a winter coat. "Why don't your mother buy you an overcoat? Won't Mama's boy catch cold?" A reporter present noted that Roosevelt ignored them until it was clear they would not let up. Finally, he confronted the three. "You—little dude," taunted one, while his companion took a swipe at Roosevelt. "But, quick as lightning, Roosevelt slipped his glasses into his side pocket, and in another second he had laid out two of the trio on the floor. The third quit cold." The story soon made the rounds in the statehouse, along with the significant fact that once the men got off the floor, Roosevelt invited them to join him in a glass of ale.

(Kearns Goodwin 2013, 69)

The ensuing invitation to a glass of ale suggests absence of resentment on Roosevelt's part, and a measured aggressive stance instead. As a boxer at Harvard, and a member of the American ruling class in a particular historical period, this form of measured aggression was available to him because he had the requisite physical ability and it met with general social approval. It might well not have been regarded with similar approval for members of subjugated groups at that time. Over the past half-century social approval for a physically aggressive response of this sort in domestic contexts has

74 DEFENSIVE HARM AND MEASURED AGGRESSION

largely dissipated; it does unfairly favor the physically strong. Use of weapons can level the playing field, but the dangers are too great. But there are other forms of measured aggression that currently do meet with social approval for the domestic context, such as verbal confrontation. At the same time, being deprived of modes of measured aggression in moral protest of one's condition, even if it is only verbal, is itself a manifestation of subjugation and oppression, and in general this should remain a serious concern in our inegalitarian social world.

Macalester Bell (2009, 166) recounts nineteenth-century African-American author and political figure Frederick Douglass's decisive angry confrontation with his slave master. Bell notes that "Douglass' anger was often remarked upon and often with approval. For example, Elizabeth Cady Stanton, abolitionist and advocate of equal rights for women, describes the first time she saw him speak: 'He stood there like an African Prince, majestic in his wrath'" (Bell 2009, 166). Douglass was born into slavery and when he was sixteen he was rented out to Edward Covey, a notorious slave breaker. By Douglass's own account, the turning point of his life came when he found himself giving into his anger and resisting one of Covey's vicious attacks on him, which Douglass describes as follows:

> This battle with Mr. Covey was the turning point in my career as a slave. It rekindled the few expiring embers of freedom, and revived within me a sense of my own manhood. It recalled the departed self-confidence, and inspired me again with a determination to be free. The gratification afforded by the triumph was a full compensation for whatever else might follow, even death itself. He only can understand the deep satisfaction which I experienced, who has himself repelled by force the bloody arm of slavery. I felt as I never felt before. It was a glorious resurrection, from the tomb of slavery, to the heaven of freedom. My longcrushed spirit rose, cowardice departed, bold defiance took its place; and I now resolved that, however long I might remain a slave in form, the day had passed forever when I could be a slave in fact. I did not hesitate to let it be known of me, that the white man who expected to succeed in whipping, must also succeed in killing me. From this time I was never again what might be called fairly whipped, though I remained a slave four years afterwards. I had several fights, but was never whipped.  (Douglass 1845/1997, 79)

"This passage," Bell remarks, "describes a pivotal moment in which Douglass stood up to Covey and, through physical resistance, made his anger felt"

THE MEASURED AGGRESSIVE STANCE    75

(Bell 2009, 166). She continues by arguing, convincingly, that Douglass's anger was appropriate in these circumstances. However, here the anger may not have been a case of resentment but instead the measured aggressive stance that presupposes that its target wrongly poses a threat. If so, then on the position I'm defending it was indeed appropriate without qualification. Moreover, even if the anger was resentful, resentment may often be practically rational upon being subjected to an abusive slavemaster, even if it has a false basic desert presupposition. One aspect of the immorality of selecting classes of people for subjugation is that the measured aggressive stance is standardly forcibly barred by the subjugating group, and often, as in the case of American slavery, with the use of violence. This in turn instills standing resentment among the abused, and instilling resentment is itself an insidious form of abuse.

It is valuable to contrast such a measured aggressive stance with resentment and a related attitude, *ressentiment*, made famous by Nietzsche in his *Of the Genealogy of Morals* (1887/1998). In Nietzsche's conception, *ressentiment* paradigmatically arises in those with ambition who have lost in a power struggle. In his genealogical account of Judeo-Christian morality, the noble warriors are the victors and the priests are the vanquished. *Ressentiment* arises primarily in the priests who are prevented from realizing the political and social power enjoyed by the nobles, and as a result "revalue" the nobles' values of acquiring and exercising power by ostensibly and by their own account devaluing them in favor of humility and egalitarianism. Crucially, at the same time they retain the noble values without explicit acknowledgment; while conceiving of themselves as rejecting those values, these "men of *ressentiment*" are in fact motivated by them. Nietzsche maintains that socially powerful people can have *ressentiment* as well.

Andrew Huddleston (2021) proposes a more general conception of ressentiment, one that abstracts away from its role in Nietzsche's genealogical and critical account of Judeo-Christian values:

> *Ressentiment* is a state of the psyche involving suffering and anger in relation to a perceived injury, slight, and/or undesirable state of affairs that one feels to have been perpetrated by some individual or group, which one resents and often regards as unjust or unfair, and which one moreover focuses on as insulting or demeaning. One desires vengeance against the felt perpetrator. One dwells on [all of this], often in an obsessive way. This psychological dynamic, in the agent in question, is such as to constitute an objectionable feature of character.    (Huddleston 2021, 677–8)

# 76  DEFENSIVE HARM AND MEASURED AGGRESSION

In Huddleston's account, *ressentiment* is a type of resentment; not all resentment in his view is an objectionable feature of character, but *ressentiment* is a kind that is. What makes *ressentiment* objectionable is that, first, it involves desiring vengeance and not just retributive justice—and we can conceive of the desire for vengeance as a desire to inflict harm more severe than can be justified on grounds of basic desert; and that, secondly, it involves dwelling on this desire, often in an obsessive way. We can add that it is also objectionable because it involves loss of control over one's psychological state typically because the slight or injury controls one's state in a suboptimal way, which is manifest in dwelling or obsessing, over an extended period of time, on exacting vengeance. In Huddleston's view, *ressentiment* is in particular characteristic of the enslavers and oppressors. It's the *ressentiment*, which in such cases often results from merely perceived slights and injuries, or only from a sense of entitlement, that gives rise to the systematic abuse. Here Huddleston cites Kate Manne's (2017) analysis of the role of men's sense of entitlement in the subjugation of women. He notes specifically Manne's account of Elliot Rodger, who shot the sorority members at the University of California at Santa Barbara, not because those he targeted in particular had not paid him the sexual attention he felt was his due, but because he believed that women more generally had objectionably failed in this regard.

Is *ressentiment*, as Huddleston contends, a species of resentment? Without committing to that thesis, I do think that all cases of resentment have at least some of the objectionable features of *ressentiment*, while those that don't quality as *ressentiment* have them to a lesser degree overall. Bernard Reginster, by contrast, aims to draw a sharp distinction between the two attitudes:

> [I]ndignation and resentment are by no means the first reactions of the man of *ressentiment* to his defeat; shame and self-contempt are [Nietzsche 1882/1887/1974, *The Gay Science* 359]. His defeat causes him shame because his fundamental aspirations include enjoying the political supremacy enjoyed by his victors [Nietzsche 1887/1998, *The Genealogy of Morals* I 15]. It is because political power matters to them that their defeat arouses *ressentiment* in the priests, and not just indignation and (moral) resentment...the fundamental difference between *ressentiment* and resentment is that resentment appears to presuppose *condemnation* of its object, and constitutes a reaction of disapproval to its occurrence, whereas *ressentiment* rests on the implicit *endorsement* of the very values embodied by those to whom it is directed.   (Reginster 1997, 296)

But on Reginster's own analysis, the man of *ressentiment* does condemn the noble values and actions that accord with them, while indeed at the same time at a not fully consciously recognized level he endorses these values and is motivated by them. So the man of *ressentiment* is a man of resentment, but also has a complex additional emotional profile.

On my account, matching the objectionable features of *ressentiment*, resentment typically involves, first, a desire to inflict basically deserved pain or harm, while there is no such thing, and in this respect it is similar to vengeance, since both attitudes involve a desire to inflict unjustified harm; second, resentment has a tendency to persist as a nagging and distressing emotion at least until the presupposed basically deserved pain or harm has been inflicted, and often beyond that point; and third, it tends to intrude on one's psychological state in a way that is difficult to control. The measured aggressive stance, by contrast, typically does not have these objectionable features: it doesn't involve the presupposition of basically deserved pain or harm; it is not a desire to inflict unjustified harm; it does not have the tendency to persist as a nagging and distressing emotion; and it does not tend to intrude on the agent's psychological state in a way that is difficult to control.

## Summary

The issue addressed in this chapter is how one might justify effectively dealing those who pose dangerous threats if they do not deserve to be harmed. I've argued that wrongly posing a threat, by contrast with deserving harm for posing the threat, is the core condition for what I call *robust liability to defensive killing*, liability that agent A has just in case A poses a threat to agent B as a result of which B and third parties are *prima facie* morally permitted to intentionally kill A to defend B from that threat. In addition, I've proposed that a non-retributive measured aggressive stance appropriately facilitates taking defensive action. Such an emotional stance may presuppose only that its target wrongly poses a threat, whereupon it accords with skepticism about basic desert. Finally, I've argued that such a stance is better for those called upon to confront injustice than the alternatives.

# 4

# Crime, Protection, and Compassion

Much seriously harmful wrongdoing perpetrated by human beings is criminal, and criminal acts and omissions are those that violate criminal law in some state and may as a result be prosecuted by that state.[1] A prominent justification for criminal punishment is retributive, which, in its classical form, invokes basic desert. The position on treatment of criminals I've proposed (Pereboom 2001, 158–86, 2013b, 2014, 153–74, 2020) rejects such retributive justification, since it presupposes that criminals are typically basically deserving of punishment that inflicts pain or harm, which I reject. Instead my position seeks to satisfy two aims: that we be protected from criminal wrongdoing, and that the well-being of the criminal be taken into serious consideration. These aims require balancing two sets of emotional attitudes: those that motivate protection against agents who pose serious threats, and those, like compassion, that are directed toward the well-being of the offender.[2]

The general skepticism I endorse about the control in action required for blame and punishment that involves basically deserved pain or harm has a role in justifying this position. But independently, our increased understanding of the neural and genetic bases for criminal behavior provides a reason to question whether criminals of certain common types have such control. The link between criminal behavior and psychopathy discussed in Chapter 3 is a case in point. On the genetic front, to cite one famous study, Avshalom Caspi and his research team analyzed data from 442 New Zealand male adults involved in a long-term study (Caspi et al. 2002). The researchers identified 154 subjects who were abused or maltreated as children, including thirty-three who were severely abused. The researchers then evaluated the influence of a particular gene on the abused children's outcomes as adults. A 'low-activity' variant of this gene which affects levels of monoamine oxidase A (MAOA), an enzyme that metabolizes the brain chemicals serotonin, dopamine, and norepinephrine, had previously been linked to

---

[1] This discussion is limited to criminal laws that are morally justified.
[2] This chapter is a revision of Pereboom (2020).

*Wrongdoing and the Moral Emotions.* Derk Pereboom, Oxford University Press. © Derk Pereboom 2021.
DOI: 10.1093/oso/9780192846006.003.0004

abnormal aggression. Caspi and his associates discovered that 85 percent of severely abused subjects with the low-activity variant of the MAOA gene developed some form of antisocial behavior. In contrast, study participants with the high-activity variant only rarely exhibited aggressive or criminal behavior in adulthood even if they had been severely abused as children. "Although individuals having the combination of low-activity MAOA genotype and maltreatment were only 12 percent of the male birth cohort," the researchers say, "they accounted for 44 percent of the cohort's violent convictions" (Caspi et al. 2002, 1–2). Adrian Raine provides a systematic treatment of our understanding of conditions of this sort in his landmark book *The Anatomy of Violence: The Biological Roots of Crime* (2013). We have reason to believe that certain common dispositions to criminal behavior are due to genetic and neural conditions, which, at least as matters currently stand, the criminal cannot control.[3]

I've argued that the optimal theory for criminal jurisprudence invokes incapacitation justified by the right to self-defense and defense of others (Pereboom 2013b, 2014, 2020), and as Gregg Caruso (2016, 2017, 2021) has proposed, embedded in a public health model.[4] In addition, I defend the claim that limited general deterrence can be justified when it is restricted by the Kantian injunction never to treat agents merely as means but always as ends in themselves (Kant 1785/1981, and that such general deterrence is likely required for a workable criminology.

## Blame as Protest with Forward-Looking Aims

In Chapters 1 and 2 I argued that the main thread of the historical free will debate issues a challenge to one aspect of our practice of holding morally responsible, the sense of moral responsibility set apart by the notion of basic desert. The practice of holding morally responsible is complex, and it features several distinct aims and justifications. One widespread justification for punishing is that the agent who has knowingly committed a crime deserves it. One conception of desert is basic in the sense that it is not grounded in distinct and more basic moral considerations, such as maximization of

---

[3] This type of consideration is consistent with those affected by these conditions having or having the potential to develop capacities to counteract their effects in relevant circumstances.

[4] Caruso (2020a) also argues that this conception of how to deal with criminal behavior fits best with the Buddhist ethical view on which compassion is a central virtue.

## 80    CRIME, PROTECTION, AND COMPASSION

good consequences. In another conception, desert is non-basic. Daniel Dennett (1984, 2003) and Manuel Vargas (2013, 2015) advocate versions of a view in which the practice-level justifications for punishment invoke desert, but that desert is not basic, because at the higher level the practice is justified by its anticipated good consequences.

In Chapter 2 I argued that there is also a largely forward-looking component to our practice of holding morally responsible, which aims at goods such as moral formation of character, reconciliation in relationships, protection from harm, and retention of integrity on the part of victims, which is not challenged by arguments in the free will debate. When a child misbehaves, a parent might blame and punish him because she believes that this is the best way to form good character, and not, or not only, to give him what he deserves. Blame in relationships that have been impaired due to bad behavior may have the aim of reconciliation. A victim of bullying might overtly blame the bully as a means to retaining his sense of integrity and as a way to protect potential future targets. One may object that blame essentially invokes desert, but in Chapter 2 I set out a notion of blame as moral protest (Hieronymi 2001; Talbert 2012; Smith 2013; Pereboom 2017a), but, distinctively, one that does not involve desert or the attendant negative reactive attitudes. Such moral protest might indeed have the aims of character formation, reconciliation in relationships, retention of integrity, and protection.

When one adopts the stance of moral protest against criminal behavior, it is appropriately accompanied by compassion. Buddhists traditionally argue that one right general attitude toward humanity generally is compassion (Goodman 2009). I agree. In her *Upheavals of Thought*, Martha Nussbaum proposes an analysis of compassion that takes Aristotle's account as its starting point. She begins by defining compassion as he did, as pain caused by the perception that someone has undeservedly suffered a misfortune that one is liable to suffer oneself.[5] On Nussbaum's view, by contrast with Aristotle's, emotions are appraisals with cognitive content, and she proposes this Aristotelian perceptual content as the basic cognitive content of compassion. She then embellishes this basis with three further specifications. First, when a subject has the emotion of compassion, she believes that the target agent's misfortune is seriously damaging to his well-being, and not merely minor. Second, she believes that the agent did not deserve this misfortune— that it was not his fault and not due to actions for which he is to blame.

---

[5] But see Rachana Kamtekar (2020) for an argument that for Aristotle the claim that the suffering must be undeserved is qualified.

# RETRIBUTIVIST THEORIES OF PUNISHMENT    81

Third, she believes that she herself is similarly vulnerable, that she could be the subject of the same misfortune (Nussbaum 2001; Deigh 2004).

In response to questions for this account raised by John Deigh (2004), Nussbaum (2004) comes close to retracting the third of these specifications. There are cases of compassion, such as those that concern animal suffering, in which one does not regard oneself as similarly vulnerable. Moreover, even with respect to beings relevantly different from oneself, imagination can arouse compassion. At this point only the first two provisions, that the misfortune be serious and that it be undeserved, remain in place. But what if there is no deserved pain or harm, at least not of the basic sort? What if we, with Śāntideva, see wrongdoing as issuing from causes beyond the agent's control, and as a result come to hold that wrongdoers never basically deserve to be harmed due to what they've done? Moreover, to be a wrong-doer is itself to be subject to a kind of misfortune. Plato maintained that it's intrinsically and non-instrumentally worse for a person to perpetrate than to suffer injustice (Gorgias 468d–79e; Kamtekar 2020), and Victor Tadros (2020) reports that in informal surveys in which the options presented are one's child being a serious wrongdoer and correctly convicted, and one's child being innocent and mistakenly convicted of the same wrongdoing, most respondents see the former as the greater misfortune. Accordingly, compassion is plausibly appropriate as an attitude for us to take toward criminals, as Plato and Tadros also maintain, and this provides motivation to see to their reform, reconciliation, and reintegration.

## Retributivist Theories of Punishment

On the classical retributivist theory for the justification of punishment, the good to be achieved by punishment is that a wrongdoer receive the pain or harm he deserves just because of his having acted wrongly or wrongly omit-ted to act, given requisite cognitive sensitivity.[6] Classical retributivism as a theory of the justification of punishment is distinct from retributivism as a penalty schedule, roughly captured by the "eye for an eye" adage, although they are related; here I focus on the theory of justification.

Classical retributivism would be undermined if the free will skeptic is right about basic desert, since this view aims to justify punishment solely on

---

[6] For examples of classical retributivism, see Kant (1797/2017), Moore (1987, 1998), Husak (2000), Kershnar (2000), Morse (2004, 2013), Berman (2008), and Alexander and Ferzan (2009).

# 82   CRIME, PROTECTION, AND COMPASSION

the grounds of basic desert, and the skeptical position contends that we lack the control in action required for punishment so conceived.[7] Compatibilists and libertarians reject this reason. But there is a powerful epistemic objection against compatibilists and libertarians who propose to justify criminal punishment on retributivist grounds. If the retributivist justification of punishment featured by our actual practice requires the rationality of the belief that compatibilism or libertarianism is true, while at the same time there are serious and unanswered objections to these positions, we cannot legitimately respond to a challenge to this part of the practice just by saying that it is supported by one of these views (contra Stephen Morse 2004, 2013). Punishment inflicts harm, and in general, justification for harm must meet a high epistemic standard. If it is significantly probable that one's justification for harming another is unsound, then, *prima facie* that behavior is seriously wrong, and one must refrain from engaging in it (Pereboom 2001, 161, 2013a, 2014, 158; Vilhauer 2009b; Caruso 2020b). A strong and credible response to the objections to compatibilism or libertarianism is required to meet this standard.

Another objection to classical retributivism derives from a generally accepted conception of the limited justifiable purview of the state. Would the legitimate role of the state include inflicting on people the pain or harm they basically deserve? Supposing that the requisite capacity for control in action is in place, and that basic desert could be secured as good or right, we nevertheless have reason to question whether the state has the right to invoke it in justifying punishment. The legitimate functions of the state are generally agreed to include protecting its citizens from significant harm, and providing a framework for constructive human interaction. These functions arguably underwrite justification that in the first instance appeals to prevention of crime. But they have no immediate connection to the aim of apportioning punishment in accord with basic desert. The concern can be made vivid by considering the proposal that the state set up institutions devoted to fairly distributing rewards on the grounds of basic desert. Wouldn't classical retributivism generalize so that the state would have as much reason to fund rewarding morally exemplary action as to fund criminal punishment (Pereboom 2013a, 2014, 159–60)?[8]

---

[7] There are views of how punishment is justified that are classified as retributivism that do not invoke basic desert (e.g., Morris 1968). I use the term 'classical retributivism' to distinguish the view under scrutiny from these alternative retributivisms.

[8] For further discussion of this issue, see Victor Tadros (2011, 69–83).

A further reason to doubt classical retributivism is that retributivist sentiments might well have their genesis in vengeful desires, and if so, retribution may be on no better footing than vengeance as a reason for punishing (Pereboom 2001, 160–1, 2013b, 2014, 158–9; Singer 2005; Greene 2008). Acting on vengeful desires may be wrong for the following reason. Although acting on vengeful desires can bring about pleasure or satisfaction, no more of a moral case can be made for the permissibility of acting on them than can be made for acting on sadistic desires. In each case, acting on the desire aims at the harm of the one to whom the action is directed, and in neither case does acting on the desire essentially aim at any good other than the pleasure of its satisfaction. But then, if retributivist motivations have their genesis in vengeful desires, acting for the sake of retribution, like acting on sadistic desires, stands to be morally wrong.

In response to this type of concern, Shaun Nichols (2013/2015) correctly points out that classical retributivist recommendations for state punishment differ importantly from practices such as the blood feud, a more direct expression of vengeful sentiments. Still, retributivist justifications, in his view, plausibly derive from such sentiments. But in defense of retributivism, Nichols writes that:

> the vast bulk of our ordinary ethical worldview likely derives from fundamentally arational emotional processes (Blair 1995, Prinz 2007, Gill and Nichols 2008). For instance, if we did not find human suffering aversive, we would likely not have the moral revulsion we do at killing. Nor would we have the moral norm of helping strangers... But notice how dramatic it would be to cast these norms out of morality. To limit our ethics to norms that have some ultimate rational justification would leave us with an ethics more barren than almost anyone would be willing to accept.
> (Nichols 2015, 133)

Nichols then considers the fact that retribution faces a competing consideration: "*ceteris paribus*, it's wrong to harm others" (Nichols 2015, 136). Relevant here is the point, made just now, that justification for harm must meet a high epistemic standard, and that if it is significantly probable that one's justification for harming another is unsound, then, *prima facie* that behavior is seriously wrong. Nichols contends that the competing consideration that it is wrong to harm others is not sufficient to overturn retributive norms generally, such as setting back cheaters at games by infliction of minor harms not fully justified by non-retributive justifications. He does

## 84   CRIME, PROTECTION, AND COMPASSION

affirm, however, that this competing consideration proscribes applying the retributive norm in support of the serious harming involved in criminal incarceration or the death penalty (Nichols 2015, 139), and on this point, the relevant one in this context, I agree with him. T. M. Scanlon (2013) endorses a similar position: there is basic desert for wrongdoing, but the most it can justify is the withdrawal of good will, and not measures as severe as paradigmatic criminal punishment, and on this last point again I agree.[9]

Michael McKenna (2020, 2021) advocates a retributive position on criminal punishment weaker than that of paradigmatic classical retributivists, but in which retributive considerations are stronger than they are for Nichols and Scanlon. McKenna's (2021) "wimpy retributivism" features, first of all, basically deserved blame and punishment, where such punishment involves an intention to harm or to set back the interests of the culpable, and the harm is conceived as a non-instrumental good. But then, to temper the harm-justifying force of this basic retributivism, McKenna cites the need to meet the high epistemic standard demanded by justifications of harming in the face of arguments for free will skepticism, the concern that many criminals are mentally ill, and the countervailing value of compassion. I differ from McKenna in that I believe the argument for free will skepticism is stronger than he thinks it is, whereupon the demanding epistemic standard for justifying harm, together with the concerns about the legitimate role of the state and about retributive sentiments being rooted in vengeance, rules it out as a legitimate justification for punishment. At the same time, tempering the force of retributive considerations as McKenna suggests stands to result in a punishment practice much closer to what I advocate than that justified by retributivism not similarly tempered.

### Deterrence Theories of Punishment

These concerns for classical retributivism suggest we turn to the prospects for justifying criminal punishment by an appeal to its deterrent effect. On deterrence theories, it is the prevention of criminal wrongdoing that serves as the good by means of which punishment is justified. Initially, it would seem that no feature of free will skepticism renders deterrence theories less

---

[9] For additional general discussions of objections to classical retributivism, see C. L. Ten (1987, 38–65), John Braithwaite and Philip Pettit (1990, 156–201), and Philip Montague (1995, 11–23, 80–90).

## DETERRENCE THEORIES OF PUNISHMENT 85

acceptable to it than to libertarianism or to compatibilism. But at least some deterrence theories are not immune to the skeptic's challenge, since they presuppose a retributivist justification. Furthermore, like classical retributivism, deterrence justifications of paradigmatic sorts of punishment face difficult objections independent of skepticism about free will.

One paradigmatic deterrence theory is Jeremy Bentham's (1823/1948). In his conception, the state's policy toward criminal behavior should aim at maximizing utility, and punishment should be administered if and only if it does so. The pain or unhappiness produced by punishment results from the restriction on freedom that ensues from the threat of punishment, the anticipation of punishment by the person who has been sentenced, the pain of actual punishment, and the sympathetic pain felt by others such as the friends and family of the criminal. The most significant value that results from punishment derives from the security of those who benefit from its capacity to deter both the criminal himself as well as other potential criminals.

Arguably the most serious misgiving raised against utilitarian deterrence theory is the *use* objection. A general problem for utilitarianism is that it allows people to be used merely as means, that is, harmed severely, without their consent, to benefit others, and this is often intuitively wrong (Kant 1785/1981). Punishing criminals for the sake of society's security would appear to be just such a practice. At this point Dana Nelkin (2019b) suggests that we combine deterrence theory with a measure of retributivism. On her proposal, the criminal's basically deserving harm functions as counterweight to the use objection, and thus we can appeal to such desert to justify treating criminals in ways that subserve general deterrence. Perhaps many who believe the point of punishment is deterrence are implicitly relying on such a retributivist assumption. But if the free will skeptic is right, this proposal's reliance on basically deserved harm is undercut, and the concern about the grounding of retributivism in vengeance counts against it as well.

The deterrence theory developed by Daniel Farrell (1985); cf., Quinn 1985; Kelly 2009) potentially avoids the use objection by justifying criminal punishment not by consequentialist considerations but by the right of self-defense (and defense of others). Farrell's theory is impressive in part because it justifies punishment on grounds that are widely accepted, and which meet a plausible epistemic standard for justifying harm. Because free will skeptics can also endorse the right to harm in self-defense, this justification of punishment is available to them as well.

## 86 CRIME, PROTECTION, AND COMPASSION

## Special Deterrence and Self-Defense

Farrell's deterrence theory highlights the distinction between special deterrence—punishment aimed at preventing the criminal, specifically, from engaging in future criminal behavior—and general deterrence—punishment aimed at preventing agents other than the targeted criminal from doing so. In his view, special deterrence is significantly easier to ground in the right to harm in self-defense than is general deterrence. In broad outline, Farrell's justification of punishment as special deterrence is as follows. Each of us has the right of direct self-defense—your right to harm an unjust aggressor to prevent him from harming you or someone else; and the right of indirect self-defense—your right to threaten an unjust aggressor with harm to prevent him from harming you or someone else. The right of direct self-defense is limited in the following way: it is the right to inflict the minimum harm on an unjust aggressor required to prevent him from harming you or someone else. The right of indirect self-defense is the right to threaten to inflict this minimum harm on a potential unjust aggressor on the condition that he attacks. The right of direct self-defense permits you to carry out this threat against the aggressor once he has violated the condition of the threat, that is, once he attacks. But furthermore, because each of us has these rights, the state, acting as proxy for us, can legitimately issue corresponding general threats to harm potential unjust aggressors, and can also legitimately carry out such threats once their conditions have been violated. In this way, the right to self-defense can justify the state's practice of criminal punishment.

This special deterrence theory avoids some, and perhaps all, of the objections to its utilitarian counterpart. On the concern for justifying punishment that is intuitively too severe, one may not, on grounds of indirect self-defense, issue a threat to inflict harm more severe than the minimum required to effectively deter the targeted crime. So, if a threat of a month in prison would be sufficient to deter auto theft, the state may not issue a threat of a two-year term. On the concern for punishing the innocent, the right to self-defense justifies harming only the unjust aggressors themselves.

Harming an unjust aggressor in self-defense does involve harming him, without his consent, for the benefit of persons other than himself, and this arguably would count as an instance of using him merely as a means to the benefit of others. But as Tadros (2017) points out, this is a case of the *use of threat elimination*, intuitively justified by the right of self-defense, by contrast with the more controversial *manipulative use*, which is not justified on the basis of this right. Farrell points out that the theory he proposes will not extend to full-fledged general deterrence, for this would involve harming someone to prevent not just his aggression but also the potential aggression of others, and that would involve use of the manipulative kind. Farrell does contend, however, that some general deterrence can be justified on the basis of his principle of distributive justice. When an agent wrongs you in such a way as to make you more vulnerable than you would otherwise be to the aggression of others, then you are justified in countering just this degree of additional vulnerability by harming him. Since this use is justified on the basis of the right of self-defense, it qualifies as the use of threat elimination, and is not an instance of manipulative use.

A concern I've raised for Farrell's line of reasoning is whether it can justify punishment, that is, treatment that involves an intention to harm, by contrast with incapacitation, such as preventative detention in the case of violent criminals who continue to pose a threat (Pereboom 2001, 172–4, 2013b, 2014, 168–9, 2020). What makes it appear as if punishment can be justified as Farrell proposes, I've argued, is the model of an unjust aggressor in circumstances in which state law enforcement and criminal justice agencies have no role—a 'state of nature' situation. A state of nature situation in which an aggressor poses immediate danger is relevantly different from the circumstances of criminals in our society who are subjected to state punishment. When the state sentences them to be punished, they are in the custody of the law. Moreover, the harms that the right of self-defense justifies in the case of aggressors in a state of nature situation are often more severe than those that this right would justify for those in custody. Suppose you confront a late-night intruder, and he clearly aims to kill you. To prevent him from killing you, the right to self-defense justifies knocking him out with the golf club you've armed yourself with. It would then be also permissible, prior to knocking him out, to threaten him with this amount of harm. Suppose he attacks anyway, but in the process, he trips over your kids' electric train set, which allows you to pin him to the ground and tie him up with an extension cord. At this point is it still legitimate for you to knock him out with the golf club? To do so would be wrong, and not be justified by the right to harm in self-defense. This right justifies only what one would reasonably believe to be the minimum harm required to prevent the aggression. Or suppose an aggressor clearly aims to kill your friend, and to protect her it is legitimate for you to knock him out with your golf club and to threaten to do so. Suppose that despite your efforts, he kills her, but that subsequently he loses his balance, falls, and you tie him up. Is it then

88   CRIME, PROTECTION, AND COMPASSION

permissible for you to knock him out? Not on the basis of the right to harm in self-defense and defense of others—he no longer poses an immediate threat. You retain the right to protect yourself and others against him, but not by carrying out a threat designed to prevent a harm that now has already occurred. So, then, it may be that a threat one might justifiably make and carry out to protect against an aggressor in a state of nature situation is not legitimately carried out in a situation in which the aggressor is in custody.

But what is the minimum harm required to protect against a violent criminal in custody? It seems evident that nothing more severe would be required than isolating him from those to whom he poses a threat. Thus, it would appear that Farrell's reasoning cannot justify the imposition of *punishment* on criminals, exactly, such as the imposition of serious physical or psychological suffering. Rather in the case of violent criminals who continue to pose a threat, this reasoning would at best justify only preventative detention. I've developed this non-punitive alternative by an analogy between the treatment of criminals and the treatment of carriers of dangerous diseases. Ferdinand Schoeman (1979) argues that if we have the right to quarantine carriers of serious communicable diseases to protect people, then for the same reason we also have the right to isolate the criminally dangerous. Quarantining a person can be justified when she is not morally responsible—in any sense—for posing a threat to others. If a child is infected with a deadly contagious virus that was transmitted to her before she was born, quarantine can still be legitimate. Imagine that a serial killer poses a grave threat to a community. Even if due to mental incapacity he is not morally responsible for his crimes or for posing a threat, the justification for preventatively detaining him is at least as strong as is quarantining a non-responsible carrier of a serious communicable disease (Pereboom 2001, 174–7, 2013b, 2014, 169–73, 2020).[10]

It would be morally wrong to treat carriers of communicable diseases more severely than is required to protect from the threat they pose. Similarly, on the self-defense justification, it would be morally wrong to treat criminals more harshly than is required to protect against the threats they pose. Just as moderately dangerous diseases may only justify measures less intrusive than quarantine, so moderately serious criminal tendencies

---

[10] Perhaps the justification for preventative detention is stronger than it is for quarantine, for the reason that it is worse for a person to be a victim of injustice than to be a victim of a natural threat. For discussion of this issue, see Derek Parfit (1984, 47), Victor Tadros (2016, 162–6), and Zofia Stemplowska (2018).

may only justify responses less intrusive than detention. The self-defense justification motivates a degree of concern for the rehabilitation and well-being of criminals that would reform current practice, and here compassion is an appropriate emotion (cf., Menninger 1968). Just as society should seek to cure the diseased it quarantines, so it should prepare criminals for reintegration.[11] Different sorts of rehabilitation programs, including some with therapeutic components, have proven to be effective, including cognitive and behavioral therapies (Pereboom 2001, 178–86), and benign biological intervention such as Omega-3 therapy and non-invasive brain stimulation (Raine 2013; Focquaert 2019; Choy et al. 2020). These achievements provide grounds for hope for higher levels of success in the near future.

Gregg Caruso (2016, 2017, 2021) embeds the account just set out within a public health model, and I welcome this development. A primary aim of the public health system is prevention of disease. In the case of dangerous communicative diseases, it is only when prevention fails that quarantine is required. Similarly, the public health approach to criminal behavior would make prevention of crime a primary aim. This approach shifts the focus to identifying and addressing the social determinants of crime, which include poverty, low social-economic status, racism, systematic disadvantage, mental illness, homelessness, educational inequity, and abuse, which would reduce the need for incapacitation. Quarantine is only needed when the public health system fails to prevent dangerous communicable diseases. Similarly, a public health approach to crime would foreground prevention, and incapacitation would be used only when we fall short of that primary aim. In Caruso's conception, the social determinants of illness and of criminal behavior are interrelated, and we should adopt a broad public health approach to address the causal factors in each case. As in the case of the social determinants of illness, it is important to identify and take action on the social determinants of criminal behavior to enhance societal well-being.

## How Much General Deterrence?

Incapacitation, and preventative detention in particular, may nevertheless involve serious harm—such as loss of liberty, personal relationships, and

---

[11] *Prima facie* duties to cure and rehabilitate are generally in place for those appropriately positioned. One might plausibly suggest that such duties are enhanced in cases in which those to be cured or rehabilitated are quarantined or preventatively detained without deserving such treatment.

# 90 CRIME, PROTECTION, AND COMPASSION

potential for career development—even if it does not qualify as punishment. In addition, plausibly the state should not conceal the fact that it detains violent criminals on such grounds, but instead make this information publicly available.[12] So even though preventative detention is justified as special deterrence, such a policy, together with a publicity provision, would yield, as a side-effect, general deterrence; it would deter others who are tempted to commit crimes. This general deterrent effect comes for free, so to speak, since it is a side-effect of the state's satisfying a publicity provision on a legitimate policy of special deterrence, justified on the basis of the right of self-defense. I call general deterrent effects justified as special deterrence by the right of self-defense *free general deterrence* (Pereboom 2020).

Free general deterrence comes with a significant limitation on how much harm can legitimately be inflicted—as I've emphasized, only the minimum harm required to protect against an aggressor is licensed. One might propose, however, that the free sort isn't enough to protect against certain sorts of wrongdoing, such as manipulation of financial markets, large-scale embezzlement, and illegal use of political influence for gain in personal wealth and power. Those who commit such crimes are typically not poor or from disadvantaged backgrounds, and the public health model, as Caruso sets it out, is not conceived to prevent crimes of this sort. Instead, many of those who commit such crimes are wealthy and well educated, but willing to free-ride for reasons of self-interest. They are often good at calculating risk, at weighing the probability of the wrongdoing being detected against the probability of significant personal gain. Free general deterrence would arguably involve the threat of loss of one's professional or political position, or say of a license to trade in financial instruments. Whether such threats are sufficient to deter the crimes at issue is an empirical matter, but, in disagreement with Caruso (2021, chapter 9), I would wager that they are not. The general deterrence in place in the United States, for example, is already much stronger than what free general deterrence would allow, and yet the incidence of such financial and political wrongdoing is fairly high. Reducing

---

[12] Kant advocates a strict publicity requirement: "All actions that affect the rights of other human beings are wrong if their maxim is not consistent with publicity" (Kant 1793/1983, 135). But there is good reason to deny the general claim. Governments are not required to publicize how their computer security systems work, even though this relates to the right of other human beings. For an overview, see Gosseries and Parr (2018).

Publicizing preventative detention, in particular in ways that don't reveal particular identities, may involve use, but involve little or any additional harm. Tadros argues (in conversation) that the legitimacy of making such measures public can be grounded in duties wrongdoers have. His more general view is discussed below.

the strength of the deterrents is thus apt to increase the incidence of such wrongdoing. As noted, public health measures that aim to reduce poverty and environmental degradation, and improve access to health care and education, are mismatched for crime of this kind. These considerations motivate an attempt to justify a stronger sort of general deterrence than the free sort already defended.

One way of justifying a stronger sort of general deterrence is on grounds of basic desert, as Nelkin (2019b) proposes. The state's function includes deterring crime, but punishment justified on general deterrence grounds is subject to the manipulative use objection. Yet as long as criminals basically deserve punishment of a particular severity, in Nelkin's view it is legitimate to recruit that punishment to the service of general deterrence. But again, this line of justification is not open to a skeptic about negative basic desert. Tadros (2017) concurs in rejecting basic desert, but aims to justify stronger general-deterrence-subserving penalties on the basis of claims about duties. In the proposal he develops, the manipulative use objection can be answered by invoking duties that wrongdoers owe to victims. Like Nelkin (2019b), I have concerns for the view as he sets it out, but I believe that the kinds of considerations he invokes serve to justify some stronger general deterrence (Pereboom 2020).

Tadros begins by arguing that wrongdoers who are not deserving of harm may sometimes be manipulatively used for the purposes of general deterrence. He does affirm that it is often intuitively wrong severely to harm one person without her consent to benefit others, a claim he illustrates with the following example:

*Bridge*: Dorabella is on a bridge with Fiordiligi. A trolley is heading on a track under the bridge towards five people who will be killed if Dorabella does nothing. Dorabella can save the five only by throwing Fiordiligi from the bridge onto the tracks. Fiordiligi's body will stop the trolley, saving the five, but Fiordiligi will be killed. (Tadros 2016, 84)

It is wrong for Dorabella to throw Fiordiligi off the bridge, knowing that he will die as a result. But Tadros contends that manipulatively using a person for a greater good is not always wrong. Consider:

*Wrongdoer on the Bridge*: As *Bridge* except Fiordiligi has wrongly started the trolley in order to kill the five, simply because he will enjoy seeing them die. (Tadros 2016, 84)

## 92    CRIME, PROTECTION, AND COMPASSION

Tadros judges that it seems permissible for Dorabella to use Fiordiligi in the way specified to save the five. But he acknowledges that the intuition might be due to the sense that Fiordiligi deserves to be harmed due to his wrongdoing. To correct for this Tadros proposes that the intuition that Fiordiligi is permissibly used withstands his being intentionally manipulated to act, as in my manipulation cases (e.g., Pereboom 2014, and set out in Chapter 1) which Tadros and I agree would rule out his deserving to be harmed:

*Manipulated Wrongdoer on the Bridge*:    As *Wrongdoer on the Bridge*, except that scientists have manipulated Fiordiligi's brain to ensure that he acts wrongly. However, Fiordiligi fulfils all plausible compatibilist conditions of responsibility—his effective first-order desire to kill the five conforms to his second-order desires; his process of deliberation from which the decision results is reason-responsive, in that it would have resulted in his refraining from posing this threat were his reasons different; his reasoning is consistent with his character, because he is egoistic; but he sometimes regulates his behavior by moral reasons; he is not constrained to act as he does, and he does not act out of an irresistible desire. (Tadros 2016, 85)

Tadros has the intuition that this use is permissible, and about it he says: "if this intuition is sound, it is plausibly sound in virtue of the fact that responsibility for wrongdoing, in the compatibilist sense, makes a difference to a person's liability to be used, even when the wrongdoing is secured through manipulation." He then provides the following diagnosis:

The manipulated wrongdoer on the bridge is heavily involved in the threat that the five face. He has a powerful reason to ensure that he is not the author of their deaths; much more powerful than the reason that innocent bystanders have to do so. If he could save their lives at some moderate cost to herself, he is required to do so. If he is thrown from the bridge to save the five, the cost that is inflicted on him is no greater than the cost that he would be required to bear in service of the end that he is used to serve. In that case, his complaint against being used in this way seems weak.    (2016, 86)

I (now) agree with Tadros that Fiordiligi is liable to defensive killing.[13] The reason is that, as I argued in Chapter 3, wrongfully posing a lethal threat

---

[13] In earlier publications I reported that in this case it was my strong sense that it is wrong to throw the manipulated man off the bridge (Pereboom 2017b, 2020). But the position on

HOW MUCH GENERAL DETERRENCE? 93

makes one thus liable, and Fiordiligi has in fact wrongfully posed a lethal threat. True, in *Manipulated Wrongdoer on the Bridge* the lethal threat, the trolley-in-motion, is in process in a way that it is not in typical examples employed to illustrate the right to defensively kill, in which killing prevents the lethal process—e.g., the shooting or the knifing—from being activated in the first place. But this is plausibly not a morally relevant difference.

However, while manipulative use by killing is sometimes justified, it may be justified largely in cases in which doing so is required to prevent another killing. We might now ask: what are the limits on manipulative use in which the right to defensively kill to prevent another killing isn't at issue? I've proposed that it is the human rights to life, liberty, and physical security of the person that have a key role in making the manipulative use objection to general deterrence intuitive (Pereboom 2020). Those rights are grounded in the more fundamental right to a life in which one's capacity for flourishing is not compromised in the long term. I've argued that there is a heavily weighted presumption (but not an absolute prohibition) against punishment as manipulative use when such use involves intentional killing, long-term confinement, and infliction of severe physical or psychological harm. But what if the proposed penalties are significantly less extreme, such as monetary penalties (Pereboom 2001, 177, 2017b, 2020)? Would it then be impermissible to use undeserving wrongdoers in ways that involve such penalties to subserve general deterrence?

As I've suggested, there may be circumstances in which effective general deterrence would require penalties more severe than can be justified on special deterrence grounds, and I cited manipulation of financial markets, large-scale embezzlement, and illegal use of political influence for gain in wealth and power. Plausibly this may also be so for less serious wrongdoing. Suppose preventing a shoplifter from future theft requires only monitoring with use of an ankle bracelet. The probability of shoplifters without monitoring devices being caught is low, and as a result, for quite a few people the expected net utility of shoplifting is relatively high. Now imagine that increasing the severity of the penalty for shoplifting to a substantial but not overly burdensome monetary penalty would reduce the incidence of shoplifting significantly relative to the threat of monitoring. Suppose also that it would reduce the cost of deterrence substantially relative to the monitoring policy. Would increasing the severity of the penalty be permissible in these

---

defensive killing that I've recently developed, in Chapter 3, changed my mind. Thanks to Carolina Sartorio for discussion of this issue.

## 94 CRIME, PROTECTION, AND COMPASSION

circumstances? Note that such a fine, by contrast with the death penalty and long-term imprisonment, need not hinder the prospects for a life lived at reasonable level of flourishing.

Moreover, if manipulative use involving fines is within bounds, should we say the same for short prison sentences, say of several months? Mark Kleiman (2016) argues that short prison sentences are often especially effective deterrents, especially in combination with a high expectation of being apprehended. This suggests that short prison sentences should also be within bounds as penalty extensions justified on general deterrence grounds. This provision would also solve a problem Tadros (in conversation) raises: what if people refuse to pay the fines they've been assessed? Here it would be helpful to have a short prison sentence as a backup, in particular given their effectiveness as deterrents.

We can add that effective general deterrence involving threats of manipulative use may sometimes require treatment less severe than what effective incapacitation would demand. Imagine someone who is guilty of insider trading, displaying a disposition to flout the regulations when it is to her advantage and the probability of getting caught is sufficiently low. Suppose that our insider trader is in fact a self-interested expected utility maximizer. What would be justified by way of incapacitation grounded in the right to self-defense? Arguably, exclusion from arrangements in which self-interested expected utility reasoning would lead to law violation of the sort at issue, such as loss of trading license and exclusion from this type of job. However, here manipulative use designed to deter such law violation might well be less harmful to her. The state might, for example, threaten and impose a substantial fine on general deterrence grounds, which on balance might well be less harmful to such offenders than the exclusion.

Schematically, the proposal is as follows:

*General Deterrence Prerogative*: If imposing a penalty on an offender on special deterrence grounds can be justified, imposing a somewhat more exacting penalty, not justified on special deterrence grounds, is justified if it (i) substantially increases general deterrence value, and/or (ii) substantially lowers the cost of deterrence, provided that the more exacting penalty doesn't hinder the prospects for a life lived at a reasonable level of flourishing. (Pereboom 2020, 94)

The rationale for this proposal has several components. First, one need not be a consequentialist to agree that consequences have weight when deciding moral and legal issues. The general deterrence prerogative specifies only that they have modest additional weight when special deterrence justification is already accounted for. Policies we all accept that would have to be justified in this way are already in place. We all accept that it's legitimate for the police to apprehend suspects of crime when there is adequate but nevertheless insufficient reason to believe that they are in fact criminals. This is a significant cost that we not infrequently impose on people who are in fact innocent, and this cost would be difficult to justify on other than consequentialist grounds.

Second, this account sets a credible standard for a weighted presumption against manipulative use: what justification might it have? Both the criminal who is given the short prison sentence for reasons of general deterrence, and the one who is made to serve life in prison or executed for this reason are being used as means for the safety of society. A pertinent question is: is each being used merely as a means? In the Kantian conception (Kant 1785/1981, this depends on whether he is also being treated as an end in himself. There are a number of accounts as to what this comes to. An attractive option is an elaboration of the idea that to treat a person as an end is to treat her in such a way as to facilitate her capacities and opportunities for developing herself as an autonomous, rational being. On capacities, we needn't privilege rationality: we can add other characteristics we value, such as the capacity for fulfilling personal relationships, the capacity to create and appreciate artistic products of culture, and the ability to excel in and value activities such as sports and physical labor. To treat someone as an end is to treat her in such a way as to allow her to flourish by developing such capacities in accordance with her preferences. Executing someone is clearly in violation of treating someone as an end in this sense, as is serving a life sentence in a standard American maximum-security prison. But a month in prison, with provision for education while confined and effective reintegration upon release, need not violate this standard. While such a short prison term is a violation of the liberty right, it is only a moderately serious violation, and will not in many cases preclude a life lived at a reasonable level of flourishing in the way that long prison terms typically do.

Might there be a non-consequentialist and non-desert-based justification for the General Deterrence Prerogative—for inflicting penalties on criminals for reasons of general deterrence that are somewhat more exacting than those justified on special deterrence grounds? As I noted above, Tadros (2016) develops a view of this sort that crucially invokes duties criminals have

## 96 CRIME, PROTECTION, AND COMPASSION

to their victims. In one of his examples, Dave, a lorry driver, involuntarily and non-culpably injures Veronica. Tadros contends, plausibly, that Dave has a more stringent duty to assist Veronica than does Xavier, a bystander. Suppose that instead Dave voluntarily injured her while satisfying the compatibilist conditions on moral responsibility. Tadros maintains that now Dave incurs even more stringent and extensive duties of this sort, even if factors beyond his control causally determine him to act, and even if he therefore doesn't basically deserve to have the cost imposed on him that carrying out these duties involves (Tadros 2016, 77–9). By analogy, it's plausible that those who commit crimes have a collective duty to compensate society that non-criminals lack, even if they don't deserve to suffer the harm involved in making this compensation. By virtue of committing crimes, criminals, as a sector of society, collectively make a costly criminal justice system necessary.

The right to self-defense justifies free general deterrence, in accord with Farrell's view. We can think of this, metaphorically, as a fence the state sets up against criminal behavior. Suppose Zoë builds a fence around her garden to prevent rampant plant-trampling. One night, Alice and Bob tear down part of the fence, enter the garden, and trample the plants. Would it be legitimate to require Alice and Bob to reconstruct the fence, on grounds other than basic desert, and not require innocent Chloë and Dan, who are also available, to help? As David Boonin (2008) and Tadros (2016) argue, duties of compensation can plausibly be supported on grounds other than desert. Suppose I accidentally break my aunt Ellen's vase, but I wasn't culpably negligent. It nevertheless seems reasonable to expect that I compensate by, for instance, replacing the vase, despite not deserving to bear this cost. By analogy, it's credible that we can reasonably expect criminals collectively to compensate, in part, for the expense of the criminal justice system, even if they don't deserve to bear that cost or to suffer the harm that such compensation may involve. As Tadros (2017) argues regarding one specific type of compensation he regards as permissibly imposed on wrongdoers: "The fact that wrongdoers wrongly lead us to be vulnerable to attack by others by undermining the credibility of our threats may be sufficient to render it permissible to use them" (Tadros 2017, 615), and this, in his view, is so regardless of considerations of desert. Note again that the objective is only to justify penalties somewhat more severe than those justifiable on special deterrence grounds alone. For this reason, such considerations needn't be especially weighty.

## A Comparison with Dennett's Position

As noted earlier, Daniel Dennett (especially in Dennett and Caruso 2020) advocates a position, like Manuel Vargas's (2013), in which the practice-level justifications for blame and punishment cite backward-looking considerations of desert, while such desert is not conceived as basic because at a higher level the practice is justified by its forward-looking aims. These aims include enhancing the ability to recognize and respond to moral considerations and protecting people from the dangers wrongdoers pose. On Dennett's account, our actual practice insofar as it involves punishing criminals because they deserve it should be retained since doing so has the best overall consequences relative to alternative practices. His view has a contractualist element: we tacitly consent to rules for behavior and for penalties imposed for crime that we, as idealized consequentialist reasoners, would formulate and endorse. Note that Dennett is also a revisionist about punishment relative to actual practice in the United States; he believes that much of it is unjust and requires reform.

As discussed in Chapter 2, Dennett employs sports analogies to confirm that his non-basic desert is genuine desert (Dennett and Caruso 2020; cf., Doris 2015; Vargas 2015). It seems legitimate to say that someone who commits a foul in basketball deserves the penalty for that foul. But such sports desert isn't basic—it's instead founded in considerations about how basketball works best as a sport. Similarly, suppose penalties for criminal behavior are justified on forward-looking, deterrence grounds, in virtue of the anticipated effect of safety. Then it similarly makes sense to say that penalties are deserved. From my perspective the crucial point of agreement with my view, and also Caruso's (2021), is that the fundamental justifications are ultimately forward looking, and justifications that appeals to basic desert are ruled out. Dennett in fact claims that 'basic desert' is an incoherent notion; in my view, attributions of basic desert to human beings are instead coherent but false. Dennett's more general view is that there is no basic desert moral responsibility and no libertarian free will, but there is deserved punishment and we do have free will. The way he puts the point is that we have all the desert and free will worth wanting, while the stronger notions are incoherent or at least clearly don't apply to us.

On deserved punishment, Dennett's view is compatible with the main claims of mine and with Caruso's. Caruso and I can allow that the player who hands the ball in soccer deserves to have the specified penalty imposed.

## 98   CRIME, PROTECTION, AND COMPASSION

Similarly, we can affirm that the insider trader deserves to have his trading license suspended, on the supposition that license suspension is the penalty that idealized forward-looking reasoners would specify for insider trading. Part of Dennett's conception is that the moral game needs knowable rules with specified penalties so that players can anticipate what will happen if they violate the rules. I agree. I don't see violent crime exactly in these terms. I say: if agents manifest a disposition to extreme violence, it is legitimate to preventatively detain them, justified on analogy with quarantine. Perhaps the meaning of 'desert' is sufficiently unrestricted for preventative detention to then count as deserved, but in my view not much depends on whether we use the term 'desert' in this context. What's key is that such measures are not justified on grounds of basic desert, and Dennett concurs.

## Objections

Let us now consider several objections, each of which is a good challenge that occasions clarification of the position I'm proposing. First, Saul Smilansky (2017) objects that the justified detention of the criminally dangerous on the quarantine analogy will yield insufficient and inadequate deterrence. He contends that on this model, those who are detained would need to be compensated for their confinement by what he calls *funishment*, a paradigm of which he once specified as equivalent to a stay in a five-star hotel (Smilanksy 2011). Neil Levy (2011) and I (Pereboom 2014, 172–3; cf., Pereboom and Caruso 2018) disagreed, and I argued that less opulent accommodations and programs for rehabilitation and reintegration would be in order. Smilansky (2017) replied that two-star accommodation would also not yield adequate deterrence, and that therefore a harsher environment, justified on retributive grounds, would be required instead.

But in addition to detention justified by analogy to quarantine, further sorts of monitoring, and programs for rehabilitation and reintegration, the model I advocate includes general deterrence by monetary penalties and short-term prison sentences. This yields a response to one example Smilansky provides, greedy relatives who murder in order to secure an inheritance. Their motive is financial gain, and it stands to reason that they would be deterred by a credible threat of dispossession. Such monetary penalties can also serve as a deterrent for the spousal killer who poses no other genuine threat, although credible examples of this phenomenon may be extremely rare. Here limited prison sentences may also be effective, in particular in combination with a high expectation of being caught.

Smilansky's inadequacy claim is empirical, and there is empirical evidence that bears on the issue. Currently there is widespread discussion of the difference between the American model for criminal justice and those that we find in countries such as Norway, Sweden, Finland, Denmark, and the Netherlands. In Norway, for example, the aim of the criminal justice system is at least largely protection and reintegration, and famously, prisons are indeed the equivalent of two-star hotels. But in these countries crime and recidivism rates are much lower than they are in the United States, whose criminal justice system is closer to what Smilansky envisions. The reasons for differential success in deterrence and prevention between these countries and the United States are undoubtedly complex, and some argue that the policy is not feasible in the American context. But the success of such a policy counsels against ready acceptance of the claim that harsher prison conditions of the sort that Smilansky advocates should generally be preferred to alternative measures.

Second, Michael Corrado (2016), John Lemos (2016), and Smilansky (2017) object that implementation of this account would draw too many people into the criminal justice system. In particular, it would lead to incapacitating those who pose threats but have not yet committed crimes. As a remedy, Smilanksy maintains that retributivism can have the role of limiting incapacitation to an intuitively plausible degree (cf., Hodgson 2012). In response, I doubt that retributivism can effectively play this role (cf., Caruso 2021), and I contend that this account has other resources to safeguard the right people from the criminal justice system.

A concern for preventative detention that I've emphasized in the past (e.g., Pereboom 2014, 170–1), is that, for example, neural tests for determining whether someone is likely to commit a crime are invasive and may seriously conflict with the right to liberty, and current neural tests are not especially reliable and frequently yield false positives (Nadelhoffer and Sinnott-Armstrong 2012; Nadelhoffer et al. 2012). But still, better tests are being developed (Nadelhoffer et al. 2012). In *Free Will, Agency, and Meaning in Life* (2014, 170) I present an example in which an agent has been given a drug without his knowledge, and we can determine that as a result he will almost certainly commit a crime within a week. After a week the effect of the drug wears off. I suggested that the state is entitled to detain him for that week. Corrado (in correspondence) allows that if the drug impairs his reasons responsiveness, preventative detention may be permissible. Smilansky

100   CRIME, PROTECTION, AND COMPASSION

might be attracted to this kind of position: if an agent is dangerous but not sufficiently reasons responsive, he may be detained. But what if someone is dangerous and sufficiently reasons responsive? Corrado's (1996) position is that then he may not be detained unless it can be shown that he has a current intention to cause harm. As Corrado indicates, delineating the particular features of intention (e.g., how specific does it need to be?) is a delicate and difficult issue. But this general sort of position seems reasonable to me.

Corrado (in correspondence) suggests that a test for the demonstrable intention model is the landmark legal case *Tarasoff* v *The Regents of the University of California* (1974). The case involves Prosenjit Poddar, who confided his desire to kill a young woman, Tanya Tarasoff, to his therapist. The therapist believed the threat to be serious enough to have Poddar preventatively detained, but the therapist was overruled by his supervisor. Prior to these events, Poddar had been civilly committed as a dangerous person but was then released when he appeared rational. Poddar then killed Tarasoff. Subsequently, the doctor and his employer, the University of California, were sued by Tarasoff's family. The Supreme Court of California decided that the defendants were liable to the family, not because they hadn't detained Tarasoff, but for the reason that they hadn't warned her of the threat that Poddar posed to her. The case established a duty on the part of therapists to warn, but only where a specific victim was targeted. A general prediction that some unspecified person would be harmed would not justify a duty to warn.

In other jurisdictions, such as Ontario, Canada, the state has the right to detain the dangerous when rationally competent, albeit under mental health legislation.[14] It seems to me that the Ontario policy, supplemented with the demonstrable intention requirement Corrado proposes, is preferable (Corrado 1996; Pereboom 2017c, 2020). Tarasoff should not have been subjected to the burden of protecting herself against someone with a demonstrable intention to kill her. Would Smilansky agree? If not, would he have allowed Tarasoff to be subjected to the burden of self-protection? But if he does agree, then retributivism cannot play the detention-limiting role he advocates for it.

A more general concern of Smilansky's is that we not treat criminals unjustly, and if they don't deserve to be harmed, it's unjust to harm them. I share this concern. He and I both believe that the arguments for free will skepticism—that we lack the control in action required to ground desert (or

---

[14] Thanks to Jennifer Chandler for this information.

at least basic desert)—are strong (Smilansky 2000; Pereboom 2001, 2014). But in his response, by contrast with mine, Smilansky (2000) advocates retaining the illusion of free will and desert, even when justifying criminal punishment. However, this involves treating people unjustly by his own standard, since he believes that arguments for free will skepticism, and thus against the view that wrongdoers deserve to be treated harshly, remain unanswered. I agree that dangerous criminals don't basically deserve to be incapacitated, but that our right to defend ourselves provides an alternative reason for incapacitation, and in a limited respect, consequentialist considerations and duties owed by wrongdoers also count. So even if harming criminals is in an important sense unjust because undeserved, and should concern us for this reason, doing so in the limited ways I've specified is nevertheless justified.

Smilansky (2017, together with others such as David Hodgson (2012), cite as a reason for adopting retributivism that it can ensure that only the guilty, and not the innocent, are punished. On this suggestion, the best way to secure this good is by way of a certain legal practice—by lawyers, judges, and juries justifying their decisions at least in part on grounds invoking desert. Notice, however, that on this conception the desert invoked won't be basic, since the practice is justified at least partly on the ground that it's the best way to secure a good consequence—that the innocent not be punished. By contrast, we might imagine someone who does think that basic desert justifications are in place and who cites this benefit only as a side-effect. But this exact view isn't available to Smilansky, since he maintains that we don't have free will, that we lack the control in action required for basic desert attributions. Again, he is, by contrast, an illusionist about free will and about basic desert. In effect, Smilansky is contending that we must maintain the illusion about free will and basic desert for the sake of a good consequence, that the innocent not be punished. Thus he is in fact invoking non-basic desert, and not basic desert, in his account. Hodgson (2012), who also cites protection of the innocent from punishment as a benefit of belief in desert, is not an illusionist about free will. He can, by contrast, consistently invoke basic desert in his proposal.

Are Hodgson and Smilansky right to think that commitment to desert-based legal justifications would have the effect of protecting the innocent from punishment? For this to be so, it must be that someone's not deserving to be harmed is sufficient reason for the state not to harm that person for the sake of a further state interest. The problem is that there is another competing state interest that justifies harm: protection from threats (Caruso

## 102 CRIME, PROTECTION, AND COMPASSION

(2021) argues similarly). Those who pose threats may uncontroversially not be deserving of harm, such as the mentally ill lethal threats we considered in Chapter 3. Or imagine someone who has been given a drug, without his knowledge, that makes him prone to extreme violence for a short time, and that the only way to stop him from killing someone is to incapacitate him with a painful taser. This is clearly legitimate. Or suppose that the drugged person is about to shoot as many students in school as he can, and the only way the police can stop him is to kill him. This is also legitimate. Thus, not being deserving of harm does not insulate a person from being justifiably harmed by the state on the basis of its interest in protection. Furthermore, and particularly troublesome for Hodgson and Smilansky's proposal, when innocent people are presumed to be threats, the belief that only the guilty should be detained or killed is often ineffectual. As Caruso (2021) points out, in the United States belief in retributivism is strong in regions in which convictions of the innocent who are believed to be threats, often unjustifiably, are also prevalent, particularly when the innocent are African-American and Latino men. This is consistent with belief in desert and in retributive justification for punishment reducing the incidence of such convictions, but it's not clear that these beliefs actually have this effect.[15]

### Summary and Conclusion

My aim was to set out a theory for treatment of criminals that rejects the retributive justification for punishment, does not fall afoul of a plausible prohibition on using people merely as means, and can actually work in the real world. The proposal is largely justified as special deterrence by the right to self-defense and defense of others, as in Farrell's (1985) theory. My account adds the quarantine analogy-based rationale for preventatively detaining criminals together with provisions for rehabilitation and reintegration, and a justification for somewhat more exacting penalties to secure effective general deterrence, measures that cannot be justified as special deterrence by the self-defense right. Here consequentialist considerations and duties of compensation have a modest, but to my mind plausible, justificatory role.

---

[15] This observation also casts doubt on the related claim that belief in retributivism has the effect of limiting the severity of punishment. For a response to this claim, see Victoria McGeer (2013, 187–8).

# 5
# Forgiveness as Renunciation of Moral Protest

When we forgive, we renounce and overcome future blaming responses to an agent in virtue of what the forgiver understands to be, and is in fact, an immoral action he has performed. Crucially, on the standard view the blaming response is understood as essentially involving a reactive attitude. In the central case in which the forgiver has been wronged by the party being forgiven, the reactive attitude is resentment, directed toward an agent due to a wrong he has done to oneself. When someone other than the forgiver has been wronged by the one being forgiven, the attitude is indignation, directed toward an agent because of a wrong he has done to a third party. Such a position was developed by Joseph Butler (1726, 2006; cf., Radzik 2014) and in more recent times endorsed by P. F. Strawson (1962), Jeffrie Murphy (1982), Jay Wallace (1994), and Charles Griswold (2007). Wallace (1994, 72) is representative when he writes: "in forgiving people we express our acknowledgment that they have done something that would warrant resentment and blame, but we renounce the responses that we thus acknowledge to be appropriate."

The standard view raises a challenge to forgiveness on the supposition of skepticism about free will. On the standard view, forgiveness involves the renunciation of an attitude, say resentment, toward a wrongdoer that one formerly regarded as appropriate. This condition is jeopardized if an agent does not resent because she believes resentment is typically unjustified due to a presupposition of basically deserved blame experienced as painful or harmful. She cannot at one point affirm and later renounce an attitude she never had, and which she never believed was justified. Suppose this agent was wronged, doubts that resentment is justified, but resents nevertheless. She can then overcome her resentment, but the forgiveness would then have the uncomfortable status of renouncing and overcoming an attitude she did not initially regard as justified. In the face of these difficulties, I propose a

---

*Wrongdoing and the Moral Emotions.* Derk Pereboom, Oxford University Press. © Derk Pereboom 2021.
DOI: 10.1093/oso/9780192846006.003.0005

104 FORGIVENESS AS RENUNCIATION OF MORAL PROTEST

sense of forgiveness that essentially features renouncing the stance of moral protest, rather than resentment or indignation.[1]

The standard view has in recent times been subjected to a number of challenges. Eve Garrard and David McNaughton (2003), Dana Nelkin (2008, 2011, 44–50, 2013), and Brandon Warmke and Michael McKenna (2013) contend that in cases in which the forgiver is the wronged party, forgiveness need not involve overcoming of resentment. On Nelkin's account, someone might not feel resentment in the first place and still forgive. She might, for instance, correctly perceive that she has been wronged, but not feel resentment, and then forgive the transgressor. The defender of the standard view may respond by arguing that in such cases resentment was nonetheless appropriate, and believed to be so by the wronged party, and what the forgiver renounces is any future resentment and its expression on her part. This exact route is not clearly available to desert skeptics, who are concerned that resentment is inappropriate due to its presupposing that the wrongdoer deserves to be the target of its expression, or due to its connection to a retributive desire (Honderich 1988; cf., Nussbaum 2016).[2] The alternative sense of forgiveness I'm proposing is that the renounced blaming response need not be an attitude such as resentment or indignation, but instead the stance of moral protest. At the same time, even for the free will skeptic, if, despite her concerns about the appropriateness of resentment, she nonetheless resents, forgiveness on her part may yet involve her renouncing it and its expressions. For this reason I agree that forgiveness can involve renunciation of different attitudes, and that in this respect it has different senses (as, for example, Santiago Amaya (2019) contends).

## Separating Blameworthiness from the Appropriateness of Anger

Forgiveness requires that the wrongdoer was in fact morally responsible—in *some* sense—for his wrongdoing, thus blameworthy for it, and is believed to be blameworthy by the forgiver. This belief would have to be retained by

---

[1] This chapter is a revision of Pereboom (2021a).
[2] In Chapter 2 I proposed an ecumenical compromise among the views on the relation of belief to emotions: when a mature, normal human subject targets another with an expression of resentment or indignation, she will typically believe that the target agent has acted wrongly, and, in my view, she will also typically believe that he basically deserves to be targeted by an expression of the reactive attitude.

the forgiver, on the pain of giving up a false belief. Hence it must not be the belief that the wrongdoer was blameworthy that the forgiver renounces. Rather, it must be attitudes and expressions of those attitudes that are justified in virtue of the wrongdoer's being blameworthy. Again, these attitudes are often specified to be reactive attitudes such as resentment and indignation. But perhaps this is a mistake. There may be examples of blameworthiness in which such attitudes, and anger more generally, are suboptimal, and in which they are in fact inappropriate. If so, supposing that wrongdoing in such cases can be forgiven, renouncing resentment or indignation, and anger more generally, will not be required for forgiveness.

On one reading of Strawson's (1962) "Freedom and Resentment," blameworthiness is a response-dependent notion, according to which it is a particular emotional, attitudinal response that makes an action blameworthy. As we saw in Chapter 2, David Shoemaker (2017) develops and defends such a Strawsonian account. On his proposal, the blameworthy (in the realm of accountability) just is whatever merits anger. What unifies all of the properties that make anger appropriate is just that they are angerworthy, and this is what makes the account genuinely response-dependent. We also saw that there is an alternative response-independent account that features anger, but as a response which is independent of the property in which blameworthiness consists. Anger is instead made appropriate in virtue of that property. On this view, blameworthiness is not essentially dependent on the response of anger, but anger is the property that fixes the reference of the term 'blameworthy.'

I raised two concerns about the choice of anger as the designated response in these accounts. First, there are cases of blameworthiness, in the context of relationships between parents and children, teachers and students, and people in professional contexts, that are not cases of angerworthiness. In the examples I set out, involving Athena the parent, Basil the teacher, and Chloe the professor, an angry response stands to be counterproductive and to undermine the effectiveness of the respondents. Even setting aside the free will skeptic's objections, in the situations imagined angry responses seem inappropriate and misplaced. The second concern I cited is that anger has a strong tendency to distort judgments of blameworthiness, and that it is dubious that to be blameworthy is to be worthy of a reactive attitude that systematically distorts judgments of blameworthiness (Alicke et al. 1994, 2012; Alicke 2000). In addition, psychological research indicates that anger, once activated, degrades subsequent reasoning processes in various ways (e.g., Lerner et al. 1998; Goldberg et al. 1999; Litvak

106　FORGIVENESS AS RENUNCIATION OF MORAL PROTEST

et al. 2010). It increases tendencies to overlook mitigating details before attributing blame, to rely on stereotypes and to discount the role of uncontrollable factors in assigning blame. Anger makes us slower to associate positive traits than negative traits with an out-group, and activates an indiscriminate tendency to punish others in unrelated situations without regard for whether their actions were intentional.

These observations call for a general characterization of blameworthiness that does not highlight anger. I cited Pamela Hieronymi (2001), Matt Talbert (2012), Angela Smith (2013), and Michael McKenna (2012) as having proposed that blame should be understood as moral protest, and follow suit for the sense of blame that I endorse, which I characterized as follows:

*Moral Protest Account of Blame*: For A to appropriately blame B is for A to adopt a stance of moral protest against B for immoral conduct B has performed and that A is epistemically justified in attributing to B, and A's adopting this stance is morally justified.

On my account, moral protest is a stance of opposition to an agent for having performed (or apparently having performed) a specific immoral action or a number of immoral actions, or for having (or apparently having) a disposition to act immorally, a posture of mind whose function in our moral practice is primarily to engage wrongdoers by communicating opposition to wrongdoing of a general type, together with moral reasons for the agent to refrain from it. This communication might appropriately be confrontational to varying degrees, depending on the circumstances. Hieronymi (2001) and the other protest theorists just mentioned tie moral protest to the negative reactive attitudes, paradigmatically resentment.[3] The notion of moral protest I propose lacks this connection. It's possible for moral protest not to involve resentment, indignation, nor any sort of anger, nor a belief in the appropriateness of such attitudes.

In accord with this sense of blame, I proposed the following amended version of the response-dependent view about the blameworthy:

*Fitting Response-Dependence about the Blameworthy*: The blameworthy (in the realm of accountability) is just is whatever merits moral protest (the

---

[3] Jean Hampton writes: "[r]esentment is a kind of anger which protests the demeaning treatment to one who could and should have known better, and this protest is frequently linked to verbal rebuke, reprimand or complaint direct at the insulter" (Murphy and Hampton 1988, 55).

## FORGIVENESS AS RENUNCIATION OF MORAL PROTEST 107

protestworthy); that is, someone is blameworthy (and so accountable) for X if and only if, and in virtue of the fact that, she merits moral protest for X,

and of its response-independent correlate:

*Fitting Protest-Response-Independence about the Blameworthy:* The blameworthy (in the realm of accountability) consists in a property (or properties) of agents that makes morally protesting their wrongdoing appropriate, a property (or properties) whose value making is ultimately independent of our responses of moral protest,

without choosing between the two. What are these properties/features of agents? In Chapter 2 (and in 2014, 134–5, 2017a) I set out a largely forward-looking conception of blame, whose objectives include moral formation of character, reconciliation in relationships, retention of integrity of a victim, and protection from harm. Blame as moral protest can be understood as having these forward-looking aims, together with a minimal backward-looking element: that the agent acted wrongly with cognitive sensitivity to the wrongness is part of what makes the protest appropriate. The agent's responsiveness to reasons is presupposed in central cases of blaming on this account, since it features blaming as engaging the wrongdoer with moral reasons.

### Forgiveness as Renunciation of Moral Protest

If in many cases of personal wrongdoing, anger is not optimal or even appropriate, forgiveness should not generally be taken to involve renunciation of anger and its expressions. Setting aside free will skepticism, in specific cases in which anger is appropriate, forgiveness may involve its renunciation. But in cases of wrongdoing in which the angry response is not optimal, and one does not in fact respond with anger but rather with moral concern, one's forgiveness cannot plausibly consist in the renunciation of anger and its expressions. This allows that forgiveness involve the renunciation of whatever blaming attitudes and their expressions are appropriate, where such attitudes differ across cases. This I accept, but even setting aside free will skepticism, I'll now contend that forgiveness fairly generally involves the renunciation of the stance of moral protest.

Imagine a friend has wronged you in some way a number of times by acting inconsiderately, and you find yourself resolved to end your friendship with

## 108 FORGIVENESS AS RENUNCIATION OF MORAL PROTEST

him. You engage in a moral conversation with him, protesting against him for the wrong he has done and for the threat that his disposition to behave this way poses. In response, he is contrite, assumes a firm disapproving stance toward that disposition, and commits himself to full elimination. You might now withdraw your protest and agree to continue the relationship on a better footing. In Hieronymi's conception, forgiveness is such a withdrawal of a protest to a threat upon acknowledgment of the offender's change of heart:

> If I ask for forgiveness, I am not asking you to understand why I did the deed, from my point of view. (I may no longer fully understand that myself. In any case, if I am properly repentant, I surely don't recommend that point of view.) To ask you to understand things from my point of view is to hope for an excuse, not to ask for forgiveness. Nor, when I ask for forgiveness, am I asking for your pity or compassion in response to the pain of my remorse. Nor am I asking you simply to acknowledge the fact of my repentance and reform. I am instead asking you to believe me when I say that I no longer see what I did to you as acceptable, to recognize and so ratify my change of heart. (Hieronymi 2001, 554)

Ratifying such a change of heart, I believe, fairly generally involves renunciation of the appropriateness of the stance of moral protest against the wrongdoer for having committed the specific wrong or wrongs that was the focus of the protest. This renunciation involves acquiring a belief that such a stance on one's own part is no longer appropriate, and a firm commitment not to engage in overt moral protest. This renunciation is compatible with the forgiver never having actually taken on the stance of moral protest, since in renouncing such a stance one may be renouncing it in the future.

Here is a case of Per-Erik Milam's that serves to illustrate several features of this proposal:

> *Infidelity.* David cheats on his partner, Donna. At first he thinks it's no big deal, but he begins to feel more and more ashamed of his behaviour and guilty about betraying her trust. David recognizes what his remorse is telling him and he recommits himself, in his own mind, to being a faithful partner. Shortly thereafter he admits to Donna what he did, apologizes to her, and assures her that it won't happen again, explaining how guilty and ashamed he feels and how much he values their relationship. Donna is understandably upset and, at first, does not know what to do. Eventually

FORGIVENESS AS RENUNCIATION OF MORAL PROTEST    109

though she comes to believe that David is sincere in his remorse and apology, that he is trustworthy, and that they can still have a healthy and fulfilling relationship together. Donna overcomes her blame and tells David that she forgives him.    (Milam 2022)

Here one might ask: in what does Donna's forgiveness consist? On my proposal, it's Donna's believing that moral protest on her part, internal and overt, against David for what he has done is no longer appropriate, and being committed to acting on this belief. This is what her renouncing the stance of moral protest amounts to. We can imagine a case in which Donna has never actually occupied the stance of protest against David's infidelity. Nevertheless, she can still renounce any future stance of moral protest against David for his wrongdoing. If Donna says at some future time, "You are such a jerk for being unfaithful; I can't believe that you did this!" this indicates that she still holds his wrongdoing against him, which is evidence that she hasn't renounced the stance of moral protest, and hasn't forgiven him.

Suppose that Emma, a student for whom Frida, her teacher, has high academic hopes, for the first time in the course is not paying attention in class and is surfing the internet instead. Protest is appropriate even if anger is not, and forgiveness, as the renunciation of the stance of moral protest and any expression of it, may be granted upon contrition and apology. Frida may say to Emma: "Your surfing the internet is distracting to other students, and it would be best for you to pay attention instead," without being angry but with a sense of duty for seeing to her education and moral formation. Suppose Emma expresses contrition and apologizes, and her subsequent behavior in the class indicates a change of heart. If at that point Frida nevertheless calls her aside to say: "You surfed the internet that day and what you did was inexcusable, you distracted the other students, and you should have been paying attention instead," it would be clear that she still holds the wrong against her, hasn't renounced the stance of moral protest, and hasn't yet responded to Emma's contrition with forgiveness. Suppose instead that in response to her contrition Frida renounces the appropriateness of the stance of moral protest on her part. This would be a case of forgiveness with renunciation of the stance of moral protest but without renunciation of resentment. On the other hand, if resentment were fairly generally appropriate, forgiveness upon contrition and apology would still involve renunciation of the stance of moral protest, even if it would also involve renunciation of resentment. Thus, I propose, renunciation of the stance of moral protest

110 FORGIVENESS AS RENUNCIATION OF MORAL PROTEST

qualifies as a fairly general feature of forgiveness, regardless of the truth of free will skepticism.

Forgiveness may often involve an occurrent belief that overtly protesting a wrongdoer's having performed an action is no longer appropriate, together with clear verbal communication to the wrongdoer that she has been forgiven. But in some cases the belief that moral protest was appropriate may be merely dispositional and not occurrent, and the indication to the wrongdoer that she has been forgiven might be understated—evident, for example, only in subtle changes in the forgiver's behavior and expression. But in any case, ruled out as inappropriate upon having forgiven is overt moral protest against the wrongdoer for having performed the act in question. Also ruled out is a continuing dispositional but uncommunicated stance of moral protest. Some overt specifications of wrongdoing on the part of the forgiver don't count as protest. In cataloging instances in which she has been wronged in the past, a forgiver might cite a wrongdoing in a way that doesn't count as moral protest against the wrongdoer. But, alternatively, she may cite the wrongdoing in such a way as to indicate that she hasn't forgiven.

When due to forgiving someone for a particular wrong it is no longer appropriate to retain the stance of protest against the wrongdoer for that particular wrongdoing, is it also no longer appropriate to retain that stance against the wrongdoer for the disposition to act in this way, and thus for wrongdoings of that general type? This depends, I think, on the history of interactions. Suppose George has a history of verbally abusing Helen, but he is regularly genuinely contrite after one particular instance. Then while it may be appropriate for Helen to renounce the stance of protest for the particular instance of verbal abuse for which George has been contrite, renunciation of the stance of moral protest against him for the disposition isn't called for, since there is substantial evidence that George retains that disposition, which persists as a threat. Or, for another type of case, imagine that what Helen has protested is specifically George's disposition, and his verbal abuse generally, and not just a single instance. In response, George is genuinely contrite about his disposition, but it's clear to Helen that the disposition persists and the abuse will continue. For her to renounce the stance of protest and its communication against George's disposition again isn't called for. The point of moral protest is forward looking, and in each of these cases moral reform is salient. Since it's clear that moral reform of the disposition to verbally abuse hasn't been achieved in either case, the value of Helen's stance of moral protest and its communication remains in place. There is, I think, a strong presumption against renouncing the stance of protest against any ongoing disposition to wrongdoing, even if the wrongdoer expresses genuine contrition for having the disposition.

One might suggest that forgiveness is essentially relationship-focused. On this account, what it is to forgive is to cease to regard the wrong done as a reason to weaken or dissolve a relationship. This feature can be seen as retracting blame in the sense T. M. Scanlon characterizes blame (Scanlon 2009, 128). My forgiving someone who has wronged me would then involve my initially having judged that what he did showed something about his attitude toward me that impairs his relationship with me, but in response to his repentance, my no longer taking this relationship to be modified in a way that this judgment of impaired relations justifies as appropriate. Upon forgiving, the judgment of impaired relations would be withdrawn because I take him to have given up the attitude toward me that impairs our relationship. A concern for this view, pressed by Susan Wolf (2011), is that relationships are often resilient to and not impaired by blameworthiness of a minor sort. Routine and expected wrongdoing, such as a spouse's snappy irritability when tired, or a child's not cleaning his room, may not be relationship impairing (Pereboom 2017a). Such wrongdoing may still be forgiven by renunciation of protest against the wrongdoer, and thus forgiveness is not essentially relationship restoring.

## Renunciation of the Stance of Moral Protest Must Be for the Right Reason

Milam (2019, 2022 cf., Fricker 2021) argues that normatively, forgiveness must respond to a perceived change of heart on the part of the wrongdoer. If blame or resentment are renounced for a reason other than change of heart, the wronged person does not forgive appropriately, if she forgives at all. Milam writes:

> A change of heart by the offender is reason to forgive because it speaks directly to one's reasons for blaming in the first place. A person is blameworthy if they are morally responsible for some wrongdoing, and moral responsibility—as opposed to mere causal responsibility—requires some particular connection between the offender and the act. A change of heart—whether evidenced by remorse, repentance, or atonement—suggests that that connection no longer exists.
>
> (Milam 2022; cf., Murphy and Hampton 1988;
> Swinburne 1989; Hieronymi 2001; Allais 2008)

## 112 FORGIVENESS AS RENUNCIATION OF MORAL PROTEST

Change of heart, or contrition, can be manifested through apology, but as noted, sometimes through other verbal and behavioral expressions. Milam argues that other sorts of reasons to cease to blame are not reasons to forgive. We might renounce the stance of moral protest because the offender had good intentions (Murphy and Hampton 1988), or because the threat incipient in the offence has been neutralized (Hieronymi 2001), or out of solidarity (Garrard and McNaughton 2003, 2010), but in Milam's view these are not cases of appropriate forgiveness. In fact, in his conception, at least some of these are cases of *letting go*, and not of forgiveness at all.[4]

Let me defend Milam's conception on the assumption that forgiveness generally involves renunciation of the stance of moral protest. We'll consider a range of cases in which moral protest is given up without contrition serving as a reason, and ask whether they plausibly count as forgiveness. One reason to renounce the stance of moral protest is discovering that the putative wrongdoer has a valid excuse. Excuses deny blameworthiness, and blameworthiness implies the lack of an excuse, that is, if the excuse is a full, by contrast with a partial excuse. Thus, as David Brink (2021, 52–4) puts it, excuse and blameworthiness are mirror images of one another. Brink points out that the criminal law in the United States recognizes two main kinds of excuse—"those that involve significant impairment of an agent's *capacities*, as reflected in cases of insanity or immaturity, and those in which an agent's circumstances compromise her fair *opportunity* to exercise these capacities free from interference, as reflected in cases involving manipulation or duress" (Brink 2021, 53). As an example of the second sort, one might protest against a fellow subway passenger for stepping on your foot, but then discover that the wrong on his part was not intentional, and that he would have avoided it had he not been crowded and jostled by other passengers. As a result, one comes to understand that he is fully excused. In response to this understanding, one may renounce the stance of moral protest one has adopted. This is not a case of forgiveness, because forgiveness requires that the wrongdoer was blameworthy and that one believes that he is, and this is not so if one believes he has a full excuse. More generally, renouncing protest due to recognition of an excuse is not forgiveness (cf., Nelkin 2013). It is also not a case of letting go. In cases in which one recognizes that one's stance of moral protest was adopted erroneously, as in the case of an excuse of which one was not initially aware, one does not let the stance go, but rather, if one's response is morally apt, one repents of having adopted it, or acknowledges its inappropriateness in some other way. Letting go does not

---

[4] For a contrary view see Santiago Amaya (2019).

involve regarding the stance of protest as being inappropriate, but rather just giving it up or allowing it to dissipate.

One may also relinquish the stance of moral protest by condoning wrongdoing, but again without forgiving. Robert Roberts (1995) characterizes condoning in terms of giving up anger, but this account can be revised to feature moral protest instead. In his conception, the condoner sees that a wrong has been done, but she gives up her anger or doesn't get angry. But, in Roberts's words, "unlike the forgiver, the condoner's failure to get angry is sub-morally motivated: by an aversion to getting 'upset,' by a fear of the consequences of angry behavior, by a distaste for effort or trouble" (Roberts 1995, 295). The condoner, on my account, gives up the stance of moral protest, or never adopts it in the first place, due to lack of resolve in confronting wrongdoing. Suppose a someone regularly indulges in bullying behavior; he berates and mocks others, particularly his rivals, in ways that harm them and is detrimental to the communal life. You initially adopt a stance of moral protest, but because you fear being targeted yourself, you give it up, and never act so as to manifest this stance. In such a case, you don't forgive the bully, but merely condone his bad behavior. One might think of this as a kind of letting go. Yet while some types of letting go are morally justified or morally neutral, condoning is morally mistaken; it is a kind of moral weakness (Roberts 1995). In Milam's words, "withholding blame in order to avoid the social burdens of blame and censure is not forgiveness because it is the wrong kind of reason" (Milam 2019, 247).

One might also relinquish the stance of moral protest when there is no change of heart, there is no excuse, and without condoning the wrongdoing. Instead, one may give up that stance because moral or prudential reasons outweigh retaining it. Imagine that a friend has certain habits that result in behavior that is morally wrong but only in minor ways—being somewhat too angry at bad drivers, somewhat too dismissive of those that disagree with him, and insufficiently restraining his irritability when tired. The friend is not contrite about such behavior even under one's initial mild protest. One might relinquish the stance of moral protest in such cases because the moral offenses are minor, and even if you see that there is some chance of expressed protest eventually being effective, you think it's not worth the disruption of the relationships to achieve the result. Maintaining that stance wears on you. So you give up the stance and its manifestations. Milam (2019, 2022) would classify this as a case of letting go, and not of forgiveness. One should exercise caution in letting go in such cases, taking care that one does not let down one's guard against wrongdoing. But it may at times be justified.

# 114 FORGIVENESS AS RENUNCIATION OF MORAL PROTEST

In summary, on the sense of forgiveness I propose, it involves renunciation of the stance of moral protest due to recognition of the wrongdoer's change of heart, where the wrongdoer was in fact blameworthy for what was being protested. Renouncing this stance due to seeing that the agent was fully excused does not qualify because forgiveness, in general, requires that one views him as blameworthy. Letting go and its subcategories, such as condoning, don't count as apt forgiveness because they involve relinquishing the stance of moral protest without the agent's change of heart. While condoning is not justified, letting go when it does not amount to condoning may sometimes be.

## An Objection to Forgiveness

Martha Nussbaum (2016, 58ff.) objects to forgiveness, at least as it is standardly conceived in the Judeo-Christian tradition. Her concern is that it is transactional in an offensive way, because it requires that the offender debase himself in confession prior to forgiveness being earned. Power is exerted over the confessor by the person receiving the confession in a way that is humiliating. As Nussbaum (2016, 70) points out, this objection is consonant with Michel Foucault's critique of the Catholic practice of confession as set out in his 1981 Louvain lectures on the topic, *Mal Faire, Dire Vrai*.

One might contend that Milam's view, which I accept, on which forgiveness should require change of heart and contrition, is subject to the same critique. I disagree. The moral life requires that wrongdoers recognize their wrongdoing, that they engage in self-directed protest against it, and that in many kinds of circumstance they convey to those they have wronged that they are sincerely engaging in such self-directed protest. This process need not and should not be debasing, and one would also recognize that engaging in self-directed protest can make a difference to how one behaves in the future by reforming one's dispositions to act.

A focal point of Nussbaum's discussion of forgiveness is the parable of the prodigal son, which we find in the Gospel of Luke. On her reading, this parable shows how we can deal with wrongdoing without transactional forgiveness, but instead with unconditional love:

> [11] Then [Jesus] said: "A certain man had two sons. [12] And the younger of them said to his father, 'Father, give me the portion of goods that falls to me.' So he divided to them his livelihood. [13] And not many days after, the

AN OBJECTION TO FORGIVENESS   115

younger son gathered all together, journeyed to a far country, and there wasted his possessions with prodigal living. [14] But when he had spent all, there arose a severe famine in that land, and he began to be in want. [15] Then he went and joined himself to a citizen of that country, and he sent him into his fields to feed swine. [16] And he would gladly have filled his stomach with the [e]pods that the swine ate, and no one gave him anything.

[17] But when he came to himself, he said, 'How many of my father's hired servants have bread enough and to spare, and I perish with hunger! [18] I will arise and go to my father, and will say to him, "Father, I have sinned against heaven and before you, [19] and I am no longer worthy to be called your son. Make me like one of your hired servants."'

[20] And he arose and came to his father. But when he was still a great way off, his father saw him and had compassion, and ran and fell on his neck and kissed him. [21] And the son said to him, 'Father, I have sinned against heaven and in your sight, and am no longer worthy to be called your son.'

[22] But the father said to his servants, 'Bring out the best robe and put it on him, and put a ring on his hand and sandals on his feet. [23] And bring the fatted calf here and kill it, and let us eat and be merry; [24] for this my son was dead and is alive again; he was lost and is found.' And they began to be merry.

[25] Now his older son was in the field. And as he came and drew near to the house, he heard music and dancing. [26] So he called one of the servants and asked what these things meant. [27] And he said to him, 'Your brother has come, and because he has received him safe and sound, your father has killed the fatted calf.'

[28] But he was angry and would not go in. Therefore his father came out and pleaded with him. [29] So he answered and said to his father, 'Lo, these many years I have been serving you; I never transgressed your commandment at any time; and yet you never gave me a young goat, that I might make merry with my friends. [30] But as soon as this son of yours came, who has devoured your livelihood with harlots, you killed the fatted calf for him.'

[31] And he said to him, 'Son, you are always with me, and all that I have is yours. [32] It was right that we should make merry and be glad, for your brother was dead and is alive again, and was lost and is found.'"[5]

---

[5] The Holy Bible, New King James Version, Copyright © 1982 Thomas Nelson, The Gospel of Luke, Chapter 10.

116  FORGIVENESS AS RENUNCIATION OF MORAL PROTEST

Nussbaum (2016, 91) draws our attention to the fact that in this parable the father expresses love for the son, which she characterizes as unconditional, prior to the son's expression of contrition, which she points out isn't clearly represented as genuine, and absent the process of transactional forgiveness. Let me note that the father's attitude to toward the son is also compassionate, and that, by contrast with what Nussbaum specifies in her earlier (2001) account, in this case the appropriateness of compassion would appear not to be challenged by the thought that the son may deserve his misfortune.

My sense is that, in general, the role of recognition of wrongdoing on the part of the wronged party should be more pronounced than what we see in Nussbaum's account of unconditional love. In her account of the parable, Nussbaum does specify that at a later time the father might talk with his son about his life's course, and that unconditional love is compatible with such guidance. I agree with Nussbaum's judgment about this particular case. But I don't believe the lesson generalizes. It doesn't indicate that that forgiveness in other similar contexts, where forgiveness is understood as requiring a change of heart and manifesting contrition to the forgiver, isn't morally apt. Without genuine contrition, the concern for the condoning of wrongdoing arises. I suspect that our reaction to the parable is in part due to the nature of the prodigal son's offense, dissolute partying, which we are perhaps inclined to see as not especially serious. What if the offense were clearly more serious—what if he had invested his money in the slave trade, and lost all due to his slave ship sinking, with all the captives drowning? If the story had then made it clear that the son did not have a change of heart, and that his expression of contrition was feigned, we would react differently to the father's expression of love. It's not that father's love and the expression of it would clearly be inappropriate, but the importance of the son's change of heart would appear much more urgent. Furthermore, the father's communication of a request for a change of heart for forgiveness for the son's dissolute behavior needn't be abasing or humiliating. It needn't be communicated angrily, which would tend to allow the son only either a humiliating or a defiant response. Rather, the father might, in a way that expresses his concern and compassion, present the son with the reasons why the behavior was wrong, and suggest the morally appropriate change of heart.

Accordingly, the moving way in which the father welcomes the son need not be interpreted as precluding forgiveness upon contrition. We may see it instead as the father's compassionately extending an offer of grace, as expressing the possibility of forgiveness and reconciliation, and a commitment to doing his part in the process required to realize this possibility. An offer of grace, when communicated in the compassionate way that the father does in this parable, itself stands to motivate a wrongdoer to contrition and to aspiring to reconciliation. When one recognizes that the person one has wronged is disposed to forgiveness and reconciliation, one may thereby be motivated to contrition and to seeking forgiveness. Thus, rather than bypassing contrition and forgiveness, the father's welcoming the son communicates and motivates that possibility, and places reconciliation within reach. The parable also inspires a more general hope for such reconciliation, showing how grace, contrition, and forgiveness might work together to achieve what many wish for in relationships that have been impaired.

## Renunciation of Resentment

I've proposed that forgiveness fairly generally features the renunciation of the stance of moral protest, where the forgiver believes that this stance was initially appropriate. Nonetheless, often the attitude toward the wrongdoer initially involves resentment, or at least anger of some type. Suppose the forgiver is angry, but doesn't believe that it was appropriate. Imagine that Ingrid is angry with her child for a minor wrongdoing, say because she is tired and stressed, but believes her anger was inappropriate, by contrast with the stance of moral protest, which she believes was appropriate and in fact was. When the child expresses remorse, forgiveness involves renouncing the stance of protest. Does it also involve renouncing anger? Perhaps in this case renouncing anger is appropriate, but doing so is not a component of forgiveness. But it is arguably a component of appropriate repentance on Ingrid's part.

Other cases are more complex. Suppose that Donna is furious with David when she finds out he's cheated on her, and angrily confronts him. Assume also that Roberts's theory of the emotions is correct, that anger is a concerned construal with a presupposition that an angry person may reject. The relevant presupposition of Donna's anger is that David basically deserves the pain involved in being a target of its expression. But imagine that she's a skeptic about desert, that skepticism about desert is true, and she believes that the presupposition of her anger is false. However, suppose in addition that her anger is inevitable in this case, that given human psychology, virtually anyone in exactly these circumstances would be angry. Moreover, its expression is practically rational for Donna because it is the optimal way for David to come to understand how deeply he has hurt her, and if she

## 118 FORGIVENESS AS RENUNCIATION OF MORAL PROTEST

weren't angry, she would be not be capable of a convincing feigned expression. Imagine that as a result of the angry confrontation, David repents and is deeply remorseful. Donna now forgives him, at least in part by renouncing her stance of moral protest. Might forgiveness in this case also involve renouncing resentment? I think so. In this case, by contrast with Ingrid's, renouncing this anger would not amount to repentance on Donna's part. The reason is that while Donna's anger does have a false basic-desert presupposition, it was practically rational. Donna's forgiveness in part consists in renouncing an emotion that was, prior to David's repentance, practically appropriate, despite it having what is, and what she regards as, a false presupposition. So even for the basic desert skeptic, supposing the view is true, forgiveness can involve renunciation of resentment.

If, as I propose, forgiveness is renunciation of the stance of moral protest, and that one can overcome anger while retaining this stance, it is possible to let go of anger without letting go of this stance, and to overcome anger without forgiving. In a case in which a wrongdoer has not had a change of heart, but one's resentful anger is psychologically debilitating, there is the possibility of letting go of the anger while still protesting the wrongdoing and not forgiving. This may be the best option in cases in which one's anger is consuming and debilitating. One would then be liberated not only from a harmful emotion, but one would also retain one's moral integrity by continuing to protest. When the wrongdoing involves a serious personal slight or attack that challenges one's self-respect, one might be freed from the harm the emotion is causing while retaining one's self-respect by maintaining the stance of protest. One way in which wrongdoers aim, at some level of conscious intention, to undermine integrity and self-respect is by inducing resentment through demeaning, hurtful interaction. A way to effectively counteract the aims of such incursions is by letting go of one's anger, while yet maintaining the stance of moral protest and not forgiving. This combination would also be a compassionate option, given that the aims of protest feature the moral formation of the offender and one's reconciliation with him.

### Forgiveness and Norm Changing

Problems noted for the standard view, notably that forgiveness does not require renunciation of actual resentment, or any other initially appropriate negative reactive attitudes, has motivated development of an alternative conception by Dana Nelkin (2013) and Brandon Warmke (2016): *the*

FORGIVENESS AND NORM CHANGING    119

*norm-changing view*. In Nelkin's conception, it is sufficient for forgiving that one choose to release an offender from certain obligations generated by his offence, whether or not one continues resenting or blaming him. In her account, blameworthy action or omission generates an obligation on the part of the wrongdoer to apologize or make amends, and for the wronged party, the victim, to forgive the wrongdoer is to release him from this obligation. Warmke (2016) contends that forgiveness changes the normative significance of the offence from one that warrants negative responses to a state in which at least some of these negative responses cease to be justified. In his conception, by forgiving a wrongdoer a victim releases the wrongdoer from personal obligations to respond in these ways, and the victim can release the wrongdoer only from those obligations over which the victim has normative authority. The victim may, for instance, communicate to the wrongdoer that no further apology or restitution are expected of her. In Warmke's view, forgiving also alters norms for the victim's behavior. The victim, most importantly, gives up certain rights to overtly blame and to punish. Accordingly, forgiveness changes norms for both wrongdoer and victim. On this conception, forgiveness resembles norm-changing actions such as debt forgiveness or waiving a promise (Twambley 1976; Nelkin 2013; Warmke 2016).

Let me point out, first of all, that renunciation of the stance of moral protest, which in my proposal forgiveness involves, is itself norm changing. All else equal, such renunciation changes the normative status of overt moral protest from being appropriate to being inappropriate, and similarly changes the status of resuming the internal stance of moral protest from being appropriate to being inappropriate. Accordingly, on this proposal forgiveness involves both the renunciation of an attitude and a change of norms.

Does forgiveness essentially involve release from an obligation to apologize or make amends? There is reason to deny this. Suppose that in the *Infidelity* example, Donna's forgiveness is a response to David's change of heart, which he expresses by apologizing and offering to make amends. Suppose that the amends consist in his making a sincere commitment to spending less time away from Donna and engaging in activities that stand to restore their relationship. Then it's implausible that Donna's forgiveness would consist even in part in Donna releasing David from the obligation to apologize and to make these amends. For David has already apologized, and in the normative case, the apology is ongoing in the sense that it's not retracted. One might imagine Donna asking for the apology to be made again overtly, and this might be consistent with her forgiveness if what she

120 FORGIVENESS AS RENUNCIATION OF MORAL PROTEST

wants is for the apology not to be retracted. The amends are also ongoing, since they involve an extended process aimed at restoration of the relationship. Here releasing David from the obligation to make these amends is also not a requirement of forgiveness. Asking him to take yet further amends may be required for the relationship to work, and Donna's requesting them would not be at odds with her having forgiven David. What remains in place, however, is her renunciation of the stance of moral protest against David, and if she is angry with him, her anger. So in this case forgiveness features renunciation of this stance, and not release from an obligation to apologize or make amends. Forgiveness may involve communication that no further apology or restitution are expected of the wrongdoer, and the inappropriateness of making such a demand on the part of the victim. But these changes in norms can be viewed as resulting from renunciation of the stance of moral protest.

Warmke argues that overcoming resentment cannot have the norm-changing function that he specifies:

> How could giving up my resentment towards someone else have an effect not only on how I am morally permitted to treat that someone, but also on how that person is morally obliged to treat me? I see no way of linking my overcoming of resentment to the inappropriateness of, say, asking for apologies or engaging in other forms of overt blame. Nor can I see how my overcoming resentment would release you from certain personal obligations to, say, apologize to me or offer me restitution. (Warmke 2016, 692)

This point can be extended to overcoming the stance of moral protest. One might now argue that if forgiveness is at its core norm changing, and if neither overcoming resentment nor overcoming the stance of moral protest can have the norm-changing function, then forgiveness is not at its core either overcoming resentment or the stance of moral protest. In response, Warmke is right that my mere *overcoming* of resentment can't affect how I am obligated to treat the wrongdoer. But my *renunciation* of resentment, since it involves a moral commitment I make not to resent, can have this function. Similarly, renunciation of the stance of moral protest can have this function, since it involves a moral commitment not to protest.

Warmke (2016) contends that releasing the wrongdoer from obligations cannot be private—it must be communicated to the wrongdoer; Santiago Amaya (2019) also emphasizes this social dimension of forgiveness. Warmke's view is plausible for paradigm cases, but not for all cases of forgiveness. If one's abusive parent sincerely repents just before he dies, one might forgive him after he dies without the possibility of communication. But in paradigm cases, as Milam (2022) points out, it is not enough to *intend* to release the offender from their obligations, since one might still abandon or in some other way fail to carry out the intention. Richard Swinburne's conception of forgiveness supplies what is needed to meet this constraint in paradigm cases. He proposes that "forgiving is a performative act achieved perhaps by saying solemnly 'I forgive you,' or perhaps by saying 'That's all right,' or maybe by just a smile" (Swinburne 1989, 85; Warmke 2016 agrees). As I remarked earlier, the indication to the wrongdoer that she has been forgiven might be evident only in subtle changes in the forgiver's behavior and expression.

Warmke also maintains that forgiveness must feature a rational and motivational mesh between the declarative act and the forgiver's mental states. The forgiver must, for instance, intend to forgive by means of the words she uses. In my view, this plausible mesh requirement serves to highlight the crucial role of the forgiver's mental state of renunciation of the stance of moral protest or resentment. Suppose I'm self-deceived in my belief that I no longer resent you for maligning me, and that my attempt to renounce my stance of moral protest is a failure. I am then mistaken when I say, "I forgive you." I utter the words, but I don't forgive. Some norms may have changed by my having said what I did, but forgiveness hasn't occurred. A pronouncement of forgiveness thus has content that can be falsified by the nature of one's attitudinal stance.

## Summary

My proposal for an account of forgiveness, like Warmke's (2016), combines elements of both the standard and the norm-changing views. Forgiveness need not be preceded by actual resentment, or indeed any actual angry emotion. Rather, the forgiver, by virtue of regarding the wrongdoer as blameworthy for a past wrongdoing, regards moral protest against him for this specific wrongdoing as having been appropriate. In forgiving, she renounces moral protest on her own part going forward, both the appropriateness of the psychological stance and its overt expressions. This renunciation is norm changing, first of all because it changes overt moral protest on her part from being appropriate to being inappropriate, and similarly changes her internal stance of moral protest from being appropriate to being inappropriate. Additional alterations in norms may also result from this renunciation. Earlier, the wronged party legitimately demanded apology and amends, while upon forgiving, the request for new apologies and additional amends may become inappropriate.

As I remarked at the outset, the standard view, on which forgiveness is the renunciation and overcoming of resentment, raises a problem for free will skepticism, since on the standard view forgiveness involves the renunciation of an attitude toward a wrongdoer that one formerly regarded as appropriate. This condition is jeopardized if an agent does not resent because she is concerned that her resentment is unjustified due to its basic desert presupposition. However, if forgiveness can instead be understood as involving renunciation of the stance of moral protest, and if that stance need not presuppose basic desert, then for the free will skeptic forgiveness is in the clear. Setting aside free will skepticism, renunciation of the stance of moral protest qualifies as a fairly general feature of forgiveness, by contrast with renunciation of resentment, which in a range of cases of wrongdoing is initially unfitting and out of place.

# 6
# Love and Freedom

In Chapters 4 and 5 we considered how a view that does not endorse basic desert, or the negative reactive attitudes, might treat serious wrongdoing. We saw that the right to harm in defense of self and others plays the decisive part, and that our having this right does not depend on an endorsement of basic desert. The virtue of compassion also has a crucial role, and it undergirds the aims of reconciliation, rehabilitation, and reintegration. We now turn to the ethics of personal relationships. Here the virtue is love, broadly construed, conceived as an emotion that has a crucial role in such relationships. How do we conceive of love without free will, basic desert, and the negative reactive attitudes as responses to wrongdoing in personal relationships?[1]

## Does Love Require Free Will?

Consider the following excerpt from John Milton's *Paradise Lost* in which God discusses the fall of Satan:

> So will fall
> He and his faithless Progeny: whose fault?
> Whose but his own? ingrate, he had of me
> All he could have; I made him just and right,
> Sufficient to have stood, though free to fall...
> Not free, what proof could they have given sincere
> Of true allegiance, constant Faith or Love,
> Where only what they needs must do, appeared,
> Not what they would? what praise could they receive?
> What pleasure I from such obedience paid,
> When Will and Reason (Reason also is choice)

[1] This chapter is a revision of Pereboom (2018).

*Wrongdoing and the Moral Emotions.* Derk Pereboom, Oxford University Press. © Derk Pereboom 2021.
DOI: 10.1093/oso/9780192846006.003.0006

Useless and vain, of freedom both despoiled,
Made passive both, had served necessity,
Not me. They therefore as to right belonged,
So were created, nor can justly accuse
Their maker, or their making, or their Fate;
As if Predestination over-ruled
Their will, disposed by absolute Decree
Or high foreknowledge; they themselves decreed
Their own revolt, not I: if I foreknew,
Foreknowledge had no influence on their fault,
Which had no less proved certain unforeknown.
So without least impulse or shadow of Fate,
Or aught by me immutably foreseen,
They trespass, Authors to themselves in all
Both what they judge and what they choose; for so
I formed them free, and free they must remain,
Till they enthrall themselves.

(Book III, 95–125, Milton 1667/2005, 58–9)

A key to Milton's vision of the meaning of our lives is that we human agents have the opportunity to freely respond to God with love. In these stanzas he contends that if divine grace were to causally determine love for God, this response would have little or no value; "what praise could they receive? What pleasure I from such obedience paid/When Will and Reason (Reason also is choice)/Useless and vain, of freedom both despoiled/Made passive both, had served necessity/Not me." In Milton's conception, love that has value must result from our free will. A number of contemporary authors have argued, with Milton, that truly valuable love indeed requires freely willed agency. As we will see, Robert Kane (1996, 86–90) defends this point of view. Yet one might disagree, as I have (Pereboom 1995, 2001, 202–4, 2009, 2014, 190–3, 2018).

## Contemporary Accounts of Love

A promising way to approach this issue is to examine the accounts of love that have been the subject of debate over the past several decades, and to test whether they presuppose or require freedom of some type. Most of these accounts contend that love, or at least valuable love, is a response to

CONTEMPORARY ACCOUNTS OF LOVE    125

reasons (Velleman 1999; Kolodny 2003; Jollimore 2011; Setiya 2014). If a view of this kind is correct, freedom may arise as a requirement for valuable love because the envisioned response to reasons on the part of the lover must itself be free, or perhaps because the responsiveness to reasons presupposed by the account itself counts as a kind of freedom. Others contend that love is not a response to reasons (e.g., Frankfurt 1999, 2004); but valuable love might nonetheless require freedom because one must be free in order to qualify as an appropriate lover or recipient of love, or else because the structure of love itself involves a kind of freedom.

Consider first the accounts on which valuable love is a response to reasons. In Troy Jollimore's view, which is a reflection of widespread opinion both contemporary and historical, "loving someone is, in large part, a kind of positive, appreciative response to her in virtue of her attractive, desirable, or otherwise valuable properties," and "love is a matter of reason, insofar as it is a response to something external that attempts to be adequate to the nature of its object" (Jollimore 2011, 25–6). This position has substantial historical precedent; Augustine (400/2008), for example, famously develops such a position (see Grau's (2004) discussion of the history of this idea).

To accounts on which reasons have a crucial role Robert Kraut (1987) objects that one does not have reason to love a counterpart who is relevantly qualitatively similar to one's beloved, for whom the reasons to love are exactly the same as the reasons in the case of one's beloved (cf., Nozick 1989). One response is that the same reasons to love the counterpart as one's beloved are in place, but in neither case do the reasons generate a requirement to love. Rather, in each case love is a rational option. Another response, advocated by Christopher Grau (2004), is that valuable love requires that the beloved is treasured as a particular instantiation of qualities, by contrast with a collection of abstract qualities that is itself abstract (cf., Ellis 2001), and as Neera Badhwar (1987) and David Velleman (1999) also contend, such love requires that this particular instantiation be valued as an end, rather than merely instrumentally (cf., Wonderly 2017). Velleman (1999) argues that such love is a kind of valuation not of qualities of a person that might also be had by others, but of her particular rational nature. Rational nature, in his conception, is a "capacity of appreciation or valuation—a capacity to care about things in that reflective way which is distinctive of self-conscious creatures like us" (Velleman 1999, 365–6). Kieran Setiya defends a broader version of this position, contending that a reason for love is "whatever property gives us the sort of status that commands respect"

126 LOVE AND FREEDOM

(Setiya 2014, 262), and such a property might be had by non-human creatures. On Niko Kolodny's proposal, it is relationships in particular that qualify as the reasons for love (Kolodny 2003; cf. Adams 1980). The fact that you are my friend or child or spouse—by contrast with a rational nature or specific non-relational qualities you might have—is the right kind of reason for love.

Kolodny and Setiya object to the kind of account Jollimore proposes on the ground that reasons for love survive the loss of qualities of the sort that in Jollimore's view serve as the reasons for love. Here Kolodny quotes Shakespeare's famous line: "Love is not love which alters as alteration finds" (Shakespeare (2008), Sonnet 116; Kolodny 2003, 140). He adds that in the case of familial love, the fact that a person is my child counts as reason for me to love her, and is enough reason for my loving her independently of any qualities she may have (Kolodny 2003, 139). He objects to Velleman's account on the ground that it yields equal reason to love anyone with rational nature, and that as far as reasons for love take us, recipients of love are interchangeable (Kolodny 2003, 175–6). Setiya objects to Kolodny by arguing that one can rationally begin to love someone even if one doesn't yet have the sort of relationship with her that qualifies as a reason for love (Setiya 2014, 259–60).

Harry Frankfurt (1999, 2004) advocates for the sharply contrasting view on which there are no reasons for love. He finds it particularly implausible that love is a response to the value, or the perceived value of the beloved. Because a qualitatively identical version of my beloved, thus someone with the same valuable qualities, need not present any reason for me to love her, valuable qualities can't be reasons for love. Instead, the proper focal point of love is the beloved's identity—just her being who she is. Frankfurt writes: "The focus of a person's love is not those general and hence repeatable characteristics that make his beloved *describable*. Rather, it is the specific particularity that makes his beloved *nameable*—something that is more mysterious than describability, and that is in any case manifestly impossible to define" (Frankfurt 1999, 170). At the same time, in Frankfurt's conception, love does have a complex psychological structure. It is a set of first-order desires involving the beloved, together with a set of second-order desires that those first-order desires be effective in moving one to action (cf., Frankfurt 1971). For instance, the lover will have a first-order desire to help the beloved in time of need, and a second-order desire that this desire be effective on appropriate occasions. This second-order desire will serve to sustain the first-order desire.

This is a sketch of a complex debate. There are other participants, other positions, and more objections and replies. But what I've set out is sufficient for my purpose here.

## Does the Nature of Love Constitutively Require Freedom?

It is widely held that reasons-responsiveness itself is a kind of freedom. Given this view, on reasons theories of valuable love, this kind of freedom may be required for such love by virtue of its very nature. If the degree of reasons-responsiveness needed for valuable love matches that required for moral responsibility, on this view valuable love would constitutively require such freedom. For defenders of reasons-responsiveness accounts of freedom, the degree of reasons-responsiveness required for moral responsibility is typically not high. Such accounts originate with John Fischer (1982, 1994; Fischer and Ravizza 1998). His core idea is that an action for which an agent is morally responsible is one that she performs as a result of recognizing reasons for it, and is such that if the reasons instead favored other incompatible options, the agent (or the relevant action-producing mechanism) would, in some such possible circumstances, have recognized and acted on those reasons instead. Fischer thinks of this reasons-responsiveness as the control condition on moral responsibility, and as an important kind of freedom. Ishtiyaque Haji (1998), Michael McKenna (2000, 2012), and Carolina Sartorio (2016) follow suit and also advance reasons-responsiveness accounts of the control condition—the free will—required for moral responsibility. In addition, Susan Wolf (1980, 1990) and Dana Nelkin (2008, 2011) accept a view on which such freedom is characterized in terms of rational action, and for them to act freely is to act in accord with the right reasons.

Fischer, McKenna, and Sartorio are compatibilists about free will and causal determinism. Their incompatibilist opponents, however, typically reject the claim that reasons-responsiveness secures the control required for moral responsibility, specifically of a sort that involves desert or basic desert. These incompatibilists often contend that the crucial sort of freedom is an ability to do otherwise that is not determinism-friendly, and they would deny that love constitutively requires the ability to do otherwise just because love requires responsiveness to reasons. But incompatibilists may nonetheless agree that reasons-responsiveness is one kind of freedom, and thus that insofar as love requires reasons-responsiveness, it may require freedom.

## 128 LOVE AND FREEDOM

As I argued in Chapter 1, to avoid merely verbal disputes it's crucial to be clear about the senses in which the terms 'free will' and 'freedom' are used. Let me briefly summarize that account. The contemporary free will debate features the following patterns of use. On one use, 'free will' refers to the ability to do otherwise, or the capacity to exercise this ability. Some, such as advocates of the Consequence Argument (e.g., Ginet 1966; van Inwagen 1975, 1983) contend that free will in this sense is incompatible with the agent's causal determination by factors beyond her control, while others argue that it is compatible (e.g., Lewis 1981; Slote 1982). On a second use, 'free will' refers to the control in action required for a core sense of moral responsibility (Mele 2006). Again, this sense of moral responsibility at issue in the free will debate is plausibly set apart by the notion of basic desert.[2] A belief that an agent is morally responsible in this sense at least typically accompanies resentment and indignation, and it is thus closely related to the notion of moral responsibility that P. F. Strawson (1962) brings to the fore. Many compatibilists argue that reasons-responsiveness secures the control required for moral responsibility in the basic desert sense, but, as noted, many incompatibilists disagree, and contend that a stronger notion of free will is required. Milton is in this incompatibilist camp. While he believes that valuable love must be freely willed, he would deny that it would be freely willed just by virtue of being responsive to reasons.

On Frankfurt's account, valuable love also requires that the lover have freedom in a sense he thinks is required for moral responsibility, and thus for him love also constitutively requires freedom of this sort. The kind of freedom at issue for Frankfurt is *acting freely and of one's own free will*, which an agent has with respect to an action just in case she wills it and she wants to will it, that is, she has a second-order volition for her desire so to act to be effective (Frankfurt 1971). Suppose Scarlet kills Mustard, and this is what Scarlet desired to do, and she wanted her desire to kill Mustard to be effective. According to Frankfurt, Scarlet then satisfies the crucial condition for acting freely in the sense required for moral responsibility. Valuable love, in Frankfurt's view, requires that the lover is disposed to act in such a

---

[2] As set out in Chapter 1, for an agent to be *morally responsible for an action in the basic desert sense* is for the action to be attributable to her in such a way that if she was sensitive to its being morally wrong, she would deserve to be blamed or punished in a way that she would experience as painful or harmful, and if she was sensitive to its being morally exemplary, she would deserve to be praised or rewarded in a way that she would experience as pleasurable or beneficial. The desert at issue is basic in the sense that the agent, to be morally responsible, would deserve such blame or punishment, praise or reward, just by virtue of having performed the action with sensitivity to its moral status, and not, for example, by virtue of consequentialist or contractualist considerations.

way that she is free in this sense. In his conception, helping the beloved when in need is a central sort of loving action. But it is crucial that the lover not only will to help, but also that this first-order volition is sustained by a second-order volition for her desire to help to be effective. When the lover's helping has this structure, she acts freely and of her own free will. We might all agree that an act with this kind of structure is free in one sense. However, accepting that valuable love requires this sort of freedom does not amount to agreeing with Milton. He has a stronger notion of freedom in mind, and he also believes that moral responsibility requires such a stronger sort of freedom.

### Must the Lover or the Beloved Be Free for the Best Kinds of Love?

We can now pose the more general question: does valuable love, or else the best kind of love, require the freedom required for moral responsibility in the sense at issue in the free will debate, that is, the sense that involves basic desert? One might argue that valuable love must be deserved, and that the reasons for love incorporate free actions that deserve a loving response. Against this, parents typically love their newborn children without their having this sort of free will, and we think that such love is highly valuable (Pereboom 1995, 41, 2001, 202–4, 2014, 190–3). Furthermore, when adults love each other it is often not due to factors that are not freely willed; appearance, intelligence, and affinities with persons or events in one's history may have a significant part. However, moral action and character are often especially important for occasioning and maintaining mature love that we value. But it would seem that such love would not be threatened if we came to believe that moral character and action do not come about through freely willed decision, for they would be loveable whether or not the beloved is thought to deserve praise for them. Valuable love involves wishing well for the other, taking on aims and projects of the other as one's own, cherishing the other for her own sake. Denying that the beloved has the free will required for desert does not threaten any of this.

Alternatively, one might argue, with Milton, that for love to be valuable, the loving response itself must be freely willed. Against this, parents' love for their children is often produced independently of the parents' will, and the same is true of romantic love, and these are kinds of love that we value highly (Pereboom 2001, 202–4, 2014). Kane agrees, but contends that "there is a *kind* of love we desire from others—parents, children (when they are old enough), spouses, lovers and friends whose significance would be

130  LOVE AND FREEDOM

diminished... by the thought that they are determined to love us entirely by instinct or circumstances beyond their control or not entirely up to them" (Kane 1996, 88). The reason the significance of this love would then be diminished is that "to be loved by others in this desired sense requires that the ultimate source of others' love lies in their own wills" (Kane 1996, 88). In response, setting aside *free* will, in what sorts of cases does the will intuitively play a role in generating love for another at all? When an intimate relationship is faltering, people sometimes make a decision to try to make it succeed, and to attempt to regain the type of relationship they once had. When a student is housed in a dormitory with a roommate she didn't select, she might choose to make the relationship work. When a marriage is arranged by parents, the partners may decide to take steps to come to love each other. In such situations we might desire that someone make a decision to love, but it is not clear that we have reason to want the decision to be *freely* willed in the sense required for desert-involving moral responsibility. A decision to love on the part of another might significantly enhance one's personal life, but it is not obvious what value the decision's being free in this sense would add. Moreover, while in these kinds of circumstances we might desire that someone else make a decision to love, we would typically prefer the situation in which the love was not mediated by decision. This is so not only for romantic attachments, but also for friendships and for relationships between parents and children.

One might propose that the will has a key role in *maintaining* love over an extended period. Søren Kierkegaard (1843/1971) suggests that a marital relationship ideally involves a commitment that is continuously renewed. Such a commitment involves a decision to devote oneself to the other, and thus, in his view, a marital relationship ideally involves a continuously repeated decision. A relationship with this sort of voluntary aspect might in fact be highly desirable. Nevertheless, it is difficult to see what value might be added by these continuously repeated decisions being freely willed in the sense required for moral responsibility, by contrast with simply being a voluntary expression of what the agent deeply cares about. Thus although one might at first have the intuition that love that is freely willed is especially valuable, it is unclear exactly how such free will might have a desirable role in producing, maintaining, or enhancing love (Pereboom 2001, 202–4, 2014, 190–3).

## Love, Wrongdoing, and the Reactive Attitudes

A further route to securing a connection between love and freedom is provided by P. F. Strawson's (1962) treatment of the reactive attitudes. Strawson

## LOVE, WRONGDOING, AND THE REACTIVE ATTITUDES    131

maintains that if our actions were causally determined and this fact did threaten reactive attitudes such as resentment, indignation, guilt, and gratitude, or, more precisely, the legitimacy of having and expressing them, we would face the prospect of an "objectivity of attitude," a stance that in his view rules out the possibility of good personal relationships, those that feature love of the sort that mutually respecting adults might have for one another. In Strawson's view, our commitment to such relationships of mutual respect or regard rules out taking this threat seriously. Relationships of this kind presuppose that the participants are legitimately susceptible to having and expressing the reactive attitudes. Furthermore, the practice of holding moral responsible actually consists in the legitimate having and expressing of the reactive attitudes, and relationships of mutual regard presuppose that participants are morally responsible insofar as they are their appropriate targets. Given the characterization of free will as the control condition on moral responsibility, relationships of mutual regard, which in paradigm cases involve love, accordingly presuppose that the participants have free will.

I agree that Strawson is right to believe that objectivity of attitude would jeopardize our personal relationships, but that he is mistaken to hold that such a stance would result or be appropriate if the causal determination of our actions by factors beyond our control undermined the legitimacy of reactive attitudes (Pereboom 2001, 2014; Sommers 2007). As we saw in Chapter 2, given free will skepticism, an expression of resentment or indignation would involve doxastic irrationality when it is accompanied by the belief that the wrongdoer basically deserves the pain or harm of being its target. But relative to certain alternative emotional attitudes available to us, these reactive attitudes and their expressions may be suboptimal for interaction in relationships when wrongdoing is at issue. The alternative attitudes I have in mind are not threatened by free will skepticism because they are not connected with beliefs that conflict with this view, while at the same time they can effectively play the requisite roles in relationships (Pereboom 2001, 2014; Nussbaum 2016).

Of the emotional attitudes associated with moral responsibility, resentment, directed toward an agent due to a wrong he has done to oneself, and indignation, directed toward an agent because of a wrong he has done to a third party, are arguably most closely connected with it. Expression of resentment and indignation has a significant communicative role in personal and societal relationships, and thus one might object that if we were to modify or eliminate these attitudes, communication in such relationships would be impeded. Against this, when we are wronged in our relationships

132   LOVE AND FREEDOM

there are other emotions available to us that are not challenged by skepticism about free will, whose expressions can also convey the relevant information. These emotions include feeling hurt or shocked or disappointed about what the offending agent has done, and sadness or sorrow and concern for him, and, most importantly, taking on the stance of moral protest against him for what he's done.

If moral protest, together with communication of sadness and sorrow, hurt and disappointment is to take the place of expressions of resentment and indignation, the former attitudes would need to be fostered and promoted at the expense of the latter. It may well be that some types and certain degrees of resentment and indignation are beyond our power to alter, and hence even supposing that the free will skeptic is committed to doing what is right and rational, she might nevertheless be unable to eradicate these attitudes. But this supposition might be contested. Shaun Nichols (2007) cites the distinction between narrow-profile emotional responses, that is, immediate emotional reactions to situations, and wide-profile responses, which are not immediate and may involve rational control. Free will skeptics might expect that we will have limited success in altering narrow-profile, immediate resentment when we are seriously wronged in our intimate personal relationships. However, in wide-profile circumstances, we may have the ability to diminish, or even eliminate resentment, or at least disavow it in the sense of rejecting any force it might be thought to have in justifying painful or harmful reactions to the wrong done. Given acceptance of free will skepticism we might take such measures for the sake of morality and rationality.

Thus I propose that love, even of the sort featured in adult relationships of mutual regard, does not require the free will required for basic desert moral responsibility, the sense of free will at issue in the traditional debate, or the conviction that we have it. Let us now consider four objections to this proposal.

First, Nichols (2007) argues that sadness together with moral resolve is not an adequate substitute for resentment and indignation in personal and social relationships. He first contends that these angry responses to wrongdoing can be shown, by way of empirical studies, to be beneficial to human beings in certain significant respects. He then argues, also on the basis of empirical work, that sadness together with resolve will be much less effective. At the time Nichols crafted this objection, and when I responded earlier (Pereboom 2009, 2014), the stance of moral protest didn't yet have the prominence in my view that it now does, and moral protest supplies a

## LOVE, WRONGDOING, AND THE REACTIVE ATTITUDES    133

significant confrontational element that was then absent. With this in place, let me emphasize that it is important to count the cost of resentment and indignation in comparison with the proposed alternative attitudes. Expression of resentment and indignation in response to wrongdoing does form an important part of human relationships as they are ordinarily conceived. It motivates resistance to abuse and oppression, and serves as a forceful mode of communication when the resented party doesn't understand that he's doing wrong, and as a result resentment can make relationships better. But expression of resentment and indignation is also apt to have harmful effects. It often fails to contribute to the well-being of those to whom it is directed. It is often intended to cause physical or emotional pain, and can give rise to destructive resistance instead of reconciliation. The stance of moral protest, together with communication of sadness and sorrow, hurt and disappointment, stands to work at least as well.

The second objection is motivated by Stephen Darwall (2006), who argues that resentment and its expressions indicate a kind of respect for the agency of another, and that resentment is valuable in this respect. In support, treating a wrongdoer as if his immoral actions are a symptom of an illness is to assimilate him to a broken machine: his wrongdoing is like the computer's crashing. Respect for the agency of those prone to acting wrongly requires being disposed to being resentful or indignant with them. In reply, expression of resentment and indignation may presuppose that its target possesses capacities that make her worthy of respect, but from this we can't conclude that these reactive attitudes actually show or express respect. Sophisticated manipulation may presuppose that its victim is practically and theoretically rational, and has a highly developed capacity for commitment to personal relationships. While these capacities may make the agent worthy of respect, the manipulation that presupposes them does not show or express it. In the case of resentment and indignation, this presupposition arguably fosters the illusion that the expression of these attitudes itself shows or expresses respect.

A more convincing Kantian theme is that we respect the agency of others by treating them as practically rational, that is, as responsive to prudential and moral reasons. On McKenna's (2012) account, it is indeed an agent's practical rationality that is engaged in the process of blaming. One might ask a wrongdoer for an explanation of his action with the intent of having him acknowledge a disposition to act this way, and if he has in fact so acted without excuse or justification, one may then present him with moral reasons for taking steps to eliminate the disposition. Here one is not treating

## 134 LOVE AND FREEDOM

wrongdoing on analogy with the malfunctioning of a machine or as a symptom of an illness, but instead as an action of a rational agent, the disposition to which can be altered by presentation and acceptance of moral reasons. This is a paradigmatic way to express respect for another's agency. Expression of resentment or indignation would not seem to be required in addition for showing respect (Pereboom 2014).

A third objection is developed by Seth Shabo (2012), who proposes that the reactive attitudes are manifestations of the kind of susceptibility to the emotions of others that is required for the best sorts of close or intimate personal relationships. We are naturally morally resentful when those with whom we have such relationships wrong us, and if in particular they thereby show disrespect or disregard for us. Avoiding resentment would appear to require making ourselves less susceptible to the emotions and actions of others, and this would tend to make our relationships less meaningful and valuable. In Shabo's account, it is the essentially personal aspect of a relationship that requires susceptibility to resentment, and conditioning ourselves to be immune to the reactive attitudes stands to render our relationships less personal or even impersonal.

The specific meaning of the term 'personal' is crucial to Shabo's objection. In his conception, 'personal' modifies in the first instance a kind of caring:

> When we care about someone's attitudes toward us in an essentially personal way, those attitudes matter to us in their own right, quite apart from what they portend for our (and others') interests. Thus, someone who hasn't received an invitation to a social event might wonder at the apparent snub, even if he or she has little desire to attend and realizes that the situation has no bearing on his or her social or professional prospects. Often in such cases, it is important to us to understand why the offending behavior has occurred, where this is precisely a question about the attitude(s) it exhibits. This type of concern with the "meaning" of others' behavior is the hallmark of such essentially personal caring.
>
> (Shabo 2012, 112)

To care about someone's attitudes personally is to care about them in their own right, or as reflections of that person's deeper attitudes. It is to care in particular about her morally significant attitudes toward oneself—in Strawson's (1962) terminology, about those that express the quality of her will. One naturally becomes resentful when a person with whom one is engaged in an intimate relationship expresses a disrespectful or demeaning

LOVE, WRONGDOING, AND THE REACTIVE ATTITUDES 135

attitude toward oneself. Shabo remarks: "it is in feelings of resentment that our susceptibility to take disregard or ill will personally is *characteristically* manifested." He contends that when the other expresses such a disrespectful or demeaning attitude, the resentment that naturally results cannot reliably be forgone or disavowed while at the same time retaining the personal nature of the caring involved in the relationship (Shabo 2012, 113–14).

Shabo characterizes the type of position I've defended as *The Containment Policy*, which in his view will fail to preserve the vulnerability required for genuine personal engagement:

> *The Containment Policy*...[W]e should strive as far as possible to take the reactive attitudes out of circulation. In the first place, this will involve trying to forestall these attitudes in the situations that normally elicit them. When a wrong or a slight occurs, we should remind ourselves that the agent isn't genuinely blameworthy for it, and that it would be unfair to harbor resentment or indignation towards her, let alone to express these attitudes in a blaming way. When this reminder isn't enough, we should continue to focus on the moral inappropriateness of our reaction so as to put it behind us as quickly as possible. When these reactions persist anyway, we should consciously disavow them...Finally, there may be times when people cannot be expected to sincerely disavow such feelings. In these cases...(when they express their resentment in blaming behavior) we won't accord their reactions any social legitimacy, treating them instead in the variety of ways we treat other inappropriate but understandable emotional responses. (Shabo 2012, 108)

I endorse a containment policy, but not exactly as Shabo describes it, as I will soon explain.

Shabo (2022) presents a number of reasons for resisting a containment policy. One is that "there will be cases where people cannot reasonably be expected to sincerely disavow their resentment, since no other response does justice to how they (reasonably) feel about how they have been treated, and since even 'soft' disavowals will ring false in these cases." But first I agree that there are situations in which an agent's resentment is practically rational even if it has a presupposition of basic desert she believes is false, and we should not then expect her to disavow their resentment. If, for example, Donna is resentful upon discovering that David has been unfaithful to her, her resentment may be practically rational even if it is doxastically irrational for her due to its basic desert presupposition which, as a free

136   LOVE AND FREEDOM

will skeptic, she is convinced is false. Still, in my view, due to the false presupposition there is a general strong prima facie reason to disavow resentment.

Shabo describes the containment policy as denying social legitimacy to expressions of resentment. This I reject. From my perspective resentment has two sides, one problematic, and another that requires negotiation. The problematic side is that at least very often resentment features the mistaken presupposition that its target basically deserves the pain or harm that being targeted by its expressions incurs, it is apt to result in false and morally objectionable beliefs about its target, and its expression tends to be destructive to relationships. The side that requires negotiation is that it is a natural, and in some cases practically rational reaction to wrongdoing. Suppose Olivia is a victim of public intellectual bullying by an envious and insecure colleague in her field, and she feels and publicly expresses resentment as a result. Should our assessment involve not granting social legitimacy to her expression of resentment? First, we should take into account that Olivia's being resentful is natural and may well be practically rational for her, as in Donna's case. Second, it may be that the way Olivia expresses her resentment would also be justified as a legitimate expression of the stance of moral protest, and my position recommends only that we refrain from expressions of resentment that would not be justified as moral protest (Chapter 3). Shabo intimates that the advocate of a containment policy is barred from "acknowledging that there is a morally significant difference between such expressions [of prima face appropriate resentment] and expressions of putatively inappropriate resentment." But on the right containment policy, expressions of such inappropriate resentment always merit rejection, while expressions of putatively appropriate resentment merit acceptance to the extent that they do not differ from justified expressions of the stance of moral protest. Shabo contends that once it is clear that people "must unreservedly own this resentment on pain of emotional dishonesty, merely withholding their endorsement is apt to seem like a mere intellectual exercise." However, it is possible to see clearly that one is resentful, acknowledge that the accompanying presupposition of basically deserved pain or harm is false, and yet affirm that being resentful is natural and practically rational in this case, and that one's expression of one's resentment can be justified as legitimate moral protest.

Shabo advances a psychological hypothesis that links disavowal of resentment to the scaling back of any manifestations of taking wrongdoing personally:

# LOVE, WRONGDOING, AND THE REACTIVE ATTITUDES    137

we could neither plan to sincerely disavow instances of resentment without a reliable way of suppressing other manifestations of our disposition to take maltreatment personally, including feeling hurt and feeling aggrieved, nor reliably suppress these other reactions without scaling back our concern with the esteem in which our coparticipants hold us, as manifested in their treatment of us...the only reliable strategy for broadly immunizing ourselves against these responses is to be significantly less emotionally attuned than we normally are to others' attitudes toward us. For when we are so attuned, our control over whether we take displays of disregard personally in these ways is at best indirect and very limited. And since we cannot control how attuned we are to others' attitudes without limiting our emotional investment in how they see us, there is an irresolvable practical tension between fostering personal relationships and making it a priority to avoid taking maltreatment personally in these ways.

(Shabo 2022)

In response, I first want to distinguish between hurt feelings on the one hand, and attitudes that presuppose desert on the other. David Shoemaker (2019) proposes that hurt feeling is a reactive attitude; Strawson (1962), he notes, includes hurt feelings in his list of reactive attitudes. Hurt feelings and resentment have something in common, but in many cases hurt feelings do not result from blameworthy behavior on the part of the other. One can feel hurt by unrequited love, by losing preferred status in friendship, and by the weakening of a collegial relationship. In each type of case, the hurt feelings are manifestations of the susceptibility Shabo contends to be required for personal relationships, but sometimes these feelings do not result from blameworthy (or praiseworthy) behavior on the part of the other. Hurt feelings do not count as reactive attitudes in the sense that they do not presuppose that the behavior that causes the hurt feelings is blameworthy (or praiseworthy).

It's instructive to consider a type of personal relationship in which it is not unusual for us to respond to expressions of disregard and disrespect with attitudes that are personal but not reactive (Pereboom 2014). Teenagers often go through a period when they have attitudes of disregard and disrespect for parents, expressions of which can cause hurt feelings. Yet for many parents, such expressions of disregard and disrespect do not occasion resentment, but rather disappointment and sadness, and the blaming response may involve moral protest without anger. Disappointment and sadness may be distinctively personal and may reveal an emotional investment in the

## 138 LOVE AND FREEDOM

relationship. When parents fit this profile, the teenager's attitudes may matter to them in their own right, apart from the consequences of these attitudes for their interests. It's an empirical question whether here lack of resentment reduces emotional investment more generally. From personal observation, my sense is that this is not so.

One might object, as Justin Coates (2013) does, that such absence of resentment is an artifact of the specific nature of the parental relationship, and that it will not carry over on a significant scale to close relationships among adults on an equal footing, relationships of mutual regard. But first, some such adult relationships are free from resentment and feature disappointment and sadness instead. A change to this sort of emotional profile may be an option for those of us who currently have the resentful reactions. The past several centuries have witnessed very significant changes in attitudes toward criminals, the insane, and children, and thus significant general emotional change over time possible for us. Second, the feature that stands to rule out the legitimacy of the reactive attitudes in parental relationships is the parents' role in the moral formation of not fully morally mature children. However, adults also stand in need of moral formation, and it's precisely the dispositions to those actions that give rise to resentment that stand in need of moral reform. When relationships are functioning properly, parents care about the moral formation of their children. Wouldn't relationships of mutual regard, when functioning properly, also involve this kind of care? In the case of children, angry responses are apt to give rise to resistance rather than reform. The same may well be true for relationships of mutual regard.

In his discussion of these issues, Per-Erik Milam (2016) has us consider an example of a difficult relationship between a parent and her adult child. As he describes it,

> the child might care deeply for her mother despite the fact that her mother has been and continues to be, at times, indifferent, emotionally manipulative, and unreasonably demanding. Such a relationship might have all the hallmarks of a personal relationship—as relationships between parents and adult children often do—even if the daughter has, over the course of her lifetime, ceased to take her mother's behavior personally.
>
> (Milam 2016, 112)

Milam proposes that not taking the mother's behavior personally may be what allows the relationship to continue. For a range of cases, this approach

LOVE, WRONGDOING, AND THE REACTIVE ATTITUDES 139

seems justified. But Milam also endorses the point at issue: when one does take wrongdoing personally, the reactive attitudes need not be in play:

> What unifies our intuitions about what it means to take personally a friend or lover's failure is the sense that, in doing so, that person has let you down. This sense of unmet expectations fits naturally with a reactive (blaming) disposition (Wallace 1994), but it does not require it. Anxiety about facing a judgmental parent, disappointment with a lover who ruins a romantic moment, frustration with a friend's thoughtless indignation— these emotional responses indicate that one has taken something personally, but not (or not necessarily) that one is disposed to the reactive attitudes.
>
> (Milam 2016, 112)

Consider now a fourth objection, due to Coates (2013). In his view, essential to love relationships of mutual regard is the normative (and not merely predictive) expectation that participants relate to each other in respectful ways. But, he contends, a normative expectation that others respect us is constituted by the reactive emotions. At this point he considers the view that non-reactive emotions such as disappointment and sadness might constitute this normative expectation instead. Against this, he argues that if emotions such as disappointment and sadness constituted these normative expectations, they would also constitute normative expectations when we are sad and disappointed due to hurricanes and cancer diagnoses (Coates 2013, 248). Moreover, it would then be legitimate for us to have normative expectations that harms due to such natural phenomena not occur. But we lack such normative expectations in these kinds of cases, and it would be inappropriate to have them. For this reason, these non-reactive emotions cannot constitute the normative expectations in question.

In response, we need not suppose that the normative expectations at issue are wholly constituted by emotions, whether they be reactive or non-reactive. They might instead be constituted partly by non-reactive emotions and partly by beliefs. When one is hurt by a loved one's behavior, one may be disappointed and saddened, as in the case of the diagnosis of an illness, but what may make the difference is that in the case of the behavior one legitimately believes that the other should not have acted as he did, while there is no analogous legitimate belief regarding the illness. Strawsonian sentimentalists about morality may hold that the normativity that pertains to relationships of mutual regard is wholly emotionally constituted, but this is a daring view, to which there is a viable alternative.

140    LOVE AND FREEDOM

Finally one might ask whether praise and gratitude, while required for good personal relationships, are threatened by skepticism about free will. As we saw in Chapter 2, Daniel Telech (2021) sets out a conversational view of praise and the related attitude of gratitude which is consistent with free will skepticism and the rejection of basic desert. On his view, praise is a kind of invitation to a praiseworthy agent, whose function it is to occasion a self-reactive attitude that mirrors the content of the praiser's attitude. That attitude Telech calls directed pride, a reflexive emotion whose evaluative focus is the meaning for another of one's manifestation of good will, a way of registering the significance for another of one's having done the right thing. When praise is accepted in this way, praiser and praiseworthy agent mutually recognize one another as standing for a common value, which serves to deepen the relationship (Telech 2021, 164-65). This in turn stands to strengthen the disposition by which the praiseworthy action is motivated, which has the additional protective function of reducing risk of harm (Pereboom 2014, 135).

## Demands, Wrongness, and Protest

In Dana Nelkin's (2011, 2014, 2022) conception, what distinguishes loving personal relationships such as friendships and marriages from mere acquaintances is a structure of demands. As Jay Wallace (2022) points out, demands also have this role in Strawson's account of personal relationships, and in his view such demands are essentially tied to being disposed to the negative reactive attitudes:

> to make a demand of this kind just is, inter alia, to be disposed to the reactive emotions in case the demand should be flouted, or to believe those emotions would be fitting or appropriate under those circumstances. Normative expectations are thus not available to be analyzed independently of the reactive emotions. Rather, the two need to be understood together. This reflects a theme in Strawson (1962). As Strawson puts the point: "attitudes of disapprobation and indignation are precisely the correlates of the moral demand in the case where the demand is felt to be disregarded. The making of the demand *is* the proneness to such attitudes."[3]

---

[3] Coleen Macnamara (2013) develops a series of objections to the link between the negative reactive attitudes and demands for which Strawson and those influenced by him argue. She cites, as advocates of such a connection, Gary Watson: "The negative reactive attitudes express

# DEMANDS, WRONGNESS, AND PROTEST 141

Wallace counsels caution here, citing the personal relationship with God:

> Reason to question whether this is the case is provided by familiar Christian characterizations of the believer's attitudes toward God, which include love and gratitude, but which do not obviously implicate the demanding stance that renders the believer susceptible to resentment or indignation toward God. This is admittedly a special case, but it suggests the coherence of love and gratitude in the absence of any susceptibility to the more narrowly reactive attitudes. (Wallace 2022)

We've already considered whether personal relationships are tied to susceptibility to the reactive attitudes. In Nelkin's analysis of demands in relationships, she focuses not on that link, but rather on their connection with moral obligation. In her view, if A and B are friends, and if A is in dire need, there is a strong prima facie moral obligation for B to help A, which in turn gives rise to a legitimate demand. However, like basic desert moral responsibility, moral obligation is threatened by a general challenge to the control we have in action. It's intuitive for many that the 'ought' of moral obligation implies 'can.' Suppose the principle is true. Then, if B does not help A, but because B is causally determined B could not have helped A, then B wasn't morally obligated to help A.[4] More generally, the freedom to do otherwise is plausibly required for demands and the moral obligations they entail to structure relationships, and such freedom is threatened by causal determination.

Nelkin (2011, 108–12) indeed finds the 'ought' implies 'can' principle for moral obligation to be intuitive, and I concur. David Copp (2008, 71) argues that because the 'ought' of moral obligation is action guiding, it applies to an agent only if his actions could be so guided, and I think he is right. Nelkin (2011, 109) also considers this rationale appealing, and in addition points

---

a moral demand, a demand for reasonable regard" (Watson 2004, 229); Stephen Darwall: "Resentment doesn't represent its object as simply contravening one's will, but as contravening some justified demand" (Darwall 2006, 81); and Margaret Urban Walker: "When we express and direct our resentment or indignation at a norm violator, we demand some rectifying response from the one who is perceived as out of bounds" (Walker 2006, 26).

[4] This is, in effect, Kant's argument for the claim that the moral law's holding for us requires that we have transcendental freedom, a type of libertarian agent-causal free will. He maintains in addition that in order to affirm that the moral law holds for us, we must believe that we are transcendentally free, despite not even being able to show that it's really (i.e., metaphysically) possible that we are free in this sense. So for him, belief that we are transcendentally free is practically, but not theoretically, justified (Kant 1781/1787/1987, A547/B575, A558/B586; Watkins 2005; Pereboom 2006b).

142    LOVE AND FREEDOM

out that this principle explains our intuitions about examples in which, upon discovering that an agent cannot fulfill what we believed to be an obligation, we retract our judgment that the obligation is in place and instead attribute a 'second-best' obligation (Nelkin 2011, 111–12; Howard-Snyder 2006, 236; Brink 1994, 231; Vranas 2007, 181–2). Suppose you promise to pick up a friend at the airport at 3 PM, but that time has now passed—you were busy with your work and forgot—and she calls and tells you she's waiting for you. Intuitively, you're no longer obligated to pick her up at 3 PM, but instead as soon as you can get there.

An initial question arises about the claim that relationships are structured by demands. Here Kant is a potential ally. Relationships are governed by morality, and Kant argues that the moral law, in general, applies to human beings in imperative form, and imperatives (at least in the context of relationships) are demands. The moral law applies to us in imperative form because we human beings have self-interested inclinations that potentially motivate us in ways contrary to the moral law. What Kant calls a holy will, by contrast, has no such motivations, and as a result, the moral law does not apply to such a being in imperative form (Kant 1785/1981, chapter 2). But human beings do not qualify.

However, if the condition for a moral principle applying in imperative form is potential contrary motivation, then for many people many moral principles do not plausibly apply in that form. Suppose Eloise is an especially kind person, and she is never motivated to be mean to anyone. Does the principle that proscribes being mean apply to her in the form of a demand? Against this, to overtly confront her with such a demand would be morally inappropriate. Because Eloise has an unopposed general disposition to act in accord with the moral principle that proscribes meanness, it would seem that for her this principle is not an imperative, and not a demand.

One might reply that given her moral personality, overtly confronting her with this demand would be inappropriate, but that does not show that for her the demand is not in place. A demand might be in place for someone and yet never be legitimately overtly expressed to her. It's legitimate to overtly express a demand to an agent only when she violates or threatens to violate the principle. However, it is always appropriate to express moral principles privately, from one's own first-person point of view, as demands. But against this, it seems that it would also be inappropriate for Eloise privately to regard the principle as a demand, given how she is actually motivated.

A resolution is that given human frailty, and thus the real possibility of contra-moral motivation, moral principles are always legitimately viewed as *conditional* demands. For Eloise, if she were motivated to be mean, the principle that proscribes being mean would confront her as a demand. If she were actually mean or threaten to be mean to someone, it would be legitimate for an appropriately situated interlocutor to express the demand overtly. Human relationships, then, might be viewed as thoroughly structured by conditional demands. Then the concern raised initially remains in place. In cases in which such a conditional demand backed by moral obligation threatens not to be met, the freedom to do otherwise is required for it to structure a relationship. Relationships would then be structured by potential or possible demands; that is, by demands legitimately made upon satisfaction of their conditions.

One way to respond to this threat to moral obligation is to contend that the 'can' in the 'ought' implies 'can' principle is not the strong 'all in' sense, that is, a sense that involves holding the entire past and all the laws fixed (e.g., Lewis 1981; Slote 1982; Campbell 1997; Perry 2004; Wedgewood 2007; Graham 2011; Nelkin 2011, 64–79). We saw in Chapter 1 that a weaker sense of 'can,' one that does not involve holding the entire past and all the laws fixed, is required to make sense of the truth of certain plausible claims about abilities. Now consider: Mario and I are in New York, he is a native speaker of Italian, we're in an Italian restaurant, the menus are in both Italian and English, and our waiter has told us he's also Italian. Although it would seem that on this occasion Mario has a fine opportunity to use his Italian, he nevertheless orders in English. I say, after the waiter has left, "You could have ordered in Italian!" Even supposing causal determinism, it's plausible that what I said in this context is true. In some contexts use of a weaker sense of can attributes only a general or global ability, such as Mario's ability to speak Italian, by contrast with a specific or local ability to exercise such an ability in particular circumstances (Mele 2003). But in this case, it's implausible that I'm merely attributing a general ability to speak Italian to Mario; that's not aptly remarked upon in this context. Rather, what I said implies that in these specific circumstances he could have exercised his general ability to speak Italian, and this is intuitively true. However, if in assessing this claim the entire past and all the laws are held fixed, the truth of "You could have ordered in Italian!" is ruled out. So it would be best to loosen what's held fixed. Here one might follow Ann Whittle (2010) in distinguishing a local ability, which holds the entire past and the laws fixed, from a *fairly* local ability, which loosens what's held fixed to a certain degree but

144  LOVE AND FREEDOM

still holds fixed particular features of the current circumstances.[5] Similarly, perhaps it would also be best to loosen what's held fixed for the sense of 'can' in 'ought' implies 'can' in order to accommodate our intuitions, and, by analogy with the restaurant example, this may secure a fairly local and not a merely general ability.[6]

This is one natural line for a compatibilist to pursue. But is it open for an incompatibilist about causal determination and basic desert, like me, to be a compatibilist about causal determination and moral obligation? An incompatibilist might begin by arguing that moral wrongness is clearly compatible with causal determination: even if some people are causally determined to knowingly kill the innocent, their actions are clearly still wrong. Next, he might claim that the following principle is plausible:

S has a moral obligation to perform A if and only if it is morally wrong for S not to perform A.   (Haji 1998, 2002)

Given this principle, if judgments of wrongness are not undermined by causal determination, neither are judgments of moral obligation. These two kinds of judgments would invariably stand and fall together. But then the 'can' in the 'ought' implies 'can' principle is not the 'all in' variety, but a weaker one that does not hold the entire past and all the laws fixed. For if the 'can' were the 'all in' variety, then the truth of judgments of moral obligation would be undermined by causal determination, while the truth of judgments of wrongness, as we're assuming, would remain in place.

---

[5] Whittle writes: "We can say that an object O has the global disposition D if O has a property complex (or one of a number of them, if the disposition is multiply-realised) in virtue of which it is true that O would D in some suitable proportion of C-cases... In contrast, an object O has the 'all-in' local disposition to D-in-W (where W is a particular type of C-case) if O instantiates a property complex in virtue of which O would (standardly) D-in-W... These 'all-in' local dispositions should be distinguished from 'fairly local' dispositions that employ a larger range of C-cases in which only some of the circumstances are held fixed. So an object O has the fairly local disposition D if O instantiates a property complex in virtue of which O would D in a suitable proportion of a range of C-cases, in which certain circumstances in that range of C-cases are held fixed" (Whittle 2010, 4–5; Whittle cites Manley and Wasserman (2008)).

[6] Note that this account does not also feature a conditional analysis of 'could have done otherwise.' Reasons why such an analysis is implausible are summarized in McKenna and Pereboom (2016), 56–62. Let me add that on the plausible supposition that the locus of moral obligation and moral responsibility is decision (or more broadly, intention formation), such conditional accounts are implausible given that that there are no mental states that generally precede decision on which to conditionalize the alternative possibility. For example, trying, contrary to what Michael Fara (2008) has suggested, is an implausible candidate for such a mental state, for as Randolph Clarke (2009, 347) points out, we never directly try to decide.

DEMANDS, WRONGNESS, AND PROTEST 145

This strategy yields one attractive response to the issue that Nelkin raises. A concern for it, however, that there would appear to be a tension in endorsing compatibilism about moral obligation while affirming incompatibilism about basically deserved pain and harm, even if there is no contradiction involved. Perhaps this tension can be resolved. David Brink, who is a compatibilist about both deserved blame and moral obligation (as is Nelkin (2011)), argues that blame and obligation nevertheless differ in their sensitivity to possibility, and that in this respect morality mirrors criminal legal practice:

> But in the criminal law capacities and opportunities condition culpability or responsibility, not wrongdoing. Excuse is an affirmative defense that concedes wrongdoing but denies responsibility for wrongdoing. Insufficient capacity or opportunity is the basis for an excuse. So, in the case of a paradigmatic excuse, the lack of morally relevant alternatives precludes blame, not wrongdoing. The excused agent violates normative requirements and demands, but is not blameworthy for doing so. This means that blame is sensitive to possibility in a way that wrongdoing and obligation are not. This is a feature of the criminal law that sounds in morality as well. In both morality and criminal law we should reject voluntarism as a principle about obligation, duty, and requirement but accept it as a principle about the conditions under which blame is appropriate.
>
> (Brink 2021, 89; cf., Nelkin 2011, 110)

The incompatibilist might agree with Brink that deserved blame is sensitive to possibility in a way that moral obligation is not—the standard of possibility for deserved blame is more exacting. The further claim is that this more exacting standard rules out (basically) deserved blame given causal determination, while moral obligation, together with wrongness, remain in place. In the terminology of Chapter 1, this combination of views involves accepting a compatibilist variety of *free will AP* (for 'alternative possibilities'), while rejecting the contentious sort of *free will MR* (for 'moral responsibility'), where the sense selected invokes basic desert.

A more resolutely incompatibilist option, which I've proposed in the past, affirms that moral obligation is undermined by causal determination, and exchanges moral obligation for axiologically based recommendation (Pereboom 2014, 142–4, 2017a). This proposal begins by replacing the role of demand in relationships with the notions of care and commitment. Care for beings with moral standing is apt to generate specific commitments in

146    LOVE AND FREEDOM

particular contexts. This kind of care would generate a commitment on the part of friends to provide help to the other when in dire need. But then how might we conceive the personal relationship between friends A and B in a situation in which there is a threat that B will not come to A's help in time of dire need, and thus not to honor his own commitment? It's natural for B to think of himself as morally obligated to help A, and for A to make a demand of moral obligation that B help her. But we might instead frame A's expectation in terms of the notion of moral wrongness: B can legitimately think that it would be wrong for him not to help A, and A can communicate to B that it would be wrong of him not to help her.

However, so far this proposal is subject to the challenge that if judgments of moral obligation are undermined by causal determination, so are judgments of wrongness. Haji (1998, 2002) contends that because of the tight connection between moral obligation and moral wrongness, the threat posed to judgments of moral obligation indeed carries over to those of moral wrongness. Essential to his argument is, again, the following principle:

S has a moral obligation to perform A if and only if it is morally wrong for S not to perform A.

If this principle were true, then if judgments of moral obligation were undermined by causal determination, judgments of moral wrongness would be ruled out as well.

But now one might argue that although this biconditional principle may be attractive viewed in the abstract, it captures only one aspect of the complex notion of moral wrongness. This can be made plausible by considering that the right-to-left half, i.e.

If it is morally wrong for S not to perform A, then S has a moral obligation to perform A

is not clearly secure. There is likely no case in which it's plausible that someone is morally obligated not to perform an action while it is not morally wrong for her to perform it. There are, however, examples in which it's intuitive that performing an action would be morally wrong for an agent, while it's at least less clear that she has a moral obligation not to perform it. Suppose that a psychopath could not have avoided an act of deception due to his psychological condition. The 'ought' implies 'can' principle provides an intuitive ground for denying that he is morally obligated not to deceive, while it remains plausible that his action was morally wrong.

## DEMANDS, WRONGNESS, AND PROTEST    147

An alternative notion of moral wrongness, one that isn't biconditionally linked to moral obligation, accommodates this intuition (Pereboom 2014, 142–4; 2017a). Alastair Norcross's (2006) suggestion for an exclusively axiological ethics involves ranking in order of value of the consequences realized, without obligation to maximize value. We can specify that actions are wrong when their axiological ranking is sufficiently low. But how low is that? Here we can again appeal to the notion of moral protest which I've already used to characterize blame:

*An axiological notion of wrongness*: An option for acting is morally wrong when its value is low enough in the axiological ranking for it to be morally appropriate for a relevantly positioned interlocutor to issue a moral protest against actions of this sort.

Moral protest can function as an axiological recommendation against performing an action. What makes such protest morally appropriate would itself consist, all else equal, in its having a relatively high ranking among available options (there might be countervailing considerations). Note also that this proposal does not characterize wrongness independently of when it is appropriate to protest, and so it cannot ground the appropriateness of protest in wrongness. Yet it does have the consequence that it's appropriate to protest a type of action only when so acting would be morally wrong, and it thus satisfies an important intuition we have about this relation.

One might think that on this conception, protest will be insufficiently forceful in some situations in which wrongdoers are aggressive or recalcitrant. But protest can be given additional force by threat of sanction. When Dave is unfaithful to Donna or is motivated to be, Donna can protest his action and the disposition that underlies it. If he is obstinate when she issues the moral protest, she can give it additional force by specifying a sanction should the protest be ignored. Accordingly, personal relationships can be viewed as structured by moral protest should the need arise, where such protest is rooted in an axiological notion of wrongness and may be backed by threat of sanction.

Thus in response to Nelkin's challenge, the free will skeptic can view personal relationships as structured by the possibility of moral protest characterized in terms of moral obligation, as Nelkin herself does, because, by contrast with basic desert, moral obligation is compatible with causal determination due to the weakness of the sense of 'can' in the 'ought' implies 'can' principle. Alternatively, moral protest can be characterized independently of moral obligation, and thus without implying freedom by way of the

148  LOVE AND FREEDOM

'ought' implies 'can' principle, because there is a notion of wrongness that can be characterized independently of moral obligation.

## Final Words

Do these proposals result in a loss in overall value relative to our ordinary beliefs about moral obligation and moral responsibility? Paul Russell (2017) argues that we must acknowledge that they do, and that this is a loss we may need to accept. The sense of loss, in Russell's view, is rooted in the assumptions and aspirations of what Bernard Williams (1985) has called "the morality system." The morality system, as Williams describes it, places emphasis on the notion of moral obligation together with what he regards as a closely allied conception of blame. Moral responsibility, as the morality system would have it, is taken to be primarily a matter of rational agents voluntarily violating their obligations and thereby being liable to retribution and to blame conceived retributivistically. In Russell's view, an optimistic aspect of free will skepticism is the rejection of the morality system's retributivist elements. He contends, however, that there is no credible exclusively optimistic response to the human predicament that results from the naturalistic threat to moral responsibility. That is, there are deeply human aspirations for agency and morality that are irrevocably frustrated by the nature of our predicament. My position is more resolutely optimistic than Russell's, but about it he writes that it is "one-sided and captures only one part of the truth about our predicament with respect to issues of agency, freedom and moral responsibility" (Russell 2017, 269) I disagree, since, as these reflections on love and personal relationships indicate, the rejected aspects of the morality system can be compensated for by what remains, together with what is available in the human repertoire to replace those rejected aspects.

# 7

# Religion and Hope

How do we see ourselves in the great scheme of things, if that scheme is deterministic, or due to the only kind of indeterminism it permits, similarly limits the control we have in action? The great theistic religions have provided answers to this question, as have non-theistic views such as Buddhism and modern descendants of orthodox theisms whose conception of the divine is impersonal. A shared theme is that such conceptions provide for greater equanimity in our lives, in particular in the face of suffering caused by wrongdoing and by natural events, and that this equanimity results from our comprehension of the scheme and our place in it. In the theistic religions the conception standardly features divine providential governance of the universe: whatever happens accords with a divine plan that aims at the good, and this provides great comfort for us. In the non-theistic views, the relevant ideas vary, as we shall see.

Conceptions of divine providence, whether or not they endorse freedom of the will, are put to the test by the existence of evils, both moral and natural, that appear not to be justified by any good to which they contribute (Flint 1998, Swinburne 1999, Hasker 2004). If an all-powerful, wholly benevolent, and providential being exists, then that being would have the power and the motivation to prevent all such evils. Yet such evils do in fact exist, so that conception faces a threat. Responses to the problem of evil are far from decisive, but I will contend that they nevertheless allow for rational hope that a providential God exists. Hope is appropriate when our interest lies in an unknown outcome due to factors completely beyond our control, as is the case if the future is rendered inevitable by theological determinism or else by the remote past in accord with the laws of nature. On either the theistic or the naturalistic conception, I will argue that a hope counterpart to John Dewey's (1934) "common faith," a faith in the survival and progress of humanity embedded in a thriving natural environment, is rational.

What is it to hope for an outcome? Most philosophers who have addressed this question agree that to hope for an outcome requires that one desire, fairly strongly, that it will come about, that to believe that it's possible

*Wrongdoing and the Moral Emotions.* Derk Pereboom, Oxford University Press. © Derk Pereboom 2021.
DOI: 10.1093/oso/9780192846006.003.0007

150   RELIGION AND HOPE

that it will. Andrew Chignell (2014) points out that Immanuel Kant (1781/1787/1987) famously asks: "What *may* I hope?" and that this connotes a concern about rational permissibility. On Chignell's analysis, the concern stems from the recognition that the desire for the outcome or the belief that it will come about might be irrational, and that if so, the hope may also be irrational. Someone might desire to be God or believe that he can be the ruler of the world, and the resulting hopes might well be irrational as a result of the irrationality of the desire and the belief. This suggests that an agent rationally hopes for an outcome only if she rationally desires it, and she is justified in believing that its coming about is possible (Chignell 2014).[1]

Mere possibility is weak, however, as Chignell notes. It is possible, in several senses, for you to become ruler of the galaxy—this conception doesn't involve a contradiction, and it's consistent, as far as we know, with the laws of nature. A potential fix is that besides rational desire, rational hope depends on rational credence, i.e., rational degree of belief, that the outcome will come about (Martin 2011, 2013; McCormick 2017; Milona 2019; Jackson 2021). Michael Milona (2019) argues that hope does not require that one's rational credence be especially high. The outcome also can't be certain; as J. M. O. Wheatley points out, "to hope, regarding the future, is in part to expect but not to be sure" (Wheatley 1958, 127). Philip Pettit agrees: "just as hope requires that one not rule out the hoped-for possibility, so it requires that one does not rule it in as a matter of absolute certainty either." (Pettit 2004, 153)

But if hope is to be rational and make a significant difference to how one acts, rational credence that the outcome will come about cannot be merely negligible (Martin 2013). If one's rational credence that one will win the lottery is one in a million, one may hope that one will win, but that hope does not rationalize contacting realtors for appointments to view expensive properties on the California coast. Victoria McGeer argues that those who maintain hopes that have no realistic chance of being realized can't be said to hope *well*. She maintains that it is "characteristic of those who hope well to resolutely shift their target of hope when the world proves adamantine with respect to some hoped-for end" (McGeer 2004, 109). This is a valuable point. But it depends on the effect of one's hope on one's actions; it's

---

[1] To distinguish hope from despair, Chignell (2021) proposes adding a disposition to focus on the desired outcome under a certain aspect—the aspect of its possibility. Despair, by contrast, is the disposition to focus on the desired outcome under the aspect of its improbability.

rationally permissible to hope that one wins that lottery, but one shouldn't be contacting the realtors. Let me propose that the more a hope has a significant and rational effect on one's actions—the more it is what I'll call a *substantial hope*—the higher the credence needs to be, all else equal. Defending rational hope in the survival and progress of humanity in a thriving natural environment, if it is to be a substantial hope, requires non-negligible evidential support, which I believe is available.

## The Stoics on Providence

In a wide range of theistic views, the understanding that everything that happens is causally determined by God in accord with a divine plan for the world is held to be a great comfort for us. We find this view expressed in ancient Stoicism, in Judaism, Christianity, and in Islam. Human lives are subject to pain, deprivation, failure, and death, which in turn makes us vulnerable to anger and despair. How do we cope with these difficulties and the suffering they occasion? Accepting a strong notion of divine providence involves the conviction that everything that happens to us, to the last detail, is in accord with God's providential will. Comfort in life may be secured by the belief that even minor harms, let alone horrendous evils, cannot befall us unless God, who is perfectly benevolent, willingly causes or allows them to happen.[2]

In the Stoic conception, God determines everything that happens in accord with the good of the entire universe, albeit that the nature of this good is incompletely understood on our part. There is an all-encompassing divine plan, and we can be assured that everything that occurs is determined by God with an aim to the realization of that plan, despite our lack of understanding of its nature and means of realization. By identifying with this all-encompassing divine plan, we can be reconciled with the world's evils. Equanimity, and, more ambitiously, gratitude, replaces anger and despair as cosmic attitudes within our reach (Inwood 1985; Pereboom 1994; Bobzien 1998; Brennan 2005).

In this conception, one should accommodate oneself to the determinism of the universe by, as the late Stoic Epictetus puts it, seeking to have things

---

[2] For a recent defense of theological determinism, see White (2019); Vicens and Kittle (2019) provide a current overview of this position, with a focus on its relation to human free will. For my views on theological determinism, see Pereboom (2005, 2012, 2016).

152   RELIGION AND HOPE

happen as they do happen (Epictetus 125/1983, §8). One should do so even if what happens may be bad from one's personal point of view, that is, from the perspective of one's ordinary human aspirations for personal survival, happiness, and success. The Stoic recommendation is that one should cease to appraise the events of one's life from one's personal point of view, and instead to evaluate them from the divine perspective. That is, one should appraise the events of one's life solely by the purposes God has in creating and preserving the universe, objectives which are distinct from, and may conflict with, one's ordinary personal concerns.

This abstracted stance towards one's life is expressed in the Stoic conception of *reservation* (Inwood 1985, 119–26; Brennan 2000). In our universe, much is not within our control in any sense, and we may find ourselves aiming to achieve goals which we will not in fact secure. This difficulty might result either from our lack of power or from absence of knowledge. If someone aspires to become head of state, she may not have the capability to achieve her end, and further, even if she will in fact succeed, she will likely not come to know this when she forms her intent. One strategy for negotiating this issue is to avoid striving for any goal one cannot be assured of acquiring. But the Stoics do not encourage this approach. Instead, they recommend acting with reservation. Whenever one acts, one does so by assenting to a proposition that corresponds to the presentation of the action. If one is to act in accordance with the will of God, the judgments one makes as a result of assenting must conform to this will. Thus if one aims to set sail tomorrow, one should not simply resolve to set sail tomorrow, but as Seneca advises in *On Tranquility*, to say "I will set sail tomorrow unless something intervenes," or "if it is so fated." (Seneca 60/1932, 13.2ff.) In the explicitly theological formulation one would resolve "I will set sail tomorrow unless it goes against the will of God." Reservation is likewise expressed in Latin as "*Deo volente,*" and in Arabic as *Inshallah*, the use of which the Quran recommends when speaking of future events. Acting with reservation involves a degree of psychological detachment from an outcome that is not up to us. As a result of this detachment we will not be (as) distressed if an attempt to secure a desired objective fails. In Seneca's view, "the suffering that comes to the mind from the abandonment of desire must necessarily be much lighter if you have not certainly promised it success." (Seneca 60/1932, 13.2ff.)

More fundamentally, acting with reservation involves assuming the divine perspective on our personal successes and failures. It ultimately requires that we evaluate the outcomes of our ventures from the point of view of divine purposes. If we supplement this stance with the belief that

DESCARTES ON PROVIDENCE    153

everything that happens is providentially ordained by God, we can aspire to accept the result of any endeavor with equanimity, and even to regard any outcome with joy. The second-century Roman emperor Marcus Aurelius recommends an outlook of this sort in his *Meditations*:

> You must consider the doing and perfecting of what the universal Nature decrees in the same light as your health, and welcome all that happens, even if it seems harsh, because it leads to the health of the universe, and the welfare and well-being of Zeus. For he would not have allotted this to anyone if it were not beneficial to the whole.
>
> (Marcus Aurelius 175/1985, V §8)

If we align our desires with the good of the whole, we will welcome anything that happens to us, even our own impending death, for "cessation of life is no evil to the individual, since... it is good if it is timely for the whole, bringing benefit to it, and benefitted by it" (Marcus Aurelius 175/1985, XII §23).

In the Stoic vision, we should align our will and judgment with the divine perspective so that we will enjoy equanimity no matter what happens, even if God's plan conflicts with the good as conceived from one's personal point of view, with one's ordinary human aspirations for personal survival, happiness, and success. Maintaining this attitude requires that we identify with a notion of the good that might well diverge significantly from our ordinary personal conception of it. One might object that such identification is too demanding given our limited capabilities. Suppose that one's role in the divine plan involves suffering miserably up to a final end to one's existence. For many theists the response is to specify that the divine plan not only aims at the good of the whole, but also at the good of the individual. Marilyn Adams proposes that God is good to every person by ensuring each a life in which all suffering contributes to a great good within that very life (Adams 1999, 55). Then it might even be, Alvin Plantinga suggests, that God would know that if I were able to make the decision whether to accept the suffering of my life, and knew enough about the divine plan, and had the right affections, I myself would accept that suffering (Plantinga 2004).

## Descartes on Providence

Descartes sets out a conception of providence that is similar to the Stoic view, but yet distinct in an important respect. In a letter to Princess

154 RELIGION AND HOPE

Elizabeth of Bohemia in the autumn of 1645 Descartes advances the view that God is the cause of everything that happens in the world:

> it seems to me that all the reasons that prove the existence of God, and that he is the first and immutable cause of all the effects that do not depend upon the free decision of men, likewise prove in the same way that he is also the cause of all those that do depend on it. For one could not demonstrate that God exists save by considering him as a being sovereignly perfect; and God could not be sovereignly perfect if something could happen in the world that did not come entirely from him...philosophy alone suffices to give us the knowledge that the least thought cannot enter the mind of man if God had not wished and willed from all eternity that it enter therein.
>
> (Descartes 1978, 162; to Elisabeth 6 October 1645, AT IV 313–14)

God is the *total cause* of everything that happens, whether it is something that depends on a free decision or whether it is not, and "thus nothing can happen without his will" (Descartes 1978, 163; AT IV 314).

In a letter to Chanut, the French ambassador to Sweden (intended for the eyes of Queen Christina of Sweden, whom Descartes would later instruct in philosophy), Descartes connects this view of God as total cause of everything that happens in the world to a strong notion of providence. In the following excerpt, he sets out "the path one ought to follow to arrive at the love of God":

> But if, in addition, we heed the infinity of his power, through which he has created so many things, of which we are the least part; the extension of his providence that makes him see in one thought alone everything that has been, is, shall be, and could be; the infallibility of his decrees, which, although they do not disturb our free will nevertheless cannot in any fashion be changed; and finally, if, on the one hand, we heed our insignificance, and if, on the other hand, we heed the grandeur of all created things, by noting the manner in which they depend on God and by considering them in a fashion that has a relationship to his omnipotence, without confining them in a globe, as do they who think the world finite: meditation upon all this so abundantly fills the man who hears it with such extreme joy that, realizing he would have to be abusive and ungrateful toward God to wish to occupy God's place, he thinks himself as already having lived sufficiently because God has given him the grace to reach

DESCARTES ON PROVIDENCE 155

such knowledge; and willingly and entirely joining himself to God, he loves God so perfectly that he desires nothing more in the world than that God's will be done. That is the reason he no longer fears either death, or pains, or disgraces, because he knows that nothing can happen to him save what God shall have decreed; and he so loves this divine decree, esteems it so just and so necessary, knows he ought so entirely to depend upon it, that even when he awaits death or some other evil, if *per impossibile* he could change that decree, he would not wish to do so. But if he does not refuse evils or afflictions, because they come to him from divine providence, he refuses still less all the goods or licit pleasures one can enjoy in this life, because they too issue from that providence; and accepting them with joy, without having any fear of evils, his love renders him perfectly happy.

(Descartes 1978, 206–7; to Chanut, 1 February 1647, AT IV 608–9)

Descartes recommends that we transcend the personal point of view, the perspective of one's ordinary human aspirations for personal survival, happiness, and success, just as Marcus Aurelius does. In Descartes's understanding, if our love for God were of the right sort, our identification with the divine perspective would be so complete that even if we could, we would not refuse our own death or other evils, since they proceed from the divine decree.

Descartes's conception of how we identify with the divine perspective differs in an important respect from the classical Stoic view. One of the most pressing issues for the Stoic conception is to provide reason and motivation for making this identification. The doctrine of reservation and Marcus Aurelius's injunctions suggest that we align ourselves with the divine perspective so that we will enjoy equanimity no matter what happens, even if what happens conflicts with the good as conceived from the personal point of view. One might doubt whether such a reason is sufficient to motivate many people. By analogy, imagine that one's sovereign has a utilitarian concern for the aggregate community which is seldom disappointed, but her scheme causes one to be poverty-stricken so that many others might be well off. Trapped in this situation, one might consider aligning with the sovereign's objectives while abandoning one's personal perspective on the good, for the reason that making these psychological moves would result in one's achieving equanimity. But very few of us are capable of being so motivated. Consequently, for Descartes's version of this strategy to be feasible, we need another proposal for a reason that might motivate us to align ourselves with the divine purposes as he conceives them.

156　RELIGION AND HOPE

In another letter to Elisabeth, Descartes argues that "it is necessary to prefer always the interests of the whole, of which one is a part, to the interest of one's own person in particular," although "this is to be done with measure and discretion." He points out that one is sometimes motivated to behave accordingly; "by considering oneself as part of the public, one takes pleasure in doing good to everyone," and as a result, one does not even fear to risk one's life to save others. Descartes then claims:

> One is naturally led to act from such a consideration when one knows and loves God as one ought: for then, abandoning oneself completely to his will, one rids oneself of one's particular interest and has no other passion save to do what one believes to be agreeable to him; in consequence of which one has satisfaction of mind and contentments incomparably more valuable than all the small fleeting joys that depend upon the senses.
> (Descartes 1978, 152; to Elisabeth, 15 September 1645, AT IV 294)

Love may be what most commonly affords reason and motivation for other-regarding actions and attitudes, and it is thus apt for Descartes to propose love for God as providing reason and motivation for identifying with the divine point of view.

To secure this role, love of God must be a very powerful sort, since it must be suited for causing a person to resign her personal concerns to the extent that Descartes envisions. Developing a love of this strength would seem unlikely if one were aware that God had no special regard for one's personal good, and all the more so if one had no hope of this attitude ever changing. There are people who on occasion develop a self-sacrificing love for someone who, although he could, has no regard for the lover's personal good. Sometimes such love arises even toward someone who shows no sign of developing such a concern. But we would not want to model love for God on such pathological cases. In non-pathological situations, a love so powerful requires that one believe that the person one loves, supposing she is able, has a genuine concern for one's personal good.

Surprisingly, Descartes does not here advocate the Pauline Christian conception by which God's concern is directed toward the good of each individual who loves God; "for in all things God works for the good of those that love him" (Romans 8:28), and even towards the good of each individual "as in Adam all die, so in Christ all will be made alive" (I Corinthians 15:22). Rather, just as in Marcus Aurelius's understanding, in the picture Descartes advances in his letters to Elisabeth and Chanut, the divine conception of the

THEOLOGICAL DETERMINISM AND THE PROBLEM OF EVIL    157

good need make little concession to the good as conceived from any individual's personal perspective. We might draw the following contrast. By the Pauline idea, one's personal good is also a concern of God's, and thus, although one might have to renounce mistaken conceptions of one's personal good in order to assume the divine point of view, one need not disengage from any personal conception of one's good whatsoever. By contrast, according to the Stoic and Cartesian picture, one must more thoroughly abandon one's ordinary personal conception of the good, and adopt instead the divine vision of the good, which may not have such a personal conception as a component. The persistent problem for the Stoic and Cartesian view is that we lack a satisfying model by which human beings, given their psychological character, will have reason and motivation to attain the sort of identification it advocates.

## Theological Determinism and the Problem of Evil

Evils that appear not to be justified by any good to which they contribute yield a challenge to the credence required for substantial hope that a providential God exists.[3] Rather than advocating a positive theodicy, an account that aims for a complete and satisfying explanation of how it is that God's existence is compatible with such evils, I prefer to focus on *skeptical theism*, a strategy proposed in recent decades by Stephen Wykstra (1984, 1996) and William Alston (1991), among others.[4] The skeptical theist contends that because of the limits of our cognitive capacities, the nature of the good might well be beyond our understanding to such a degree that we should not rationally expect to understand how God's governance of the universe accords with divine perfect goodness. An advantageous way of casting the issue is in terms of the extent to which the world's evils reduce the probability of God's existence, and thus our rational credence that God exists. Let E be a proposition that specifies the types and amounts of evil that the world actually features, and G be the hypothesis that God exists. What is the probability of G given E? According to the skeptical theist, given the limits of our cognitive capacities to understand the good, for us E does not reduce the probability of G, at least not so much as to make G less likely than not-G

---

[3] This section is based on Pereboom (2016).
[4] These skeptical theist accounts were occasioned by Rowe (1979). The term 'skeptical theism' can seem a bit puzzling, given the view it represents, but it's become standard.

158    RELIGION AND HOPE

(Pereboom 2004, 2016). On an importantly distinct strategy, advocated by Peter van Inwagen, due to the limitations of our cognitive capacities and of our actual knowledge and understanding, we are not even in a position to assess the probability of G on E. Van Inwagen's version is continuous with his more general skepticism about probability assessments—in particular about our ability to assess probabilities is scant in domains substantially removed from the concerns of ordinary life (van Inwagen 2006).

Different statements of skeptical theism agree that we might well possess only limited cognitive capacities for understanding the nature of the good. These statements sometimes diverge in their formulation of the upshot this limitation has for rational credence concerning the existence of the requisite God-justifying purposes. In one version, because it's open that our ability to understand the nature of the good is limited, *we are in no position to deny* (or, equivalently, *we are in no position to rule out*) that there exist sufficient moral reasons for God's allowing the world's evils to occur, even if we have no sense for what these reasons might be, and as a result we lack good reason to believe that not-G is more likely on E than G is. But this statement of the position is vulnerable, since, by analogy, a skeptic about a well-confirmed scientific theory would then have an easy argument against her quarry. Is the claim that classical electromagnetic theory (CET) is approximately true well supported by the evidence (EV) that physicists currently have for it? One might contend: because our cognitive capacities for understanding physics are limited, we are in no position to deny that there is a currently unspecified theory distinct from CET that is more plausible and that explains EV as well, and as a result we have no reason to believe that CET is more likely on EV than not. Skepticism about historical claims can also easily be generated in this way. Our cognitive capacity to ascertain historical truths is limited, but often we reasonably judge some historical claim to be more likely than not on the evidence, while we also are in no position actually to deny or rule out the existence of some as yet unspecified alternative hypothesis. The general problem is that rationally assigning a high probability to P is compatible with not being a position to deny the existence of some unspecified alternative hypothesis. Accordingly, being in no position to deny that there is some unspecified God-justifying good for some evil's occurrence is compatible with rationally assigning a high probability to there being no such good. This, in turn, threatens the rationality of a substantial hope that a providential God exists.

A reasonable solution is to supplement skeptical theism with more thoroughly developed skeptical hypotheses—more specific and filled-out

THEOLOGICAL DETERMINISM AND THE PROBLEM OF EVIL    159

suggestions that support the truth of the skeptical claim (Pereboom 2004, 2016). Such hypotheses should focus on especially horrendous evils—Marilyn Adams (1999) persuasively argues that such evils should be the focal point of this discussion, since they are most difficult to account for and yield the strongest challenge to theism. Two leading possibilities for such partially specified skeptical hypotheses are one that cites the value of free will and one that invokes the good of a process of development. Richard Swinburne's version of the free will theodicy yields an impressive example of the former, and for the latter I'll turn to John Hick (1978), Eleonore Stump (1985), and Adams (1999). I will argue that partially specified hypotheses that invoke free will are ineffective in the case of horrendous evils, while hypotheses that cite the good of a developmental process are more promising for securing the rationality of substantial hope that a providential God exists.

The free will theodicy in systematized form dates back at least to Augustine (354–430) and remains the most popular of all theodicies. On the most common contemporary version of the free will theodicy, God had the option of creating or refraining from creating what Alvin Plantinga calls *significantly free beings*.[5] By his characterization, a being is *free* with respect to a decision to perform an action, if, holding fixed the entire history of the universe up to the time of the decision, it is causally possible both that she make or else refrain from making this decision. Plantinga has in mind free will as characterized by the libertarian, according to which if a being is causally determined to make a choice, then by definition she is not free with respect to that decision. Further, an action is *morally significant* for a person at a time if it would be wrong for her to perform the action then, and right to refrain, or vice versa. A person is *significantly free* at a time if she is then free with respect to an action that is morally significant for her. Again, a risk incurred by creating such beings is that they might freely choose evil while God cannot prevent that choice. Benefits include creatures having moral responsibility for action and being creators in their own right. But since the benefits outweigh the risks, God is morally justified in creating significantly free beings, and not to blame when they choose immorally.

In accord with skeptical theism, we'll now evaluate this free will account not as a theodicy but as a partially filled-out skeptical hypothesis. One problem is that many of the more serious evils would not seem to be freely willed

---

[5] Plantinga (1974, 65–7); note that Plantinga does not advocate a free will theodicy, but rather a less ambitious free will defense, which is more akin to a partially filled-out skeptical hypothesis.

160    RELIGION AND HOPE

decisions or to result from them. When people are harmed by earthquakes, volcanic eruptions, and diseases, their suffering is not plausibly a consequence of evil free choices, and thus would not seem to be addressed by the free will hypothesis. Evils of this kind are natural by contrast with moral evils. Sometimes evil decisions result from mental illnesses and are unfree as a result, and the free will theodicy does not address these either. The free will theodicy can therefore only be partial, and it would need to be supplemented by other considerations—and most advocates of this theodicy agree.

A further concern, raised by David Lewis (1993), is that even if we have free will of the libertarian sort, and many of our choices are freely willed in the libertarian sense, God could still have acted so as to prevent the consequences of those decisions.[6] As consequences of a decision we can count the bodily movements that result from it, and the changes in the world that in turn result from these bodily movements. After the Nazis freely decided to perpetrate genocide, God might have caused the means they used, for example the rifles or the gas chambers, to fail. Or more radically, one might argue that the value of the continued existence of beings with free will, given how they have freely decided, can sometimes be outweighed, and that God might justifiably arrange for people to die or be incapacitated before they can act on their evil decisions. God might thus have prevented Nazi genocide by having their officials die of illnesses before being able to act on their decisions, or by arranging circumstances differently so that prior to acting on these decisions would-be assassins had succeeded rather than failed.

It does seem that if a free will account is to answer this type of objection, it must be not only that the capacity for freely willed decision is significantly valuable, but also that the freely willed decisions themselves are significantly valuable, whether they be morally right or wrong. In addition, not only freely willed decisions themselves, but also their being carried out in action must have significant value. Swinburne sets out a version of the free will account that meets these specifications. He contends that it is not just freely willed decision *tout court* that has relevantly high intrinsic value, but two characteristics in addition: agents' freely willed decisions accomplishing what they intend, which Swinburne denominates *efficacious* free will, and freely willed decisions adjudicating between good and evil options, each of which motivate the agent; *serious* free will, in his vocabulary. Swinburne argues that it is efficacious and serious free will that often has intrinsic value

---

[6] Similarly, J. L. Mackie remarks: "Why should [God] not leave men free to will rightly, but intervene when he sees them beginning to will wrongly." (Mackie 1955, 34)

# THEOLOGICAL DETERMINISM AND THE PROBLEM OF EVIL    161

high enough to justify God in not preventing the evil consequences of immoral decisions. In his view, first of all, "the very fact of the agent having a free choice is a great good for the agent; and a greater good the more serious the kind of free will, even if it is incorrectly used" (Swinburne 1999, 87). In addition, an agent "is an ultimate source in an even fuller way if the choices open to him cover the whole moral range, from the very good to the very wrong" (Swinburne 1999, 85), Moreover, "an agent who has serious, efficacious free will is in a much fuller way an ultimate source of the direction of things in the world than one who does not."

Furthermore, in his development of this account, Swinburne proposes that:

> It is a good for us if our experiences are not wasted but are used for the good of others, if they are the means of a benefit which would not have come to others without them, which will at least in part compensate for those experiences. It follows from this insight that it is a blessing for a person if the possibility of his suffering makes possible the good for others of having the free choice of hurting or harming them…and of choosing to show or not show sympathy.   (Swinburne 1999, 103)

He illustrates this proposal with the example of the slave trade from Africa in the eighteenth century:

> But God allowing this to occur made possible innumerable opportunities for very large numbers of people to contribute or not to contribute to the development of this culture; for slavers to choose to enslave or not; for plantation-owners to choose to buy slaves or not and to treat them well or ill; for ordinary white people and politicians to campaign for its abolition or not to bother, and to campaign for compensation for the victims or not to bother; and so on.   (Swinburne 1999, 245)

A pressing concern for this line of thought is that it conflicts with core features of our moral practice when horrendous evil is at issue (Pereboom 2004, 2016). First, as Lewis (1993) points out, for us the wrongdoer's freedom is a weightless consideration, not merely an outweighed consideration. That is, when one is deliberating about whether to prevent or allow evil, a wrongdoer's free will has no value that we take into consideration. For example, if the inhabitants of a town decide to resist a group of soldiers threatening them with annihilation, we would not expect the townspeople to take

162   RELIGION AND HOPE

into account the (purported) value of their attackers' freely willed actions successfully executed. But this value would have to be immense if this kind of consideration were sufficient to justify God in permitting rather than preventing the slave trade, allowing horrendous suffering on the part of a Black population in order to realize a purported benefit largely for slave traders, slave owners, and their beneficiaries. More abstractly, if Swinburne were right, then when 100 soldiers are freely deciding to perpetrate mass murder, twice as much value is at stake as when there are just fifty. Moreover, there would be significantly less reason to harm in self-defense an attacker who has free will than someone who is not capable of free choice due to mental illness.[7]

Another problem for the free will theodicy is occasioned by Swinburne's view that to choose freely to do what is right in a serious and valuable way one must have an appreciably strong countervailing desire to do what is wrong, strong enough that it might actually motivate a free choice (Swinburne 1999, 86–9). He thinks that this point supports the free will theodicy, since it can explain why God allows us to have desires to do evil, and, by extension, to make choices in accord with those desires. But this point rather serves to undermine the force of the free will theodicy as an explanation for many evils. We have no tendency to believe that the value of a free choice outweighs the disvalue of having desires to perform horrendously evil actions that are strong enough to result in choice. For example, the proposal that it is appreciably valuable for people to have a serious desire to kill young children for the reason that this provides them with the opportunity to choose freely to refrain from doing so has no purchase on us. Our recommendation for people with desires of this sort is to have them undergo therapy to eliminate such desires. We have no tendency to believe that the value of making a free decision not to kill made in the struggle against a desire to do so carries any weight against the proposal to provide this sort of therapy (Wolf 1990).[8] Furthermore, were we to come across someone with a strong desire to reinstate slavery but who nevertheless resisted actively seeking to do so, we would not think that his condition has more value overall than one in which he never had the desire to reinstate slavery in the first place. Moreover, I would guess that a significant proportion of people alive

---

[7] Thanks to Mark Moyer for this point.

[8] Susan Wolf (1990) argues that there isn't value in being able to choose badly. What is valuable is being able to choose rationally and for the good. Thus, given that free will is valuable, it must not be an ability to choose both well and badly.

THEOLOGICAL DETERMINISM AND THE PROBLEM OF EVIL 163

today—well over 90 percent—has neither intentionally chosen a horrendous evil nor had a genuine struggle with a desire to do so—they have never, for instance, tortured, maimed, or murdered, nor seriously struggled with desires to do so. But we do not believe that their lives would have been more valuable had they instead possessed such desires even if every struggle against them was successful. For these reasons it is implausible that God would allow people to have such desires in order to realize the value of certain free choices for the good. This aspect of Swinburne's theodicy may have some credibility in the case of evils that are not horrendous, but has none in the case of those that are. In summary, Swinburne's proposed value for efficacious and serious free will has no traction for us when it comes to horrendous evils, and thus for such evils it can't function as a plausible partially filled-out skeptical hypothesis.

Alternatively, one might turn to partially filled-out skeptical hypotheses that invoke instead the value of developmental process (Pereboom 2005, 2012, 2016). For many participants in the historical discussion, such value is at least part of the story, but in recent times John Hick (1978) has most prominently foregrounded this consideration. According to Hick's soul-building account, evil is required for the best sort of human intellectual, technological, moral, and spiritual development. Evil is valuable because it occasions freely chosen efforts whereby it might be overcome, and because improvement of character—both within an individual and throughout human history—results from such efforts. Without evil there would be no stimulus to the development of economic, technological, and social structures, which lie at the core of human civilization. Without evil there would be no occasion for care for others, devotion to the public good, courage, self-sacrifice, for the kind of love that involves bearing one another's burdens, or for the kind of character that is built through these qualities.

It's of interest given the views for which I've argued in this book that this soul-building hypothesis can be endorsed by the free will skeptic. While our wills arguably must have a role in the soul-building process he describes, free will in the sense required for moral responsibility in the basic desert sense need not. The process of educating and developing our characters, sensitivities, and abilities, even conceived without such freedom, is a great good. The development from cowardice to courage, from immorality to morality, from ignorance to enlightenment, is valuable, even if these processes are causally determined by God, or else naturally determined, in such a way as to exclude free will. Hick argues that such processes are more

164    RELIGION AND HOPE

valuable if they involve libertarian free will, but that is consistent with the claim that they have value even if causally determined.

The main difficulty for this proposal, which Hick is concerned to address, is that evils often do not yield the specified goods, and in fact sometimes destroy lives rather than contribute to salutary development. His response is that such evils are only apparently without purpose. In a world without such evils,

> human misery would not evoke deep personal sympathy or call forth organized relief and sacrificial help and service. For it is presupposed in these compassionate reactions both that the suffering is not deserved and that it is bad for the sufferer...in a world that is to be the scene of compassionate love and self-giving for others, suffering must fall upon mankind with something of the haphazardness and inequity that we now experience. It must be apparently unmerited, pointless, and incapable of being morally rationalized.    (Hick 1978, 334)

To this one might object that evils on the order of World War II or the fourteenth-century plague are not required to occasion virtuous responses of these kinds or the attendant personal development. But still, it might be argued that these and similar horrors did provide unusually challenging opportunities for virtuous responses, and that they did in fact result in especially valuable instances of such responses. Yet one might doubt whether refraining from preventing these calamities could be justified by the expected benefit. Thus it seems that here too, nothing in our experience or in our ordinary values allows for the horrendous evil-balancing weight that would have to be attributed to personal or societal development, and that we don't yet have an effective partially filled-out skeptical hypothesis.

Eleonore Stump (1985) argues that suffering from moral and natural evil contributes to a humbling recognition of oneself as having a defective will, which in turn can motivate one to turn to God to fix the defect in the will. The defect in the will is that one has a bent toward evil, so that one has a diminished capacity to will what one ought to will. This account can perhaps be recruited as a partially filled-out skeptical hypothesis. In this case as well, no feature of this account demands libertarian free will, nor even a notion of free will of the sort required for moral responsibility. Note that this process, as Stump describes it, does not require an indeterministic conception of free will, nor does it require that the agent be morally responsible in the basic desert sense for turning to God on the occasion of suffering. It

THEOLOGICAL DETERMINISM AND THE PROBLEM OF EVIL 165

is sufficient that this change is highly valuable, and that it results in a more intimate relationship with God.

This is a promising proposal, and the skeptical theist who is also a free will skeptic can agree. But do we have the beginning of an explanation for the horrendous evils? This is a task that Marilyn Adams takes on. Her strategy is to specify a possible scenario in which God is good to all persons by ensuring each a life that is a great good to the person on the whole, not merely by balancing off but also by *defeating* her participation in horrendous evils within the context of the world as a whole and of that individual's life (Adams 1999). On Roderick Chisholm's characterization, an evil is balanced off within a larger whole just in case that whole features goods that equal or outweigh it; while an evil is defeated within a larger whole just in case it actually contributes to a greater good within that whole (Chisholm 1968). In Adams's account, balancing off horrendous evil might be guaranteed by an afterlife in an environment in which we live in beatific intimacy with God. But defeat of such evil is also possible, for it may be that God will defeat all human suffering by empathetically identifying with it, since this would allow human beings to re-envision their suffering as a point of identification with God; "by virtue of endowing horrors with a good aspect, Divine identification makes the victim's experience of horrors so meaningful that she would not retrospectively wish it away" (Adams 1999, 167). Since this account invokes the suffering of God, Adams thinks of it as specific to Christianity.

Adams denies, however, that participation in horrors is necessary for an individual's incommensurate good, for "a horror-free life that ended in beatific intimacy with God would also be one in which the individual enjoyed incommensurate good" (Adams 1999, 167). One might accordingly question why God would allow anyone at all to suffer horrendous evil. Adams claims to be able to provide only partial reasons in response to this question (Adams 1999, 165–6). But skeptical theism requires no more than partial reasons, for it demands only partially filled-out skeptical hypotheses. This account of the defeat of evil also does not involve our having free will in the sense required for moral responsibility in the basic desert sense, and thus can be endorsed by the free will skeptic.

The problem with the suggestion that the value of efficacious and serious free will balances off horrendous evil was that nothing in our experience or ordinary values allows for it, so it can't effectively serve as a partially filled-out skeptical theist hypothesis. We need to keep in mind, however, that the standard does not require thorough but only partial understanding of the

166   RELIGION AND HOPE

proposal. The elements of Adams's account are inspired by the widespread sacrificial aspects of human religion, and this provides some reason to think that the criticism raised for Swinburne's suggestion doesn't apply in this case. There are common features in human experience that lend support to the proposal, although we don't understand them thoroughly. Sacrifice of animals and humans is foreign to us in a way that it wasn't to our ancestors, and this makes understanding the view difficult. The element of the value of identification in suffering is more familiar. For these reasons, Adams's account yields a more effective partially filled-out hypothesis.

Do these reflections secure the credence required to support the rationality of a substantial hope that a providential God exists? The precise level of credence that would be rational may well vary across subjects. If someone has had particularly vivid religious experiences, a higher credence may be rational for her than it would be, all else equal, for someone who hasn't. Note again that evidential standards for hope, even substantial hope, are lower than they are for belief or acceptance, or even for faith. Elizabeth Jackson (2021) provides a particularly lucid account of this landscape. Her interest is in hope that is substantial in the sense I've set out. In her view such hope crucially features what she calls acceptance, that is, a commitment to act as if some proposition is true, and a desire that the proposition be true. Hope contrasts with belief, i.e., regarding a proposition as true, which need not involve a desire that the proposition be true, and faith, which entails a stronger credence than hope but not as strong as belief, but also a desire that the proposition be true:

[A]gents can be justified in accepting [proposition] p even if they get significant counterevidence that drastically lowers the probability of p, as long as it doesn't lower the probability of p to 0. They do so by relying on their belief that p, then their faith that p, and then their hope that p. For example, suppose someone is a committed religious believer and both believes and accepts that God exists. Then, they gain counterevidence, e.g. they experience serious evil in the world and see that this counts against the existence of an all-powerful, all-good God. Their credence that God exists might decrease and this evidence might even require that they give up their belief that God exists, but they can nonetheless have faith that God exists and continue to accept that God exists. Suppose they gain even more counterevidence, such that their credence is, say, 0.2. Nonetheless, they still maintain that there is a chance that God exists and that God's existing would be a very good thing. Even though they think that God

# TRANSCENDENT HOPE FOR HUMANITY    167

probably does not exist, they also believe that if they were wrong and God did exist, knowing God would be a very valuable thing. Thus, they continue to accept that God exists and act as if God exists...This can be rational for them, despite the fact their credence is quite low, due to the fact that they think God's existing would be valuable and there would be a huge benefit to doing those things if God turns out to exist.

(Jackson 2021, sect. 4.1; cf. Mann 1993; Martin 2013)

I don't want to argue for a verdict on the rationality of theistic belief or faith. Instead, my focus is on the rationality of substantial hope.

## Transcendent Hope for Humanity

Let us now turn to a hope that is not specifically theistic. One of the earliest figures in modern Western philosophy to reject divine providence is Spinoza. As we saw in Chapter 1, Spinoza is a determinist and a free will skeptic, who maintains that everything that happens is necessitated by the divine essence. The crucial commitment of Stoic and Cartesian theology Spinoza rejects is that God acts for the sake of ends or purposes (1677/1985, *Ethics* I Appendix, 439–46). He contends that if God did act for the sake of ends, this would imply divine imperfection, for God would then aim at remedying something that is lacking (1677/1985, *Ethics* I Appendix, 442–3). Because divine providence involves God's acting for the sake of ends—the well-being of the universe and the benefit of human beings—in Spinoza's conception there is no divine providence. We cannot be motivated to identify with God's point of view by reflecting on divine providence, because there is no such thing.

In the place of the comfort of divine providence, Spinoza proposes an intellectual form of consolation in the face of evil (1677/1985, *Ethics* V, 594–617). In his conception, God or Nature (*Deus sive Natura*) is the only substance, and we are modes of God. But although God is eternal, our existence appears to be thoroughly temporally qualified. Our temporality renders us vulnerable to causes that are contrary to our nature, and as a result we can be affected by debilitating passions. We can also die. Nevertheless, there is a respect in which we are eternal as God is, and in this respect we are exempt from the harmful passions and from death. Spinoza reasons as follows. Everything that happens follows from the divine essence by necessity. Since by reason we can come to know how all follows from the divine

168   RELIGION AND HOPE

essence, reason allows us to identify with the divine point of view. The joy, and the resulting intellectual love of God (*amor intellectus Dei*) occasioned by this employment of reason reinforces our identification with the divine perspective. To the extent that we so align ourselves with God, we are actually, non-metaphorically, identical with aspects of his essence:

> The mind's intellectual love of God is the very love of God by which God loves himself, not insofar as he is infinite, but insofar as he can be explained by the human mind's essence, considered under a species of eternity (*sub specie aeternitatis*); i.e. the mind's intellectual love of God is part of the infinite love by which God loves himself.
>
> (1677/1985, Ethics V, Proposition 36, 612)

To the extent that we are fused with the divine essence, we are eternal, and because it makes no sense for something to be contrary to the nature of an eternal entity (1677/1985, *Ethics* V, Propositions 37 and 38, 613–14), to the degree we are eternal we are immune from the harmful passions and from death (Pereboom 1994).

Spinoza's intellectualist religious vision met with considerable resistance in the century after it became known, at least in part due to the absence of providence (a story Jonathan Israel tells admirably in his book *Radical Enlightenment*). An alternative, pursued especially from the mid-eighteenth century onward, retains Spinoza's pantheist determinism, but shifts the focus of the good of the universe to humanity. In the late eighteenth and early nineteenth centuries, humanity comes to be viewed as a force for inevitable and sustained progress on multiple fronts. This theme is pursued by the German Idealists, of which Hegel is representative. One idea in Hegel is crucial in this context. He reworks Spinoza's vision by supplementing it with a deterministic process of human rational development over the course of history, recapturing the providential aspect of the deterministic scheme by conceiving this human development itself as divine. For Spinoza, God or Nature, independently of individual human subjects, contributes nothing to the goodness of the universe; the goodness of the universe, for us, derives solely from the intellectual joy and subsequent intellectual love we can experience upon understanding that the nature of the universe flows by necessity from the divine essence. For Hegel, by contrast, the divine is a historical process of realizing an ideal, and human beings and their history are a central component. This historical process is structured (in a dialectical way that Hegel calls a process of Spirit (*Geist*)) and multi-faceted; it realizes

## TRANSCENDENT HOPE FOR HUMANITY    169

potential in the sciences, the arts and letters, social and political development, and, of all of which we become conscious through philosophical reflection.[9] In Hegel's view, philosophical reflection on human history reveals it as a theodicy, showing how history is providential despite apparent evil. At the close of his *Philosophy of History* Hegel writes:

> our mode of treating the subject is, in this aspect, a theodicy—a justification of the ways of God—which Leibniz attempted metaphysically in his method, i.e., in indefinite abstract categories—so that the ill that is found in the world may be comprehended, and the thinking Spirit reconciled with the fact of the existence of evil. Indeed, nowhere is such a harmonizing view more pressingly demanded than in universal history.
>
> (Hegel 1824/1956, 48)

Hegel's notion of the progress of human history as a theodicy met with serious resistance in the twentieth century. Adorno's retort, "No universal history leads from savagery to humanitarianism, but there is one leading from the slingshot to the megaton bomb" (Adorno 1970, 312), is characteristic. But the theme that continues to attract is Hegel's notion of religion as focused on human progress in actual history. This idea was taken up in the nineteenth century by American transcendentalists such as Ralph Waldo Emerson and Henry Thoreau, and later by pragmatists, notably John Dewey in the first part of the twentieth century. Dewey advocated a "common faith," a religious attitude broader than traditional theism. Its core feature is a "sense of nature as the whole of which we are parts, while it also recognizes that we are parts that are marked by intelligence and purpose, having the capacity to strive by their aid to bring conditions into greater consonance with what is humanly desirable" (Dewey 1934, 25). Dewey echoes a theme of the transcendentalists by focusing not exclusively on the community of rational beings of which we are members, but on such a community embedded in nature, "the enveloping world that the imagination feels is a universe" (Dewey 1934, 53).

To claim actual knowledge of continued human survival and progress in a thriving natural environment is ambitious. The rationality of substantial hope in this outcome, however, can be defended. The objective in the present context is to secure the rationality of this hope in a scheme in which we

---

[9] See Charles Taylor's *Hegel* (1976) for a classic account.

170  RELIGION AND HOPE

do not exercise ultimate control. If causal determinism is true, then the entire history and future of humanity is rendered inevitable by virtue of causal factors beyond our control, by states of the universe that precede humanity's existence, together with the laws of nature. As we saw in Chapter 1, there is nevertheless a sense in which how humans deliberate and choose makes a difference to the future—if we had deliberated differently, the future would have been different. Still, factors beyond our control render inevitable how we deliberate, the choices that result, and the effects these choices have. Even if there is quantum indeterminacy, that is, metaphysical indeterminacy in how the wave function collapses, it's at least a stretch to believe that our free choices determine those outcomes.

Hope is the right attitude to invoke for humanity's survival and progress in a thriving natural environment, despite human wrongdoing and irrationality. This is partly because we're not assured of this outcome, while it is an open possibility. Hope is apt in contexts in which we are dependent on how factors beyond our control turn out, which is so whether determinism is true or if there is quantum indeterminacy. As Katie Stockdale points out, hope reminds us of "the kinds of creatures we are: we are creatures who, because of the constraints we necessarily and contingently face as agents, must depend on factors external to ourselves for many of our desires to be fulfilled." (Stockdale 2019, 30)

Some of our hopes are personal. When we protest against the wrongdoing of a loved one, we may appropriately place our hope in the possibility that he might have an appropriate change of heart and undergo moral reform. More generally, the very fact that we can employ compassionate moral protest to powerful effect provides us with a reason to be hopeful in our common humanity. The hope for humanity is not personal, but impartial. One may ask whether such impartial hope is easy or difficult for us to attain. Martha Nussbaum (2001) asks a similar question for compassion; we are more likely to feel compassion for friends and relatives with whom we are on good terms than for people in other parts of the world we've never visited and who we don't know at all. The same problem has been raised for related notions such as empathy and sympathy (very recently by Paul Bloom in his *Against Empathy*). David Hume, in his *Treatise of Human Nature* (1739/1978), expresses this concern as an objection to his claim that moral judgment is founded in sympathy: "But as this sympathy is very variable, it may be thought that our sentiments of morals must admit of all the same variations. We sympathize more with persons contiguous to us, than with persons remote from us: With our acquaintance, than with strangers: With our countrymen, than with foreigners." However, he also notes that "notwithstanding this variation of our sympathy, we give the same approbation to the same moral qualities in China as in England. They appear equally virtuous, and recommend themselves equally to the esteem of a judicious spectator." Hume then provides a famous solution: "In order, therefore, to prevent those continual contradictions, and arrive at a more stable judgment of things, we fix on some steady and general points of view; and always, in our thoughts, place ourselves in them, whatever may be our present situation" (Hume 1739/1978, Book III, Part III, Section I). Elevating oneself to a point of view that transcends differences among persons affords an elegant way forward. Some authors, such as Kant (1785/1991, 1788/1996) and Rawls (1971), identify such transcendence with a kind of rationality or reasonability.

Recall that Nussbaum maintains that "emotions are evaluative appraisals that ascribe high importance to things and people that lie outside the agent's own sphere of control" (Nussbaum 2004, 443; see also 2001). On her account, these appraisals are eudaimonistic, that is, made from the perspective of its subject's aims. On the conception of compassion that Buddhists, for example, invoke, those aims are conceived as impartially fair. Accordingly, John Deigh (2004, 468) proposes the following for compassion's cognitive content: "the thought that it was a bad thing for x to have undeservedly suffered serious misfortune," conceived as "conditioned on one's interest in fairness and in preserving the moral order one's sense of fairness implies." I'm subtracting the "undeservedly," and I propose that to be compassionate in the impartially fair sense involves the appraisal that an agent has been harmed or disadvantaged in some way, together with the eudaimonistic perceptual take of a caring and impartial concern for well-being that addresses that harm or disadvantage. Ordinary compassion is often partial; to become impartial, compassion must transcend that ordinary partiality. It's thus fitting to call the result *transcendent* compassion. Alongside transcendent compassion, we can advocate transcendent love, which is broader than transcendent compassion in that it aims not just at relief of misfortune, but at well-being more generally. We can also endorse transcendent hope, which projects successes of transcendent compassion and transcendent love into the future.

Can we secure the rational credence required for a substantial transcendent hope for human survival and progress in a thriving natural

## 172 RELIGION AND HOPE

environment? The practical stakes for this hope are in one respect less ambitious than they are for orthodox versions of monotheism, since they aspire to individual lives, and not only the larger scheme, being providentially governed. A problem of evil does exist for this hope, since there are counterindications to the realization of the hoped-for outcome. But such transcendent hope is, on balance, less rationally demanding than hope in personal survival after death. Theists and atheists alike can endorse the transcendent hope for human survival and progress in a thriving environment. Theists may be inclined to believe that without divine assistance, it cannot be realized, and also that it is by itself insufficient due to the absence of hope for personal survival. But these concerns do not preclude theists and atheists from having this transcendent hope in common.

Theodore Parker, American transcendentalist, expresses the idea of continued human progress in its moral dimension in his reflections on the abolition of slavery, using a now-familiar metaphor:

> We cannot understand the moral Universe. The arc is a long one, and our eyes reach but a little way; we cannot calculate the curve and complete the figure by the experience of sight; but we can divine it by conscience, and we surely know that it bends toward justice. Justice will not fail, though wickedness appears strong, and has on its side the armies and thrones of power, the riches and the glory of the world, and though poor men crouch down in despair. Justice will not fail and perish out from the world of men, nor will what is really wrong and contrary to God's real law of justice continually endure.   (Parker 1853, 84–5)

In his speeches, Martin Luther King also exhorted us to envision, quoting Parker, that "the arc of the moral universe is long, but it bends toward justice." Here Parker claims knowledge, but transcendent hope is less demanding and more accessible, even if it is substantial and accordingly has a significant effect on how we act.

What evidence do we have to support Parker's optimism? In the last century humanity faced extremely serious challenges: two worldwide wars, mass genocide, terrorism, diseases, and epidemics. But we repeatedly confronted these challenges with impressive success. Many of the most oppressive regimes that that century had witnessed have vanished, medical science made tremendous progress, technology advanced spectacularly, and knowledge in many fields saw immense expansion. On balance, threats were effectively confronted, and advance was achieved. Let me emphasize

TRANSCENDENT HOPE FOR HUMANITY 173

again that my concern is not with knowledge, belief, or even faith, but solely with hope, albeit of the substantial sort.[10]

Consider the threat that the Covid-19 pandemic poses (as I write). While the human response has involved much wrongful and irrational behavior, medical workers worldwide worked tirelessly to impede the spread of the disease, and researchers developed vaccines in record time. Or consider the threat of climate change to our natural environment and to the flourishing of humanity, with the prospect of melting polar ice inundating land, and the planet becoming too hot to sustain the life of many of its current inhabitants, a threat which resulted at least in part from failure of stewardship. Hope can be grounded in the growth of climate activism, large-scale reaffirmation of international agreements, the advancement of renewable energy, increase in reforestation and climate-friendly methods in agriculture, and the distinct possibility of feasible direct carbon capture within a decade. Human intelligence, skill, and moral resolve in these cases provide evidence to ground the rationality of the hope that we will be successful in meeting such challenges more generally.[11]

So what may we hope? We may hope that human intelligence, skill, and moral resolve is sufficient for overcoming the challenges we will face. The feature of this conception that provides inspiration and comfort is that we, embedded in our natural world, form a system whose future is survival and progress, and whose arc tends toward justice. Human experience, despite the irrationality and injustice that we see, secures the rationality of this transcendent hope, in the adoption of which we can all unite.

---

[10] The case Steven Pinker (2018) makes for overall human progress has endured criticism on the basis of his neglect of reasons for pessimism. However, the evidence he cites might be claimed to successfully justify hope rather than belief or high credence.

[11] www.sierraclub.org/sierra/10-reasons-feel-hopeful-about-climate-change-2019.

# Bibliography

Adams, Marilyn McCord. (1999). *Horrendous Evils and the Goodness of God*, Ithaca, NY: Cornell University Press.

Adams, Robert M. (1980). "Pure Love," *The Journal of Religious Ethics* 8 (1), pp. 83–99.

Adorno, Theodor W. (1970). *Negative Dialektik*, Frankfurt am Main: Suhrkamp.

Alexander, Lawrence, and Kimberly Kessler Ferzan. (2009). *Crime and Culpability*, Cambridge: Cambridge University Press.

Alexander, Lawrence, and Michael Moore. (2016). "Deontological Ethics," *Stanford Encyclopedia of Philosophy*, Winter Edition, Edward N. Zalta, ed., https://plato.stanford.edu/entries/ethics-deontological/.

Alicke, Mark D. (2000). "Culpable Control and the Psychology of Blame," *Psychology Bulletin* 126, pp. 556–74.

Alicke, Mark. D., Teresa. L. Davis, and Mark. V. Pezzo. (1994). "A Posteriori Adjustment of A Priori Decision Criteria," *Social Cognition* 8, pp. 286–305.

Alicke, Mark D., David Rose, and Dori Bloom. (2012). "Causation, Norm Violation and Culpable Control," *Journal of Philosophy* 106, pp. 587–612.

Allais, Lucy. (2008). "Wiping the Slate Clean: The Heart of Forgiveness," *Philosophy and Public Affairs* 36 (1), pp. 33–68.

Alston, William. (1991). "The Inductive Argument from Evil and the Human Cognitive Condition," *Philosophical Perspectives* 5, pp. 29–67.

Amaya, Santiago. (2019). "Forgiveness as Emotional Distancing," *Social Philosophy and Policy* 36 (1), pp. 6–26.

Anscombe, G. E. M. (1956/1981). "Mr. Truman's Degree," in *Ethics, Religion, and Politics, The Collected Philosophical Papers of G. E. M. Anscombe*, vol. 3. Minneapolis, MN: University of Minnesota Press, pp. 51–71.

Arneson, Richard. (2018). "Self-Defense and Culpability: Fault Forfeits First," *San Diego Law Review* 55, pp. 231–63.

Arpaly, Nomy. (2006). *Meaning, Merit, and Human Bondage*, Princeton, NJ: Princeton University Press.

Augustine (400/2008). *Saint Augustine: Confessions*, tr. Henry J. Chadwick, Oxford: Oxford University Press, 2008.

Ayer, Alfred J. (1954). "Freedom and Necessity," in *Philosophical Essays*, London: Macmillan, pp. 271–84.

Badhwar, Neera. (1987). "Friends as Ends in Themselves," *Philosophy and Phenomenological Research* 48, pp. 1–23.

Baker, Lynne R. (2006). "Moral Responsibility without Libertarianism," *Noûs* 40, pp. 307–30.

Balaguer, Mark. (2010). *Free Will as an Open Scientific Problem*, Cambridge, MA: MIT Press.

## 176 BIBLIOGRAPHY

Balaguer, Mark. (2014). "Replies to McKenna, Pereboom, and Kane," *Philosophical Studies* 169 (1), pp. 71–92.

Bell, Macalester. (2009). "Anger, Virtue, and Oppression," *Feminist Ethics and Social and Political Philosophy*, Lisa Tessman, ed., Dordrecht: Springer, pp. 165–83.

Bentham, Jeremy. (1823/1948). *An Introduction to the Principles of Morals and Legislation*, New York: Macmillan.

Bergson, Henri. (1889/1910). *Essai sur les données immédiates de la conscience*, Paris: F. Alcan; *Time and Free Will*, tr. F. L. Pogson, London: Allen and Unwin, 1910.

Berman, Mitchell. (2008). "Punishment and Justification," *Ethics* 18, pp. 258–90.

Björnsson, Gunnar, and Derk Pereboom. (2014). "Free Will Skepticism and Bypassing," in *Moral Psychology*, vol. 4, W. Sinnott-Armstrong, ed., Cambridge, MA: MIT Press, pp. 27–35.

Björnsson, Gunnar, and Derk Pereboom. (2016). "Traditional and Experimental Approaches to Free Will," in *The Blackwell Companion to Experimental Philosophy*, Wesley Buckwalter and Justin Sytsma, eds., Oxford: Blackwell Publishers, pp. 142–57.

Björnsson, Gunnar, and Karl Persson. (2012). "The Explanatory Component of Moral Responsibility," *Noûs* 46, pp. 326–54.

Blair, R. J. R. (1995). "A Cognitive Developmental Approach to Morality: Investigating the Psychopath," *Cognition* 57, pp. 1–29.

Bloom, Paul. (2016). *Against Empathy: The Case for Rational Compassion*, New York: Harper Collins.

Blumer, Herbert. (1958). "Race Prejudice as a Sense of Group Position," *Pacific Sociological Review* 1 (1), pp. 3–7.

Bobo, Lawrence D. (1999). "Prejudice as Group Position: Microfoundations of a Sociological Approach to Racism and Race Relations," *Journal of Social Issues* 55 (3), pp. 445–72.

Bobzien, Suzanne. (1998). *Determinism and Freedom in Stoic Philosophy*, Oxford: Oxford University Press.

Bok, Hilary. (1998). *Freedom and Responsibility*, Princeton, NJ: Princeton University Press.

Boonin, Daniel. (2008). *The Problem of Punishment*, Cambridge: Cambridge University Press.

Borg, Jana Schaich, and Walter P. Sinnott-Armstrong. (2013). "Do Psychopaths Make Moral Judgments?", in *Handbook on Psychopathy and Law*, Kent A. Kiehl and Walter P. Sinnott-Armstrong, eds, New York: Oxford University Press, pp. 107–28.

Braithwaite, John, and Philip Pettit. (1990). *Not Just Deserts*, Oxford: Oxford University Press.

Brandenburg, Daphne. (2019). "Inadequate Agency and Appropriate Anger," *Ethical Theory and Moral Practice* 22, pp. 169–85.

Brennan, Tad. (2000). "Reservation in Stoic Ethics," *Archiv für Geschichte der Philosophie*, 82 (2), pp. 149–77.

Brennan, Tad. (2005). *The Stoic Life: Emotions, Duties, and Fate*, Oxford: Oxford University Press.

## BIBLIOGRAPHY 177

Briggs, Jean. L. (1970). *Never in Anger: Portrait of an Eskimo Family*, Cambridge, MA: Harvard University Press.

Brink, David. (1994). "Moral Conflict and Its Structure," *The Philosophical Review* 103, pp. 215–47.

Brink, David. (2021). *Fair Opportunity, Responsibility and Excuse*, Oxford: Oxford University Press.

Brink, David, and Dana Nelkin. (2013). "Fairness and the Architecture of Responsibility," in *Oxford Studies in Agency and Responsibility* 1, David Shoemaker, ed., Oxford: Oxford University Press, pp. 31–54.

Broad, C. D. (1952). "Determinism, Indeterminism, and Libertarianism," in *Ethics and the History of Philosophy*, London: Routledge and Kegan Paul, pp. 195–217.

Butler, Joseph. (1726). *Fifteen Sermons Preached at the Rolls Chapel*, London: J. and J. Knapton.

Butler, Joseph. (2006). *The Works of Bishop Butler*, D. White, ed., Rochester, NY: University of Rochester Press.

Campbell, Joseph. (1997). "A Compatibilist Theory of Alternative Possibilities," *Philosophical Studies* 88, pp. 319–30.

Capes, Justin. (2013). "Mitigating Soft Compatibilism," *Philosophy and Phenomenological Research* 87, pp. 640–63.

Carlsson, Andreas B. (2017). "Blameworthiness as Deserved Guilt." *Journal of Ethics* 21, pp. 89–115.

Caruso, Gregg D. (2012). *Free Will and Consciousness: A Determinist Account of the Illusion of Free Will*, Lanham, MD: Lexington Books.

Caruso, Gregg D. (2016). "Free Will Skepticism and Criminal Behavior: A Public Health Quarantine Model," *Southwest Philosophy Review* 32 (1), pp. 25–48.

Caruso, Gregg D. (2017). *Public Health and Safety: The Social Determinants of Health and Criminal Behavior*, ResearchLinks Books.

Caruso, Gregg D. (2018). "Skepticism about Moral Responsibility", *Stanford Encyclopedia of Philosophy*, Spring Edition, Edward N. Zalta, ed., https://plato.stanford.edu/entries/skepticism-moral-responsibility/.

Caruso, Gregg D. (2020a). "Buddhism, Free Will, and Punishment: Taking Buddhist Ethics Seriously," *Zygon* 55 (2), pp. 474–96.

Caruso, Gregg D. (2020b). "Justice without Retribution: An Epistemic Argument against Retributive Criminal Punishment," *Neuroethics* 13 (1), pp. 13–28.

Caruso, Gregg D. (2021). *Rejecting Retributivism: Free Will, Punishment, and Criminal Justice*, Cambridge: Cambridge University Press.

Caruso, Gregg. (forthcoming). "On the Compatibilism of Rational Deliberation and Determinism: Why Deterministic Manipulation Is Not a Counterexample," *Philosophical Quarterly*.

Caspi, Avshalom, J. McClay, T. E. Moffitt, J. Mill, J. Martin, I. W. Craig, A. Taylor, and R. Poulton. (2002). "Role of Genotype in the Cycle of Violence in Maltreated Children," *Science* 297, pp. 851–4.

Castañeda, Hector-Neri. (1975). *Thinking and Doing*, Dordrecht: D. Reidel.

Chalmers, David. (2011). "Verbal Disputes," *The Philosophical Review* 120, pp. 515–66.

## 178 BIBLIOGRAPHY

Chignell, Andrew. (2014). "Rational Hope, Possibility, and Divine Action," in *Kant's Religion within the Bounds of Mere Reason: A Critical Guide*, Gordon Michalson, ed., Cambridge: Cambridge University Press, pp. 98–117.

Chignell, Andrew. (2021). "The Focus Theory of Hope," ms.

Chisholm, Roderick. (1964). "Human Freedom and the Self," The Lindley Lecture, Department of Philosophy, University of Kansas, 1964; reprinted in *Free Will*, Gary Watson, ed., Oxford, Oxford University Press, 1982, pp. 24–35.

Chisholm, Roderick. (1968). "The Defeat of Good and Evil," *Proceedings and Addresses of the American Philosophical Association* 42, pp. 21–38.

Chisholm, Roderick. (1976). *Person and Object*, La Salle, PA: Open Court.

Chislenko, Eugene. (2019). "Blame and Protest," *Journal of Ethics* 23 (2), pp. 163–81.

Choy, Olivia, Farah Focquaert, and Adrian Raine. (2020). "Benign Biological Interventions to Reduce Offending," *Neuroethics* 13 (1), pp. 29–41.

Clarke, Randolph. (1992). "Deliberation and Beliefs about One's Abilities," *Pacific Philosophical Quarterly* 73, pp. 101–13.

Clarke, Randolph. (1993). "Toward a Credible Agent-Causal Account of Free Will," *Noûs* 27, pp. 191–203.

Clarke, Randolph. (1996). "Agent Causation and Event Causation in the Production of Free Action," *Philosophical Topics* 24, pp. 19–48.

Clarke, Randolph. (2003). *Libertarian Theories of Free Will*, New York: Oxford University Press.

Clarke, Randolph. (2009). "Dispositions, Abilities to Act, and Free Will: The New Dispositionalism," *Mind* 118, pp. 323–51.

Clarke, Randolph. (2013). "Some Theses on Desert," *Philosophical Explorations* 16, pp. 153–64.

Clarke, Randolph. (2019). "Free Will, Agent Causation, and 'Disappearing Agents'," *Noûs* 53 (1), pp. 76–96.

Coates, D. Justin. (2013). "In Defense of Love Internalism," *Journal of Ethics* 17, pp. 233–55.

Coffman, E. J., and Ted Warfield. (2005). "Deliberation and Metaphysical Freedom," *Midwest Studies in Philosophy* 29, pp. 25–44.

Cohen, Yishai. (2018). "Deliberation in the Presence of Manipulation," *Canadian Journal of Philosophy* 48, pp. 85–105.

Copp, David. (2008). "'Ought' Implies 'Can' and the Derivation of the Principle of Alternative Possibilities," *Analysis* 68, pp. 67–75.

Corrado, Michael L. (1996). "Punishment and the Wild Beast of Prey: The Problem of Preventive Detention," *Journal of Criminal Law and Criminology* 86, pp. 1–32.

Corrado, Michael L. (2016). "Two Models of Criminal Justice," SSRN. http://ssrn.com/abstract=2757078.

Corrado, Michael L. (2017). "Punishment and the Burden of Proof," UNC Legal Studies Research Paper. https://ssrn.com/abstract=2997654; http://dx.doi.org/10.2139/ssrn.2997654.

Cyr, Taylor. (2020). "Manipulation Arguments and Libertarian Accounts of Free Will," *Journal of the American Philosophical Association* 6 (1), pp. 57–73.

BIBLIOGRAPHY 179

D'Arms, Justin, and Daniel Jacobson. (2003). "The Significance of Recalcitrant Emotions (Or Anti-QuasiJudgmentalism)," in *Philosophy and the Emotions*, Anthony Hatzimoysis, ed., Cambridge: Cambridge University Press, pp. 127–45.

D'Arms, Justin, and Daniel Jacobson. (2021). *Rational Sentimentalism*, Oxford: Oxford University Press.

d'Holbach, Paul-Henri Thiry. (1770). *Système de la Nature, ou Des Loix du Monde Physique et du Monde Moral*, Amsterdam: Marc-Michel Rey.

Darwall, Stephen. (2006). *The Second-Person Standpoint: Morality, Respect, and Accountability*, Cambridge, MA: Harvard University Press.

Davidson, Donald. (1963). "Actions, Reasons, and Causes," *Journal of Philosophy* 60, pp. 685–700.

De Leersnyder, Jozefien, Marcus Boiger, and Batja Mesquita. (2013). "Cultural Regulation of Emotion: Individual, Relational, and Structural Sources," *Frontiers in Psychology*, 4, Article 55. https://doi.org/10.3389/fpsyg.2013.00055.

DeCaro, Mario. (2021). "Machiavelli's Lucretian View of Free Will," in *Lucretius, Poet and Philosopher: Background and Fortunes of the De Rerum Natura*, V. Prosperi and D. Zucca, eds, Berlin: De Gruyter.

Deery, Oisín, and Eddy Nahmias. (2017). "Defeating Manipulation Arguments: Interventionist Causation and Compatibilist Sourcehood," *Philosophical Studies* 174 (5), pp. 1255–76.

Deigh, John. (2004). "Nussbaum's Account of Compassion," *Philosophy and Phenomenological Research*, 68(2), pp. 465–72.

Demetriou, Kristin. (2010). "The Soft-Line Solution to Pereboom's Four-Case Argument," *Australasian Journal of Philosophy* 88, pp. 595–617.

Dennett, Daniel C. (1984). *Elbow Room*, Cambridge, MA: MIT Press.

Dennett, Daniel C. (2003). *Freedom Evolves*, New York: Viking Press.

Dennett, Daniel C., and Gregg D. Caruso. (2020). *Just Deserts*, Cambridge: Polity Press.

Descartes, René. (1978). *Descartes, His Moral Philosophy and Psychology*, John J. Blom, ed. and tr., New York: New York University Press.

Dewey, John. (1934). *A Common Faith*, New Haven, CT: Yale University Press.

Doggett, Tyler. (2018). "Killing Innocent People," *Noûs* 52, pp. 645–66.

Doris, John. (2015). "Doing without (Arguing about) Desert," *Philosophical Studies* 172, pp. 2625–34.

Doris, John, and Dominic Murphy. (2022). "Atrocity, Evil, and Responsibility," in *The Oxford Handbook of Moral Responsibility*, Dana Nelkin and Derk Pereboom, eds, New York: Oxford University Press.

Douglass, Frederick. (1845/1997). *Narrative of the Life of Frederick Douglass, An American Slave, Written by Himself*, W. L. Andrews and W. S. McFeeling, eds, New York: Norton Critical Edition.

Duggan, Austin P. (2018). "Moral Responsibility as Guiltworthiness," *Ethical Theory and Moral Practice* 21, pp. 291–309.

Duggan, Austin P. (2020). "A Genealogy of Retributive Intuitions," ms.

Ekstrom, Laura W. (2000). *Free Will: A Philosophical Study*, Boulder, CO: Westview.

Ekstrom, Laura W. (2019). "Toward a Plausible Event-Causal Indeterminist Account of Free Will," *Synthese* 196, pp. 127–44.

180 BIBLIOGRAPHY

Ellis, Fiona. (2001). "The Ethics of Love: A Paradox Dispelled," *Journal of Value Inquiry* 35, pp. 242–62.

Epictetus. (125/1983). *The Handbook (The Encheiridion)*, Nicholas F. White, tr., Indianapolis: Hackett Publishing Company.

Fara, Michael. (2008). "Masked Abilities and Compatibilism," *Mind* 117, pp. 843–65.

Farrell, Daniel M. (1985). "The Justification of General Deterrence," *The Philosophical Review* 104, pp. 367–94.

Feinberg, Joel. (1970). "Justice and Personal Desert," in *Doing and Deserving*, Princeton, NJ: Princeton University Press.

Feltz, Adam. (2013). "Pereboom and Premises: Asking the Right Questions in the Experimental Philosophy of Free Will," *Consciousness and Cognition* 22(1), pp. 53–63.

Ferzan, Kimberly Kessler. (2012). "Culpable Aggression: The Basis for Liability to Defensive Killing," *Ohio State Journal of Criminal Law* 9, pp. 669–97.

Fischer, John Martin. (1982). "Responsibility and Control," *Journal of Philosophy* 79, pp. 24–40.

Fischer, John Martin. (1994). *The Metaphysics of Free Will*, Oxford: Blackwell.

Fischer, John Martin. (2003). " 'Ought-Implies-Can,' Causal Determinism, and Moral Responsibility," *Analysis* 63, pp. 244–50.

Fischer, John Martin. (2004). "Responsibility and Manipulation," *Journal of Ethics* 8, pp. 145–77.

Fischer, John Martin. (2007). " 'Compatibilism' and 'Response to Kane, Pereboom, and Vargas,'" in *Four Views on Free Will*, John Martin Fischer, Robert Kane, Derk Pereboom, and Manuel Vargas, eds, Oxford: Blackwell, pp. 44–84, 184–90.

Fischer, John Martin. (2016). "How do Manipulation Arguments Work?" *Journal of Ethics* 20, pp. 47–67.

Fischer, John Martin. (2021). "Initial Design, Manipulation, and Moral Responsibility," *Criminal Law, Philosophy*, https://doi.org/10.1007/s11572-021-09561-0.

Fischer, John Martin, and Mark Ravizza. (1998). *Responsibility and Control: A Theory of Moral Responsibility*, Cambridge: Cambridge University Press.

Fischer, John Martin, and Neal A. Tognazzini. (2011). "The Physiognomy of Moral Responsibility," *Philosophy and Phenomenological Research* 82 (2), pp. 381–417.

Fischer, John Martin, Robert Kane, Derk Pereboom, and Manuel Vargas. (2007). *Four Views on Free Will*, Oxford: Blackwell.

Flint, Thomas P. (1998). *Divine Providence: The Molinist Account*, Ithaca, NY: Cornell University Press.

Focquaert, Farah. (2019). "Neurobiology and Crime: A Neuro-Ethical Perspective," *Journal of Criminal Justice* 65, 10.1016/j.jcrimjus.2018.01.001.

Focquaert, Farah, Andrea L. Glenn, and Adrian Raine. (2018). "Free Will Skepticism, Freedom, and Criminal Behavior," in *Neuroexistentialism: Meaning, Morals, and Purpose in the Age of Neuroscience*, Gregg D. Caruso and Owen Flanagan eds, New York: Oxford University Press, pp. 235–50.

Forth, Adelle E., Sune Bo, and Mickey T. Kongerslev. (2013). "Assessment of Psychopathy: The Hare Psychopathy Checklist Measures", in *Handbook on Psychopathy and Law*, Kent A. Kiehl and Walter Sinnott-Armstrong, eds., New York: Oxford University Press, pp. 5–33.

BIBLIOGRAPHY 181

Foucault, Michel. (1981). *Mal Faire, Dire Vrai*, Lectures presented at Louvain.

Frank, Robert H. (2011). *The Darwin Economy: Liberty, Competition, and the Common Good*, Princeton, NJ: Princeton University Press.

Frank, Robert H. (2020). *Under the Influence: Putting Peer Pressure to Work*, Princeton, NJ: Princeton University Press.

Frankfurt, Harry G. (1969). "Alternate Possibilities and Moral Responsibility," *Journal of Philosophy* 66, pp. 829–39.

Frankfurt, Harry G. (1971). "Freedom of the Will and the Concept of a Person," *Journal of Philosophy* 68, pp. 5–20.

Frankfurt, Harry G. (1999). "On Caring," in his *Necessity, Volition, and Love*, Cambridge: Cambridge University Press, pp. 155–80.

Frankfurt, Harry G. (2004). *The Reasons of Love*, Princeton, NJ: Princeton University Press.

Franklin, Christopher. (2011). "Farewell to the Luck (and Mind) Arguments," *Philosophical Studies* 156(2), pp. 199–230.

Franklin, Christopher. (2018). *A Minimal Libertarianism: Free Will and the Promise of Reduction*, New York: Oxford University Press.

Fricker, Miranda. (2016). "What's the Point of Blame? A Paradigm Based Explanation," *Noûs* 50, pp. 165–83.

Fricker, Miranda. (2021). "Forgiveness: An Ordered Pluralism," *Australasian Philosophical Review*.

Frowe, Helen. (2014). *Defensive Killing*, Oxford: Oxford University Press.

Frowe, Helen. (2015). "Claim Rights, Duties, and Lesser-Evil Justifications," *Proceedings of the Aristotelian Society*, Supplementary volume 89, pp. 267–85.

Frowe, Helen. (2020). "The Duty to Save and the Duty to Minimise Harm," *Oxford Studies in Political Philosophy* 7, David Sobel, Peter Vallentyne, and Steven Wall, eds, Oxford: Oxford University Press.

Garrard, Eve, and David McNaughton. (2003). "In Defence of Unconditional Forgiveness," *Proceedings of the Aristotelian Society* 100, pp. 39–60.

Garrard, Eve, and David McNaughton. (2010). *Forgiveness*, Durham: Acumen.

Gill, Michael, and Shaun Nichols. (2008). "Sentimentalist Pluralism," *Philosophical Perspectives* 18, pp. 143–63.

Ginet, Carl. (1966). "Might We Have No Choice?" in *Freedom and Determinism*, Keith Lehrer, ed., New York: Random House, pp. 87–104.

Ginet, Carl. (1990). *On Action*, Cambridge: Cambridge University Press.

Ginet, Carl. (1997). "Freedom, Responsibility, and Agency," *Journal of Ethics* 1, pp. 85–98.

Ginet, Carl. (2007). "An Action Can Be Both Uncaused and up to the Agent," in *Intentionality, Deliberation, and Autonomy*, Christoph Lumer and Sandro Nannin eds, Farnhnam: Ashgate, pp. 243–56.

Goetz, Stewart. (2008). *Freedom, Teleology, and Evil*, London: Continuum.

Goldberg, Julie H., Jennifer S. Lerner, and Philip E. Tetlock. (1999). "Rage and Reason: The Psychology of the Intuitive Prosecutor," *European Journal of Social Psychology* 29, pp. 781–95.

Goodman, Charles. (2009). *The Consequences of Compassion*, New York: Oxford University Press.

# 182 BIBLIOGRAPHY

Gordon-Solmon, Kerah. (2018). "What Makes a Person Liable to Defensive Harm?" *Philosophy and Phenomenological Research* 92, pp. 543–67.

Gosseries, Axel, and Tom Parr. (2018). "Publicity," *Stanford Encyclopedia of Philosophy*, Winter Edition, Edward N. Zalta, ed., https://plato.stanford.edu/archives/win2018/entries/publicity/.

Graham, Peter. (2011). "'Ought' and Ability," *The Philosophical Review* 120, pp. 337–82.

Grau, Christopher. (2004). "Irreplaceability and Unique Value," *Philosophical Topics*, pp. 111–29.

Greene, Joshua. (2008). "The Secret Joke of Kant's Soul," in *Moral Psychology*, vol. 3, Walter P. Sinnott-Armstrong, ed., Cambridge, MA: MIT Press, pp. 35–79.

Greene, Joshua. (2014). *Moral Tribes: Emotion, Reason, and the Gap between Us and Them*, London: Penguin.

Greene, Joshua, and Jonathan D. Cohen. (2004). "For the Law, Neuroscience Changes Nothing and Everything," *Philosophical Transactions of the Royal Society of London*, Series B-Biological Sciences 359, pp. 1775–85.

Greenspan, Patricia. (1988). *Emotions and Reason: An Inquiry into Emotional Justification*, London: Routledge and Kegan Paul.

Greenspan, Patricia. (1992). "Subjective Guilt and Responsibility," *Mind* 101, pp. 287–303.

Griffith, Meghan. (2010). "Why Agent-Caused Actions Are Not Lucky," *American Philosophical Quarterly* 47, pp. 43–56.

Griffiths, Paul E. (1997). *What Emotions Really Are: The Problem of Psychological Categories*, Chicago, IL: University of Chicago Press.

Griswold, Charles. (2007). *Forgiveness: A Philosophical Exploration*, Cambridge: Cambridge University Press.

Haas, Daniel. (2013). "In Defense of Hard-line Replies to the Multiple-Case Manipulation Argument," *Philosophical Studies* 163, pp. 797–811.

Haji, Ishtiyaque. (1998). *Moral Appraisability*, New York: Oxford University Press.

Haji, Ishtiyaque. (2000). "Libertarianism and the Luck Objection," *Journal of Ethics* 4 (4), pp. 329–37.

Haji, Ishtiyaque. (2002). *Deontic Morality and Control*, Cambridge: Cambridge University Press.

Haji, Ishtiyaque. (2012). *Reason's Debt to Freedom*, New York: Oxford University Press.

Hanser, Matthew. (2005). "Permissibility and Practical Inference," *Ethics* 115, pp. 443–70.

Hare, Robert D., Leslie M. McPherson, and Adelle E. Forth. (1988). "Male Psychopaths and Their Criminal Careers," *Journal of Consulting and Clinical Psychology* 56 (5), pp. 710–14.

Harris, Sam. (2012). *Free Will*, New York: Free Press.

Hartman, Robert J. (2016). "Against Luck-Free Moral Responsibility," *Philosophical Studies* 173 (10), pp. 2845–65.

Hasker, William. (2004). *Providence, Evil, and the Openness of God*, London: Routledge.

BIBLIOGRAPHY    183

Hegel, G. W. F. (1824/1956). *The Philosophy of History*, J. Sibree, tr., New York: Dover, 1956.

Hick, John. (1978). *Evil and the God of Love*, New York: Harper and Row.

Hieronymi, Pamela. (2001). "Articulating an Uncompromising Forgiveness," *Philosophy and Phenomenological Research* 62, pp. 529–55.

Hobbes, Thomas. (1654). *Of Libertie and Necessity: A treatise, wherein all controversie concerning predestination, election, free-will, grace, merits, reprobation, &c., is fully decided and cleared, in answer to a treatise written by the Bishop of London-Derry, on the same subject*, London, printed by W. B. for F. Eaglesfield.

Hodgson, David. (2012). *Rationality + Consciousness = Free Will*, New York: Oxford University Press.

Hohfeld, Wesley Newcombe. (1919). *Fundamental Legal Conceptions as Applied in Judicial Reasoning*, W. W. Cooke, ed., New Haven, CT: Yale University Press.

Honderich, Ted. (1988). *A Theory of Determinism*, Oxford: Oxford University Press.

Honderich, Ted. (1996). "Compatibilism, Incompatibilism, and the Smart Aleck," *Philosophy and Phenomenological Research* 56, pp. 855–62.

Howard-Snyder, Frances. (2006). "'Cannot' Implies 'Ought Not,'" *Philosophical Studies* 130, pp. 233–46.

Huddleston, Andrew. (2021). "Ressentiment," *Ethics* 131 (4), pp. 670–96.

Hume, David. (1739/1978). *A Treatise of Human Nature*, Oxford: Oxford University Press.

Hume, David. (1748/2000). *An Enquiry Concerning Human Understanding*, Oxford: Oxford University Press.

Husak, Douglas. (2000). "Holistic Retributivism," *California Law Review* 88, pp. 991–1000.

Inwood, Brad. (1985). *Ethics and Human Action in Early Stoicism*, Oxford: Oxford University Press.

Israel, Jonathan. (2001). *Radical Enlightenment: Philosophy and the Making of Modernity 1650–1750*, Oxford: Oxford University Press.

Jackson, Elizabeth. (2021). "Belief, Faith, and Hope: On the Rationality of Long-Term Commitment," *Mind*.

Jackson, Frank C. (1998). *From Metaphysics to Ethics*, Oxford: Oxford University Press.

James, William. (1884). "The Dilemma of Determinism," *The Unitarian Review*; reprinted in William James, *The Will to Believe and Other Essays in Popular Philosophy*, New York: Longmans Green and Co., 1907, pp. 145–83.

Jefferson, Anneli. (2019). "Instrumentalism about Moral Responsibility Revisited," *Philosophical Quarterly* 69, pp. 555–73.

Jeppsson, Sofia. (2020). "The Agential Perspective: A Hard-Line Reply to the Four-Case Manipulation Argument," *Philosophical Studies* 177 (7), pp. 1935–51.

Jeppsson, Sofia. (2022). "Accountability, Answerability and Attributability: On Different Kinds of Moral Responsibility," in *The Oxford Handbook of Moral Responsibility*, Dana Nelkin and Derk Pereboom, eds, New York: Oxford University Press.

Jollimore, Troy. (2011). *Love's Vision*, Princeton, NJ: Princeton University Press.

Kamm, Frances. (1993). *Creation and Abortion*, Oxford: Oxford University Press.

184 BIBLIOGRAPHY

Kamtekar, Rachana. (2020). "Platonic Pity, or Why Compassion Is Not a Platonic Virtue," in *Emotions in Plato*, Laura Candiotto and Olivier Renaut, eds, Leiden: Brill, pp. 308–29.

Kane, Robert. (1985). *Free Will and Values*, Albany, NY: SUNY Press.

Kane, Robert. (1996). *The Significance of Free Will*, New York: Oxford University Press.

Kane, Robert. (2007). "Libertarianism" and "Response to Fischer, Pereboom, and Vargas," in *Four Views on Free Will*, John Martin Fischer, Robert Kane, Derk Pereboom, and Manuel Vargas, eds, Oxford: Blackwell, pp. 5–43, 184–90.

Kant, Immanuel. (1781/1787/1987). *Critique of Pure Reason*, Paul Guyer and Allen Wood, trs, Cambridge: Cambridge University Press.

Kant, Immanuel. (1785/1981). *Grounding for the Metaphysics of Morals*, J. Ellington, tr., Indianapolis, IN: Hackett.

Kant, Immanuel. (1788/1996). *Critique of Practical Reason*, Mary Gregor, tr., Cambridge: Cambridge University Press.

Kant, Immanuel. (1795/1983). *Towards Perpetual Peace: A Philosophical Sketch*, tr. Ted Humphrey, Indianapolis, Hackett Publishing Company.

Kant, Immanuel. (1797/2017). *The Metaphysics of Morals*, Mary Gregor, tr., Cambridge: Cambridge University Press.

Kapitan, Tomis. (1986). "Deliberation and the Presumption of Open Alternatives," *Philosophical Quarterly* 36, pp. 230–51.

Kapitan, Tomis. (1996). "Modal Principles in the Metaphysics of Free Will," *Philosophical Perspectives* 10, pp. 419–46.

Kearns, Stephen. (2012). "Aborting the Zygote Argument," *Philosophical Studies* 160, pp. 379–89.

Kearns Goodwin, Doris. 2013. *The Bully Pulpit: Theodore Roosevelt, William Howard Taft, and the Golden Age of Journalism*, New York: Simon and Schuster.

Kelly, Erin. (2009). "Criminal Justice without Retribution," *Journal of Philosophy* 106, pp. 440–62.

Kershnar, Stephen. (2000). "A Defense of Retributivism," *International Journal of Applied Philosophy* 14 (1), pp. 97–117.

Khoury, Andrew. (2014). "Manipulation and Mitigation," *Philosophical Studies* 168 (1), pp. 283–94.

Kierkegaard, Søren. (1843/1971). *Either/Or*, vol. 2, Walter Lowrie, tr., Princeton, NJ: Princeton University Press.

Kiehl, Kent A. (2014). *The Psychopath Whisperer: The Science of Those Without Conscience*, New York: Broadway Books.

Kilner, Peter. (2017). "Know Thy Enemy," *Association of the United States Army*, www.ausa.org/articles/know-thy-enemy.

King, Matthew. (2013). "The Problem with Manipulation," *Ethics* 124 (1), pp. 65–83.

Kleiman, Mark. (2009). *When Brute Force Fails: How to Have Less Crime and Less Punishment*, Princeton, NJ: Princeton University Press.

Kolodny, Niko. (2003). "Love as Valuing a Relationship," *The Philosophical Review* 123, pp. 251–80.

Kraut, Robert. (1987). "Love De Re," *Midwest Studies in Philosophy* 10 (1), pp. 413–30.

BIBLIOGRAPHY 185

Latham, Noa. (2004). "Determinism, Randomness, and Value," *Philosophical Topics* 32 (1/2), pp. 153–67.

Lazar, Seth. (2009). "Responsibility, Risk, and Killing in Self-Defense," *Ethics* 119, pp. 699–728.

Lazarus, Richard. (1991). *Emotion and Adaptation*, Oxford: Oxford University Press.

Leiter, Brian. (2007). "Nietzsche's Theory of the Will," *Philosophers' Imprint* 7, pp. 1–15.

Lemos, John. (2016). "Moral Concerns about Responsibility Denial and the Quarantine of Violent Criminals," *Law and Philosophy* 35 (5), pp. 461–83.

Lenman, James. (2006). "Compatibilism and Contractualism: The Possibility of Moral Responsibility," *Ethics* 117, pp. 7–31.

Lerner, Jennifer S., Julie H. Goldberg, and Philip E. Tetlock. (1998). "Sober Second Thought: The Effects of Accountability, Anger, and Authoritarianism on Attributions of Responsibility," *Personality and Social Psychology Bulletin* 24 (6), 563–74.

Levy, Neil. (2006). "Determinist Deliberations," *Dialectica* 60, pp. 453–59.

Levy, Neil. (2007). "The Responsibility of the Psychopath Revisited," *Philosophy, Psychiatry and Psychology* 14, pp. 129–38.

Levy, Neil. (2010). "Psychopathy, Responsibility and the Moral/Conventional Distinction," in *Responsibility and Psychopathy*, L. Malatesti and J. McMillan, eds, Oxford: Oxford University Press, pp. 213–26.

Levy, Neil. (2011). *Hard Luck: How Luck Undermines Free Will and Moral Responsibility*, Oxford: Oxford University Press.

Levy, Neil. (2012). "Skepticism and Sanction: The Benefits of Rejecting Moral Responsibility," *Law and Philosophy* 31, pp. 477–93.

Lewis, David. (1981). "Are We Free to Break the Laws?" *Theoria* 47, pp. 113–21.

Lewis, David. (1986). "Events," in his *Philosophical Papers*, vol. 2, New York: Oxford University Press, pp. 241–69.

Lewis, David. (1993). "Evil for Freedom's Sake?" *Philosophical Papers* 22, pp. 149–72.

Litvak, Paul M., Jennifer S. Lerner, Larissa Z. Tiedens, and Katherine Shonk. (2010). "Fuel in the Fire: How Anger Impacts Judgment and Decision-Making," in *International Handbook of Anger*, Michael Potegal, Gerhard Stemmler, and Charles Spielberger, eds, New York: Springer, pp. 287–310.

Lowe, E. Jonathan. (2008). *Personal Agency: The Metaphysics of Mind and Action*, Oxford: Oxford University Press.

Lucretius. (50 BCE/1998). *On the Nature of the Universe*, Ronald Melville, tr., Oxford: Oxford University Press.

Lycan, William G. (1997). *Consciousness*, Cambridge, MA: MIT Press.

Mackie, John L. (1955). "Evil and Omnipotence," *Mind* 64, pp. 200–12.

Macnamara, Coleen. (2013). "Taking Demands out of Blame," in *Blame: Its Nature and Norms*, D. Justin Coates and Neal A. Tognazzini, eds, New York: Oxford University Press, pp. 141–61.

Macnamara, Coleen. (2015a). "Reactive Attitudes as Communicative Entities," *Philosophy and Phenomenological Research* 90, pp. 546–69.

Macnamara, Coleen. (2015b). "Blame, Communication, and Morally Responsible Agency," in *The Nature of Moral Responsibility: New Essays*, Randolph Clarke,

186  BIBLIOGRAPHY

Michael McKenna, and Angela M. Smith, eds, New York: Oxford University Press, pp. 211–35.

Mahon, James Edwin. (2008). 'Two Definitions of Lying,' *International Journal of Applied Philosophy* 22, pp. 211–30.

Mahon, James Edwin. (2016). "The Definition of Lying and Deception," *Stanford Encyclopedia of Philosophy*, Winter Edition, Edward N. Zalta, ed., https://plato.stanford.edu/archives/win2016/entries/lying-definition/.

Maibom, Heidi. (2018). "What Can Philosophers Learn from Psychopathy?" *European Journal of Analytic Philosophy* 14, pp. 63–78.

Manley, David, and Ryan Wasserman. (2008). "On Linking Dispositions and Conditionals," *Mind* 117, pp. 59–84.

Mann, William E. (1993). "Hope," in *Reasoned Faith*, Eleanor Stump, ed., Ithaca, NY: Cornell University Press, pp. 251–80.

Manne, Kate. (2017). *Down Girl*, Oxford: Oxford University Press.

Marcus Aurelius. (175/1985). *Meditations*, G. M. A. Grube, tr., Indianapolis, IN: Hackett.

Markovits, Julia. (2010). "Acting for the Right Reasons," *The Philosophical Review* 119 (2), pp. 201–42.

Martin, Adrienne M. (2011). "Hopes and Dreams," *Philosophy and Phenomenological Research* 83, pp. 148–73.

Martin, Adrienne M. (2013). *How We Hope*, Princeton, NJ: Princeton University Press.

Mason, Elinor. (2019). *Ways to Be Blameworthy: Rightness, Wrongness, and Responsibility*, Oxford: Oxford University Press.

Matheson, Benjamin. (2016). "In Defense of the Four-Case Argument," *Philosophical Studies* 173 (7), pp. 1963–82.

McCann, Hugh. (1998). *The Works of Agency*, Ithaca, NY: Cornell University Press.

McCormick, Miriam. (2017). "Rational Hope," *Philosophical Explorations* 20 (S1), pp. 127–41.

McGeer, Victoria. (2004). "The Art of Good Hope," *Annals of the American Academy of Political and Social Sciences* 592, pp. 100–27.

McGeer, Victoria. (2013). "Civilizing Blame," in *Blame: Its Nature and Norms*, D. Justin Coates and Neal. A. Tognazzini, eds, Oxford: Oxford University Press, pp. 162–88.

McGeer, Victoria. (2014). "P. F. Strawson's Consequentialism," in *Oxford Studies in Agency and Responsibility* 2, David Shoemaker and Neal A. Tognazzini, eds, Oxford: Oxford University Press, pp. 64–92.

McGeer, Victoria. (2015). "Building a Better Theory of Responsibility," *Philosophical Studies* 172, pp. 2635–49.

McGeer, Victoria, and Philip Pettit. (2015). "The Hard Problem of Responsibility," *Oxford Studies in Agency and Responsibility* 3, David Shoemaker, ed., Oxford: Oxford University Press, pp. 160–88.

McKenna, Michael. (2000). "Assessing Reasons-Responsive Compatibilism," *International Journal of Philosophical Studies* 8, pp. 89–114.

McKenna, Michael. (2008). "A Hard-Line Reply to Pereboom's Four-Case Argument," *Philosophy and Phenomenological Research* 77, pp. 142–59.

# BIBLIOGRAPHY 187

McKenna, Michael. (2012). *Conversation and Responsibility*, New York: Oxford University Press.

McKenna, Michael. (2014). "Resisting the Manipulation Argument: A Hard-Liner Takes it on the Chin," *Philosophy and Phenomenological Research* 89, pp. 467–84.

McKenna, Michael. (2019). "Basically Deserved Blame and Its Value," *Journal of Ethics and Social Philosophy* 15, pp. 255–82.

McKenna, Michael. (2020). "Punishment and the Value of Deserved Suffering," *Public Affairs Quarterly* 34 (2), pp. 97–123.

McKenna, Michael. (2021). "Wimpy Retributivism and the Promise of Moral Influence Theories," *The Monist*.

McKenna, Michael, and Derk Pereboom. (2016). *Free Will: A Contemporary Introduction*, New York: Routledge.

McMahan, Jeff. (2009). *Killing in War*, Oxford: Oxford University Press.

Mele, Alfred. (2002). "Review of John Searle's Rationality in Action," *Mind* 111, pp. 905–9.

Mele, Alfred. (2003). "Agents' Abilities," *Noûs* 37, pp. 447–70.

Mele, Alfred. (2005). "A Critique of Pereboom's 'Four-Case' Argument for Incompatibilism," *Analysis* 65, pp. 75–80.

Mele, Alfred. (2006). *Free Will and Luck*, New York: Oxford University Press.

Mele, Alfred. (2008). "Manipulation, Compatibilism, and Moral Responsibility," *Journal of Ethics* 12, pp. 263–86.

Mele, Alfred. (2017). *Aspects of Agency: Decisions, Abilities, Explanations, and Free Will*, New York: Oxford University Press.

Menninger, Karl. (1968). *The Crime of Punishment*, New York: Penguin.

Milam, Per-Erik. (2016). "Reactive Attitudes and Personal Relationships," *Canadian Journal of Philosophy* 42(1), pp. 102–22.

Milam, Per-Erik. (2019). "Reasons to Forgive." *Analysis* 79 (2), pp. 242–51.

Milam, Per-Erik. (2022). "Forgiveness," in *The Oxford Handbook of Moral Responsibility*, Dana K. Nelkin and Derk Pereboom, eds, Oxford: Oxford University Press.

Miller, Dale E. (2014). "'Freedom and Resentment' and Consequentialism: Why 'Strawson's Point' Is Not Strawson's Point," *Journal of Ethics and Social Philosophy* 8 (2), pp. 1–22.

Milona, Michael. (2019). "Finding Hope." *Canadian Journal of Philosophy* 49 (5), pp. 710–29.

Milton, John. (1667/2005). *Paradise Lost*, Gordon Teskey, ed., New York: W. W. Norton and Company.

Mokros, Andreas, Robert D. Hare, Craig S. Neumann, Pekka Santtila, Elmar Habermeyer, and Joachim Nitschke. (2015). "Variants of Psychopathy in Adult Male Offenders: A Latent Profile Analysis," *Journal of Abnormal Psychology* 124 (2), pp. 372–86.

Montague, Philip. (1995). *Punishment as Societal Defense*, Lanham, MD: Rowman and Littlefield.

Moore, Michael. (1987). "The Moral Worth of Retribution," in *Responsibility, Character, and the Emotions*, Ferdinand Schoeman, ed., Cambridge: Cambridge University Press, pp. 179–219.

188  BIBLIOGRAPHY

Moore, Michael. (1998). *Placing Blame*, Oxford: Oxford University Press.

Morris, Herbert. (1968). "Persons and Punishment," *The Monist* 52, pp. 475–501.

Morris, Stephen. (2018). "The Implications of Rejecting Free Will: An Empirical Analysis," *Philosophical Psychology* 31 (2), pp. 299–321.

Morse, Stephen J. (2004). "Reasons, Results, and Criminal Responsibility," *University of Illinois Law Review*, pp. 363–444.

Morse, Stephen J. (2013). "Common Criminal Law Compatibilism, in *Neuroscience and Legal Responsibility*, Nicole A. Vincent, ed., Oxford: Oxford University Press, pp. 29–52.

Murphy, Jeffrie E. (1982). "Forgiveness and Resentment," *Midwest Studies in Philosophy* 7, pp. 503–16.

Murphy, Jeffrie E. (1998). "Jean Hampton on Immorality, Self-Hatred, and Self-Forgiveness," *Philosophical Studies* 89 (2), pp. 215–36.

Murphy, Jeffrie E. (2004). *Getting Even: Forgiveness and Its Limits*, New York: Oxford University Press.

Murphy, Jeffrie E., and Jean Hampton. (1988). *Forgiveness and Mercy*, Cambridge: Cambridge University Press.

Murray, Dylan, and Tania Lombrozo. (2017). "Effects of Manipulation on Attributions of Causation, Free Will, and Moral Responsibility," *Cognitive Science* 41, pp. 447–81.

Nadelhoffer, Thomas. (2006). "Bad Acts, Blameworthy Agents, and Intentional Actions: Some Problems for Jury Impartiality," Philosophical Explorations 9, pp. 203–20.

Nadelhoffer, Thomas. (2011). "The Threat of Shrinking Agency and Free Will Disillusionism," in *Conscious will and Responsibility*, Lynne Nadel and Walter Sinnott-Armstrong, eds, Oxford: Oxford University Press, pp. 173–88.

Nadelhoffer, Thomas, and Walter Sinnott-Armstrong. (2012). "Neurolaw and Neuroprediction: Potential Promises and Perils," *Philosophy Compass* 7 (9), pp. 631–42.

Nadelhoffer, Thomas, Stephanos Bibas, Scott Grafton, Kent A. Kiehl, Andrew Mansfield, Walter Sinnott-Armstrong, and Michael Gazzaniga. (2012). "Neuroprediction, Violence, and the Law: Setting the Stage," *Neuroethics* 5, pp. 67–99.

Nagel, Thomas. (1986). *The View from Nowhere*, Oxford: Oxford University Press.

Nahmias, Eddy. (2011). "Intuitions about Free Will, Determinism, and Bypassing," in *The Oxford Handbook of Free Will*, second edition, Robert Kane, ed., New York: Oxford University Press, pp. 555–76.

Nelkin, Dana K. (2004a). "The Sense of Freedom," in *Freedom and Determinism*, J. Campbell, M. O'Rourke, and D. Shier, eds, Cambridge, MA: MIT Press, pp. 105–34.

Nelkin, Dana K. (2004b). "Deliberative Alternatives," *Philosophical Topics* 32, pp. 215–40.

Nelkin, Dana K. (2008). "Responsibility and Rational Abilities: Defending an Asymmetrical View," in *Pacific Philosophical Quarterly* 89, pp. 497–515.

Nelkin, Dana K. (2011). *Making Sense of Freedom and Responsibility*, Oxford: Oxford University Press.

BIBLIOGRAPHY    189

Nelkin, Dana K. (2013). "Freedom and Forgiveness," in *Free Will and Moral Responsibility*, Ishtiyaque Haji and Justin Caouette, eds, Newcastle: Cambridge Scholars Press.

Nelkin, Dana K. (2014). "Symposium Contribution on Free Will," *Agency, and Meaning in Life*, in *Science, Religion and Culture* 1, pp. 209–17.

Nelkin, Dana K. (2015). "Psychopaths, Incorrigible Racists, and Faces of Responsibility," *Ethics* 125, pp. 357–90.

Nelkin, Dana K. (2019a). "Frontotemporal Dementia and the Reactive Attitudes: Two Roles for the Capacity to Care?" *Journal of Applied Philosophy* 36, pp. 817–37.

Nelkin, Dana K. (2019b). "Duties, Desert, and the Justification of Punishment," *Criminal Law and Philosophy* 13 (3), pp. 425–38.

Nelkin, Dana K. (2019c). "Guilt, Grief, and the Good," *Social Philosophy and Policy* 36 (1), pp. 173–91.

Nelkin, Dana K. (2022). "Relationships and Responsibility," in *The Oxford Handbook of Moral Responsibility*, Dana Nelkin and Derk Pereboom, eds, New York: Oxford University Press.

Nichols, Shaun. (2004). *Sentimental Rules: On the Natural Foundations of Moral Judgment*, Oxford: Oxford University Press.

Nichols, Shaun. (2007). "After Compatibilism: A Naturalistic Defense of the Reactive Attitudes," *Philosophical Perspectives* 21, pp. 405–28.

Nichols, Shaun. (2013). "Brute Retributivism," in *The Future of Punishment*, Thomas Nadelhoffer, ed., New York: Oxford University Press, pp. 65–88.

Nichols, Shaun. (2015). *Bound*, Oxford: Oxford University Press.

Nichols, Shaun, and Joshua Knobe. (2007). "Moral Responsibility and Determinism: The Cognitive Science of Folk Intuitions," *Noûs* 41, pp. 663–85.

Nietzsche, Friedrich. (1882/1887/1974). *The Gay Science*, Walter Kaufmann, tr., New York: Viking.

Nietzsche, Friedrich. (1887/1998). *On the Genealogy of Morality*, Maudemarie Clark and Alan Swensen, trs, Indianapolis, IN: Hackett.

Nietzsche, Friedrich. (1888/1954). *Twilight of the Idols*, Walter Kaufmann, tr., New York: Viking.

Norcross, Alastair. (2006). "Reasons without Demands: Rethinking Rightness," in *Blackwell Contemporary Debates in Moral Theory*, Jamie Dreier, ed., Oxford: Blackwell, pp. 38–54.

Nowell-Smith, Patrick. (1948). "Free Will and Moral Responsibility," *Mind*, *57*, pp. 45–61.

Nozick, Robert. (1974). *Anarchy, State and Utopia*, New York: Basic Books.

Nozick, Robert. (1989). "Love's Bond," in *The Examined Life: Philosophical Meditations*, New York: Simon and Schuster, pp. 68–86.

Nussbaum, Martha C. (1997). "Emotions as Judgments of Value and Importance," in *Relativism, Suffering and Beyond*, P. Bilimoria and J. Mohanty, eds, New Delhi: Oxford University Press, pp. 271–83.

Nussbaum, Martha C. (2001). *Upheavals of Thought: The Intelligence of Emotions*, New York: Cambridge University Press.

Nussbaum, Martha C. (2004). "Précis of *Upheavals of Thought*," *Philosophy and Phenomenological Research* 58 (2), pp. 443–9.

190 BIBLIOGRAPHY

Nussbaum, Martha C. (2016). *Anger and Forgiveness*, Oxford: Oxford University Press.

O'Connor, Timothy. (1995). "Agent Causation," in *Agents, Causes, and Events*, Timothy O'Connor, ed., New York: Oxford University Press, pp. 170–200.

O'Connor, Timothy. (2000). *Persons and Causes*, New York: Oxford University Press.

O'Connor, Timothy. (2008). "Agent-Causal Power," in *Dispositions and Causes*, Toby Handfield, ed., Oxford: Oxford University Press, pp. 189–214.

Otsuka, Michael. (1994). "Killing the Innocent in Self-Defense," *Philosophy and Public Affairs* 23, pp. 74–94.

Palmer, David. (2021). "Free Will and Control: A Noncausal Approach," *Synthèse*.

Parfit, Derek. (1984). *Reasons and Persons*, Oxford: Oxford University Press.

Parker, Theodore. (1853). "Of Justice and the Conscience," in *Ten Sermons of Religion by Theodore Parker*, Boston, MA: Crosby, Nichols and Company.

Pereboom, Derk. (1994). "Stoic Psychotherapy in Descartes and Spinoza," *Faith and Philosophy* 11, pp. 592–625.

Pereboom, Derk. (1995). "Determinism *Al Dente*," *Noûs* 29, pp. 21–45.

Pereboom, Derk. (2001). *Living without Free Will*, Cambridge: Cambridge University Press.

Pereboom, Derk. (2004). "The Problem of Evil," in *The Blackwell Guide to Philosophy of Religion*, William E. Mann, ed., Oxford: Blackwell.

Pereboom, Derk. (2005). "Free Will, Evil, and Divine Providence," in *God and the Ethics of Belief: New Essays in Philosophy of Religion*, Andrew Chignell and Andrew Dole, eds, Cambridge: Cambridge University Press.

Pereboom, Derk. (2006a). "Reasons Responsiveness, Alternative Possibilities, and Manipulation Arguments against Compatibilism; Reflections on John Martin Fischer's My Way," Philosophical Books 47, pp. 198–212.

Pereboom, Derk. (2006b). "Kant on Transcendental Freedom," *Philosophy and Phenomenological Research* 73, pp. 537–67.

Pereboom, Derk. (2007a). "'Hard Incompatibilism' and 'Response to Kane, Fischer, and Vargas,'" in *Four Views on Free Will*, John Martin Fischer, Robert Kane, Derk Pereboom, and Manuel Vargas, eds, Oxford: Blackwell, pp. 85–125, 191–203.

Pereboom, Derk. (2007b). "On Mele's *Free Will and Luck*," *Philosophical Explorations* 10, pp. 163–72.

Pereboom, Derk. (2008a). "A Hard-Line Reply to the Multiple-Case Manipulation Argument," *Philosophy and Phenomenological Research* 77, pp. 160–70.

Pereboom, Derk. (2008b). "A Compatibilist Account of the Epistemic Conditions on Rational Deliberation," *Journal of Ethics* 12, pp. 287–307.

Pereboom, Derk. (2009). "Free Will, Love, and Anger," *Ideas y Valores: Revista de Colombiana de Filosofía* 141, pp. 5–25.

Pereboom, Derk. (2012). "Theological Determinism and Divine Providence," in *Molinism: The Contemporary Debate*, Ken Perszyk, ed., Oxford: Oxford University Press, pp. 262–79.

Pereboom, Derk. (2013a). "Free Will Skepticism and Criminal Punishment," in *The Future of Punishment*, Thomas Nadelhoffer, ed., New York: Oxford University Press, pp. 49–78.

## BIBLIOGRAPHY 191

Pereboom, Derk. (2013b). "Free Will Skepticism, Blame, and Obligation," in *Blame: Its Nature and Norms*, D. Justin Coates and Neal A. Tognazzini, eds, New York: Oxford University Press, pp. 189–206.

Pereboom, Derk. (2014). *Free Will, Agency, and Meaning in Life*, Oxford: Oxford University Press.

Pereboom, Derk. (2015). "A Notion of Moral Responsibility Immune to the Threat from Causal Determination," in *The Nature of Moral Responsibility*, Randolph Clarke, Michael McKenna, and Angela Smith, eds, New York: Oxford University Press, pp. 281–96.

Pereboom, Derk. (2016). "Libertarianism and Theological Determinism," in *Free Will and Theism: Connections, Contingencies, and Concerns*, Daniel Speak and Kevin Timpe, eds, New York: Oxford University Press, pp. 112–31.

Pereboom, Derk. (2017a). "Responsibility, Regret, and Protest," *Oxford Studies in Agency and Responsibility* 4, David Shoemaker, ed., Oxford: Oxford University Press, pp. 121–40.

Pereboom, Derk. (2017b). "A Defense of Free Will Skepticism: Replies to Commentaries by Victor Tadros, Saul Smilansky, Michael McKenna, and Alfred R. Mele on *Free Will, Agency, and Meaning in Life*," *Criminal Law and Philosophy* 11 (3), pp. 617–36.

Pereboom, Derk. (2017c). "Responsibility, Agency, and the Disappearing Agent Objection," in *Le Libre-Arbitre, approches contemporaines*, Jean-Baptiste Guillon, ed., Paris: Collège de France, pp. 1–18.

Pereboom, Derk. (2018). "Love and Freedom," in *The Oxford Handbook of the Philosophy of Love*, Christopher Grau and Aaron Smuts, eds, New York: Oxford University Press.

Pereboom, Derk. (2019). "Free Will Skepticism and Prevention of Crime," in *Free Will Skepticism in Law and Society*, Gregg Caruso, Elizabeth Shaw, and Derk Pereboom, eds, Cambridge: Cambridge University Press.

Pereboom, Derk. (2020). "Incapacitation, Reintegration, and Limited General Deterrence," *Neuroethics* 13, pp. 87–97.

Pereboom, Derk. (2021a). "Forgiveness as Renunciation of Moral Protest," in *Forgiveness*, Michael McKenna, Dana Kay Nelkin, and Brandon Warmke, eds, New York: Oxford University Press.

Pereboom, Derk. (2021b). "A Forward-Looking Account of Self-Blame," in *Self Blame*, Andreas Carlsson, ed., Cambridge: Cambridge University Press.

Pereboom, Derk, and Gregg D. Caruso. (2018). "Hard-Incompatibilist Existentialism: Neuroscience, Punishment, and Meaning in Life, in *Neuroexistentialism: Meaning, Morals, and Purpose in the Age of Neuroscience*, Gregg D. Caruso and Owen Flanagan, eds, New York: Oxford University Press, pp. 193–222.

Pereboom. Derk, and Michael McKenna. (2022). "Manipulation Arguments," in *The Oxford Handbook of Moral Responsibility*, Dana Nelkin and Derk Pereboom, eds, New York: Oxford University Press.

Perry, John. (2004). "Compatibilist Options," in *Freedom and Determinism*, J. K. Campbell, M. O'Rourke, and D. Shier, eds, Cambridge, CA: MIT Press.

Pettit, Philip. (1989). "Determinism with Deliberation," *Analysis* 49, pp. 42–44.

## 192 BIBLIOGRAPHY

Pettit, Philip. (2004). "Hope and Its Place in Mind," *Annals of the American Academy of Political and Social Science* 592 (1), pp. 152–65.

Pinker, Steven. (2018). *Enlightenment Now: The Case for Reason, Science, Humanism, and Progress*, London: Allen Lane.

Plantinga, Alvin. (1974). *God, Freedom, and Evil*, Grand Rapids, MI: Eerdmans.

Plantinga, Alvin. (2004). "Supralapsarianism, or 'O Felix Culpa,'" In *Christian Faith and the Problem of Evil*, Peter van Inwagen, ed., Grand Rapids, MI: Eerdmans.

Plato. (1997). *Plato: Complete Works*, J. M. Cooper and D. S. Hutchinson, eds, Indianapolis, IN: Hackett.

Priestley, Joseph. (1788/1965). *A Free Discussion of the Doctrines of Materialism and Philosophical Necessity, In a Correspondence between Dr. Price and Dr. Priestley*, Part III. Reprinted in Joseph Priestley, *Priestley's Writings on Philosophy, Science, and Politics*, John Passmore, ed., New York: Collier.

Prinz, Jesse J. (2007). *The Emotional Construction of Morals*, New York: Oxford University Press.

Prinz, Jesse J., and Shaun Nichols. (2010). "Moral Emotions," in *The Moral Psychology Handbook*, John. M. Doris and The Moral Psychology Research Group, eds, New York: Oxford University Press, pp. 111–46.

Quinn, Warren. (1985). "The Right to Threaten and the Right to Punish," *Philosophy and Public Affairs* 14, pp. 327–73.

Quong, Jonathan. (2012). "Liability to Defensive Harm," *Philosophy and Public Affairs* 40, pp. 45–77.

Quong, Jonathan. (2016). "Agent-Relative Prerogatives to Do Harm," *Criminal Law and Philosophy* 10, pp. 815–29.

Quong, Jonathan. (2020). *The Morality of Defensive Force*, Oxford: Oxford University Press.

Radzik, Linda. (2014). "Joseph Butler on Forgiveness," in *Vergebung: Philosophische Perspektiven auf ein Problemfeld der Ethik*, Johannes Brachtendorf and Stephan Herzberg, eds, Munster: Mentis, pp. 139–47.

Raine, Adrian. (2013). *The Anatomy of Violence: The Biological Roots of Crime*, London: Allen Lane.

Rawls, John. (1955). "Two Concepts of Rules," *The Philosophical Review* 64, pp. 3–32.

Rawls, John. (1971). *A Theory of Justice*, Cambridge, MA: Harvard University Press.

Reginster, Bernard. (1997). "Nietzsche on *Ressentiment* and Valuation," *Philosophy and Phenomenological Research* 57 (2), pp. 281–305.

Reid, Thomas. (1788/1983). *Essays on the Active Powers of Man*, in *The Works of Thomas Reid, D. D.*, Sir William Hamilton, ed., Hildesheim: G. Olms Verlagsbuchhandlung.

Renzo, Massimo. (2017). "Rights Forfeiture and the Liability to Harm," *Journal of Political Philosophy* 25, pp. 324–42.

Roberts, Robert C. (1995). "Forgivingness," *American Philosophical Quarterly* 32 (4), pp. 289–306.

Roberts, Robert C. (1988). "What an Emotion Is: A Sketch," *The Philosophical Review* 97, pp. 183–209.

Roberts, Robert C. (2003). *Emotions: An Essay in Aid of Moral Psychology*, Cambridge: Cambridge University Press.

BIBLIOGRAPHY 193

Roberts, Robert C. (2013). *Emotions in the Moral Life*, Cambridge: Cambridge University Press.

Rosch, Eleanor. (1972). "Universals in Color Naming and Memory," *Journal of Experimental Psychology* 93, pp. 10–20.

Rosch, Eleanor. (1973). "Natural Categories," *Cognitive Psychology* 4, pp. 328–50.

Rosen, Gideon. (2003). "Culpability and Ignorance," *Proceedings of the Aristotelian Society* 103, Part 1, pp. 61–84.

Rosen, Gideon. (2004). "Skepticism about Moral Responsibility," *Philosophical Perspectives* 18, pp. 295–313.

Rowe, William L. (1979). "The Problem of Evil and Some Varieties of Atheism," *American Philosophical Quarterly* 16, pp. 335–41.

Russell, Paul. (2017). "Free Will Pessimism," in *Oxford Studies in Agency and Responsibility* 4, David Shoemaker, ed., Oxford: Oxford University Press, pp. 93–120.

Russell, Paul. (2020). "Hume on Free Will", *Stanford Encyclopedia of Philosophy*, Fall Edition, Edward N. Zalta, ed., https://plato.stanford.edu/entries/hume-freewill/.

Śāntideva. (700/1995). *The Bodhicaryāvaātra*, Kate Crosby and Andrew Skilton, tr., New York: Oxford University Press.

Sapolsky, Robert M. (2017). *Behave: The Biology of Humans at Our Best and Worst*, London: Penguin.

Sartorio, Carolina. (2014). "The Problem of Determinism and Free Will Is Not the Problem of Determinism and Free Will," in *Surrounding Free Will*, Alfred Mele, ed., New York: Oxford University Press.

Sartorio, Carolina. (2016). *Causation and Free Will*, Oxford: Oxford University Press.

Scanlon, Thomas M. (1998). *What We Owe to Each Other*, Cambridge, MA: Harvard University Press.

Scanlon, Thomas M. (2009). *Moral Dimensions*, Cambridge, MA: Harvard University Press.

Scanlon, Thomas M. (2013). "Giving Desert Its Due," *Philosophical Explorations* 16, pp. 101–16.

Schlick, Moritz. (1939). "When Is a Man Responsible?" in *Problems of Ethics*, D. Rynin, tr., New York: Prentice-Hall, pp. 143–56.

Schoeman, Ferdinand D. (1979). "On Incapacitating the Dangerous," *American Philosophical Quarterly* 16, pp. 27–35.

Schopenhauer, Arthur. (1818/1961). *The World as Will and Idea* (later translated as *The World as Will and Representation*), R. B Haldane and J. Kemp, trs, Garden City, NY: Doubleday, 1961.

Schwitzgebel, Eric. (2013). "A Dispositional Approach to Attitudes: Thinking outside the Belief Box," in *New Essays on Belief: Constitution, Content and Structure*, Nikolaj Nottleman, ed., London: Palgrave Macmillan, pp. 75–99.

Searle, John. (2001). *Rationality in Action*, Cambridge, MA: MIT Press.

Sekatskaya, Maria. (2019). "Double Defence against Multiple-Case Manipulation Arguments," *Philosophia* 47 (4), pp. 1283–95.

Seneca, Lucius A. (60/1932). *On Tranquility of Mind*, in Seneca, Moral Essays, Volume II, John W. Basore, tr., Loeb Classical Library, Cambridge MA: Harvard University Press.

194 BIBLIOGRAPHY

Setiya, Kieran. (2014). "Love and the Value of a Life," *The Philosophical Review* 112, pp. 135–9.

Shabo, Seth. (2012). "Where Love and Resentment Meet: Strawson's Interpersonal Defense of Compatibilism," *The Philosophical Review* 121, pp. 95–124.

Shabo, Seth. (2022). "Responsibility, Personal Relationships, and the Significance of the Reactive Attitudes," in *The Oxford Handbook on Moral Responsibility*, Dana Nelkin and Derk Pereboom, eds, New York: Oxford University Press.

Shakespeare, William. (2008). *The Oxford Shakespeare, The Complete Sonnets and Poems*, Oxford: Oxford University Press.

Shaw, Elizabeth. (2016). "Psychopathy, Moral Understanding and Criminal Responsibility," *European Journal of Current Legal Issues* 22 (2), pp. 1–25.

Shaw, Elizabeth. (2019). "Justice without Moral Responsibility?" *Journal of Information Ethics* 28 (1), pp. 95–114.

Sher, George. (2006). *In Praise of Blame*, New York: Oxford University Press.

Shoemaker, David. (2011). "Attributability, Answerability, and Accountability: Toward a Wider Theory of Moral Responsibility," *Ethics* 121, pp. 602–32.

Shoemaker, David. (2015). *Responsibility from the Margins*, Oxford: Oxford University Press.

Shoemaker, David. (2017). "Response-Dependent Responsibility," *The Philosophical Review* 126, pp. 481–527.

Shoemaker, David. (2019). "Hurt Feelings," *Journal of Philosophy* 116(3), pp. 125–48.

Shoemaker, David. (2021). "The Trials and Tribulations of Tom Brady: Self-Blame, Self-Talk, and Self-Flagellation," in *Self Blame*, Andreas Carlsson, ed., Cambridge: Cambridge University Press.

Singer, Peter. (2005). "Ethics and Intuitions," *Journal of Ethics* 9, pp. 331–52.

Slattery, 'Trick. (2014). *Breaking the Free Will Illusion for the Betterment of Humankind*, Working Matter Publishing.

Slote, Michael. (1982). "Selective Necessity and the Free-Will Problem," *Journal of Philosophy* 79, pp. 5–24.

Slote, Michael. (1990). "Ethics without Free Will," *Social Theory and Practice* 16, pp. 369–83.

Smart, J. J. C. (1961). "Free Will, Praise, and Blame," *Mind* 70, pp. 291–306.

Smilansky, Saul. (1997). "Can a Determinist Help Herself?" in *Freedom and Moral Responsibility: General and Jewish Perspectives*, C. H. Manekin and M. Kellner, eds, College Park, MD: University of Maryland Press, pp. 85–98.

Smilansky, Saul. (2000). *Free Will and Illusion*, New York: Oxford University Press.

Smilansky, Saul. (2011). "Hard Determinism and Punishment: A Practical Reductio," *Law and Philosophy* 30, pp. 353–67.

Smilansky, Saul. (2017). "Pereboom on Punishment: Funishment, Innocence, Motivation, and Other Difficulties," *Criminal Law and Philosophy* 11 (3), pp. 591–603.

Smith, Angela. (2008). "Control, Responsibility, and Moral Assessment," *Philosophical Studies* 138 (3), pp. 367–92.

Smith, Angela. (2012). "Attributability, Answerability, and Accountability: In Defense of a Unified Account," *Ethics* 122 (3), pp. 575–89.

BIBLIOGRAPHY 195

Smith, Angela. (2013). "Moral Blame and Moral Protest," in *Blame: Its Nature and Norms*, D. Justin Coates and Neal A. Tognazzini, eds, New York: Oxford University Press, pp. 27–48.

Solnick, Sara J., and David Hemenway. (1989). "Is More Always Better? A Survey on Positional Concerns," *Journal of Economic Behavior and Organization* 37 (3), pp. 373–83.

Solomon, Robert. (1988). "On Emotions as Judgments," *American Philosophical Quarterly* 25 (2), pp. 183–91.

Sommers, Tamler. (2007). "The Objective Attitude," *Philosophical Quarterly* 57, pp. 321–41.

Sommers, Tamler. (2009). "More Work for Hard Incompatibilism," *Philosophy and Phenomenological Research* 79, pp. 511–21.

Sommers, Tamler. (2012). *Relative Justice: Cultural Diversity, Free Will, and Moral Responsibility*, Princeton, NJ: Princeton University Press.

Speak, Daniel. (2004). "Toward an Axiological Defense of Libertarianism," *Philosophical Topics* 3, pp. 353–69.

Spinoza, B. (1677/1985). *The Collected Works of Spinoza*, vol. 1, Edwin Curley, ed. and tr., Princeton, NJ: Princeton University Press.

Sripada, Chandra. (2012). "What Makes a Manipulated Agent Unfree?" *Philosophy and Phenomenological Research* 85, pp. 563–93.

Stemplowska, Zofia. (2018). "Should Coercive Neurointerventions Target the Victims of Wrongdoing?" in *Treatment for Crime: Philosophical Essays on Neurointerventions in Criminal Justice*, David Birks and Thomas Douglas, eds, Oxford: Oxford University Press.

Stockdale, Katie. (2019). 'Social and Political Dimensions of Hope," *Journal of Social Philosophy* 50(1), pp. 28–44.

Strawson, Galen. (1986). *Freedom and Belief*, Oxford: Oxford University Press.

Strawson, Galen. (1994). "The Impossibility of Moral Responsibility," *Philosophical Studies* 75, pp. 5–24.

Strawson, Peter F. (1962/2003). "Freedom and Resentment," *Proceedings of the British Academy* 48, pp. 187–211. Reprinted in Free Will, Gary Watson, ed., 2nd edition, Oxford: Oxford University Press, 2003, pp. 72–93.

Stump, Eleonore. (1985). "The Problem of Evil," *Faith and Philosophy* 2, pp. 392–418.

Swinburne, Richard. (1989). *Responsibility and Atonement*, Oxford: Oxford University Press.

Swinburne, Richard. (1999). *Providence and the Problem of Evil*, Oxford: Oxford University Press.

Swinburne, Richard. (2013). *Mind, Brain, and Free Will*, Oxford: Oxford University Press.

Tadros, Victor. (2011). *The Ends of Harm*, Oxford: Oxford University Press.

Tadros, Victor. (2016). *Wrongs and Crimes*, Oxford: Oxford University Press.

Tadros, Victor. (2017). "Doing without Desert," *Criminal Law and Philosophy* 11, pp. 605–16.

Tadros, Victor. (2020). "Distributing Responsibility," *Philosophy and Public Affairs* 48 (3), pp. 223–61.

## 196 BIBLIOGRAPHY

Talbert, Matthew. (2012). "Moral Competence, Moral Blame, and Protest," *Journal of Ethics* 16, pp. 89–101.

Taylor, Charles. (1976). *Hegel*, New York: Cambridge University Press.

Taylor, Richard. (1966). *Action and Purpose*, Englewood Cliffs, NJ: Prentice-Hall.

Taylor, Richard. (1974). *Metaphysics*, fourth edition, Englewood Cliffs, NJ: Prentice-Hall.

Telech, Daniel. (2021). "Praise as Moral Address," *Oxford Studies in Agency and Responsibility*, vol. 7, David Shoemaker, ed., Oxford: Oxford University Press, pp. 154–81.

Ten, Chin Liew. (1987). *Crime, Guilt, and Punishment*, Oxford: Oxford University Press.

Thomson, Judith Jarvis. (1990). *The Realm of Rights*, Cambridge, MA: Harvard University Press.

Thomson, Judith Jarvis. (1991). "Self-Defense," *Philosophy and Public Affairs* 20, pp. 283–310.

Tierney, Hannah. (2013). "A Maneuver around the Modified Manipulation Argument," *Philosophical Studies* 165, pp. 753–63.

Tierney, Hannah. (2014). "Taking It Head-On: How to Best Handle the Modified Manipulation Argument," *Journal of Value Inquiry* 48, pp. 663–75.

Tierney, Hannah, and David Glick. (2020). "Desperately Seeking Sourcehood," *Philosophical Studies* 177 (4), pp. 953–70.

Todd, Patrick. (2011). "A New Approach to Manipulation Arguments," *Philosophical Studies* 152, pp. 127–33.

Todd, Patrick. (2013). "Defending (a Modified Version of the) Zygote Argument," *Philosophical Studies* 164, pp. 189–203.

Tognazzini, Neal A. (2014). "The Structure of a Manipulation Argument," *Ethics* 124 (2), pp. 358–69.

Twambley, Paul. (1976). "Forgiveness," *Analysis* 36 (2), pp. 84–90.

Usher, Marius. (2020). "Agency, Teleological Control and Robust Causation," *Philosophy and Phenomenological Research* 100 (2), pp. 302–24.

van Inwagen, Peter. (1975). "The Incompatibility of Free Will and Determinism," *Philosophical Studies* 27, pp. 185–99.

van Inwagen, Peter. (1983). *An Essay on Free Will*, Oxford: Oxford University Press.

van Inwagen, Peter. (2006). *The Problem of Evil*, New York: Oxford University Press.

Vargas, Manuel. (2007). "'Revisionism' and 'Response to Fischer, Kane, and Pereboom,'" in *Four Views on Free Will*, John Martin Fischer, Robert Kane, Derk Pereboom, and Manuel Vargas, eds, Oxford: Blackwell, pp. 126–65, 204–19.

Vargas, Manuel. (2013). *Building Better Beings*, New York: Oxford University Press.

Vargas, Manuel. (2015). "Desert, Responsibility, and Justification: A Reply to Doris, McGeer, and Robinson," *Philosophical Studies* 172, pp. 2659–78.

Vargas, Manuel. (2022). "Instrumentalist Theories of Moral Responsibility," in *The Oxford Handbook of Moral Responsibility*, Dana Nelkin and Derk Pereboom, eds, New York: Oxford University Press.

Velleman, J. David. (1999). "Love as a Moral Emotion," *Ethics* 109, pp. 338–74.

Vicens, Leigh, and Simon Kittle. (2019). *God and Human Freedom*, Cambridge: Cambridge University Press.

BIBLIOGRAPHY 197

Vihvelin, Kadri. (2017). *Causes, Laws, and Free Will: Why Determinism Doesn't Matter*, Oxford: Oxford University Press.

Vilhauer, Benjamin. (2004). "Hard Determinism, Remorse, and Virtue Ethics," *Southern Journal of Philosophy* 42, pp. 547–64.

Vilhauer, Benjamin. (2008). "Hard Determinism, Humeanism, and Virtue Ethics," *Southern Journal of Philosophy* 46, pp. 121–44.

Vilhauer, Benjamin. (2009a). "Free Will Skepticism and Personhood as a Desert Base," *Canadian Journal of Philosophy* 39, pp. 489–511.

Vilhauer, Benjamin. (2009b). "Free Will and Reasonable Doubt," *American Philosophical Quarterly* 46, pp. 131–40.

Vilhauer, Benjamin. (2012). "Taking Free Will Skepticism Seriously," *Philosophical Quarterly* 62, pp. 833–52.

Vilhauer, Benjamin. (2013). "Persons, Punishment, and Free Will Skepticism," *Philosophical Studies* 162, pp. 143–63.

Vranas, Peter. (2007). "I Ought, Therefore I Can," *Philosophical Studies* 136, pp. 167–216.

Walker, Margaret Urban. (2006). *Moral Repair: Reconstructing Moral Relations after Wrongdoing*, Cambridge: Cambridge University Press.

Wallace, R. Jay. (1994). *Responsibility and the Moral Sentiments*, Cambridge, MA: Harvard University Press.

Wallace, R. Jay. (2011). "Dispassionate Opprobrium: On Blame and the Reactive Sentiments," in *Reasons and Recognition: Essays on the Philosophy of T. M. Scanlon*, R. Jay Wallace, Rahul Kumar, and Samuel Freeman, eds, New York: Oxford University Press, pp. 348–72.

Wallace, R. Jay. (2022). "Reactive Attitudes," in *The Oxford Handbook of Moral Responsibility*, Dana Nelkin and Derk Pereboom, eds, New York: Oxford University Press.

Waller, Bruce. (1985). "Deliberating about the Inevitable," *Analysis* 45, pp. 48–52.

Waller, Bruce. (1990). *Freedom without Responsibility*, Philadelphia, PA: Temple University Press.

Waller, Bruce. (2011). *Against Moral Responsibility*, Cambridge, MA: MIT Press.

Waller, Bruce. (2015). *The Stubborn System of Moral Responsibility*, Cambridge, MA: MIT Press.

Warmke, Brandon. (2016). "The Normative Significance of Forgiveness," *Australasian Journal of Philosophy* 94 (4), pp. 687–703.

Warmke, Brandon, and Michael McKenna. (2013). "Moral Responsibility, Forgiveness, and Conversation," in *Free Will and Moral Responsibility*, Ishtiyaque Haji and Justin Caouette, eds, Newcastle upon Tyne: Cambridge Scholars Press, pp. 189–212.

Watkins, Eric. (2005). *Kant and the Metaphysics of Causality*, Cambridge: Cambridge University Press.

Watson, Gary. (1987). "Responsibility and the Limits of Evil," in *Responsibility, Character, and the Emotions*, Ferdinand Schoeman, ed., Cambridge: Cambridge University Press, pp. 256–86.

Watson, Gary. (1996). "Two Faces of Responsibility," *Philosophical Topics* 24, pp. 227–48.

## BIBLIOGRAPHY

Watson, Gary. (2004). *Agency and Answerability: Selected Essays*, New York: Oxford University Press.

Watson, Gary. (2011). "The Trouble with Psychopaths," in *Reasons and Recognition: Essays on the Philosophy of T. M. Scanlon*, R. Jay Wallace, Rahul Kumar, and Samuel Freeman, eds, New York: Oxford University Press, pp. 307–31.

Watson, Gary. (2014). "Peter Strawson on Responsibility and Sociality," *Oxford Studies in Agency and Responsibility* 2, David Shoemaker, ed., Oxford: Oxford University Press, pp. 15–32.

Wedgwood, Ralph. (2007). *The Nature of Normativity*, Oxford: Oxford University Press.

Wegner, Daniel. (2002). *The Illusion of Conscious Will*, Cambridge, MA: MIT Press.

Wheatley, J. M. O. (1958). "Wishing and Hoping," *Analysis* 18, pp. 121–31.

White, Heath. (2019). *Fate and Free Will: A Defense of Theological Determinism*, Notre Dame, IL: Notre Dame University Press.

Whittle, Ann. (2010). "Dispositional Abilities," *Philosophers' Imprint* 10, pp. 1–23.

Widerker, David. (2000). "Frankfurt's Attack on Alternative Possibilities: A Further Look," *Philosophical Perspectives* 14, pp. 181–201.

Widerker, David. (2019). "Pereboom's Defense of Deliberation-Compatibilism: A Problem Remains," *Journal of Ethics* 23, pp. 333–45.

Williams, Bernard. (1985). *Ethics and the Limits of Philosophy*, London: Routledge.

Wolf, Susan. (1980). "Asymmetrical Freedom," *Journal of Philosophy* 77, pp. 151–66.

Wolf, Susan. (1990). *Freedom within Reason*, Oxford: Oxford University Press.

Wolf, Susan. (2011). "Blame, Italian Style," in *Reasons and Recognition: Essays on the Philosophy of T. M. Scanlon*, R. Jay Wallace, Rahul Kumar, and Samuel Freeman, eds, New York: Oxford University Press, pp. 332–47.

Wonderly, Monique. (2017). "Love and Attachment," *American Philosophical Quarterly* 33 (4), pp. 339–56.

Wykstra, Stephen J. (1984). "The Human Obstacle to Evidential Arguments from Suffering: On Avoiding the Evils of 'Appearance,'" *International Journal for Philosophy of Religion* 16, pp. 73–94.

Wykstra, Stephen J. (1996). "Rowe's Noseeum Arguments from Evil," in *The Evidential Argument from Evil*, Daniel Howard-Snyder, ed., Bloomington, IN: Indiana University Press, pp. 126–50.

# Index of Authors

For the benefit of digital users, indexed terms that span two pages (e.g., 52–53) may, on occasion, appear on only one of those pages.

Adams, Marilyn McCord 153, 158–9, 165–6
Adams, Robert Merrihew 125–6
Adorno, Theodor W. 169
Alexander, Lawrence 54–5, 59n.6, 81n.6
Alicke, Mark D. 3n.3, 42–3, 105–6
Allais, Lucy 111
Alston, William 157–8
Amaya, Santiago 36n.8, 104, 112n.4, 120–1
Anscombe, G. E. M. 56n.1
Arneson, Richard 56–7, 64–5
Arpaly, Nomy 36–7, 58–9
Augustine 125, 159
Ayer, Alfred J. 15

Badhwar, Neera 124–6
Baker, Lynne R. 18n.16
Balaguer, Mark 18–19, 19n.17
Bell, Macalester 74–5
Bentham, Jeremy 85
Bergson, Henri 21–2
Berman, Mitchell 81n.6
Björnsson, Gunnar 17–18, 18n.16
Blair, R. J. R. 83
Blumer, Herbert 4n.5
Bloom, Paul 170–1
Bobo, Lawrence D. 4n.5
Bobzien, Suzanne 151
Bok, Hilary 14, 49–51
Boonin, Daniel 96
Borg, Jana Schaich 64n.11
Braithwaite, John 84n.9
Brandenburg, Daphne 36n.7
Brennan, Tad 151–2
Briggs, Jean L. 6
Brink, David 2, 11, 40, 141–2, 145
Broad, Charlie Dunbar 13n.14
Butler, Joseph 103

Campbell, Joseph 143–4
Capes, Justin 18n.16
Carlsson, Andreas B. 27–8, 49–50
Caruso, Gregg D. 5, 13n.14, 18n.16, 24n.22, 29–31, 79, 79n.4, 81–2, 89–91, 97–102
Caspi, Avshalom 78–9
Castañeda, Hector-Neri 24n.22
Chalmers, David 9
Chignell, Andrew 149–50, 150n.1, 157n.4
Chisholm, Roderick 19n.17, 165
Chislenko, Eugene 45
Choy, Olivia 88
Clarke, Randolph 12–13, 19n.17, 24n.22, 27, 49, 144n.6
Coates, D. Justin 138–9
Coffman, E. J. 24n.22
Cohen, Jonathan D. 13n.14
Cohen, Yishai 24n.22
Copp, David 141–2
Corrado, Michael L. 99–100
Cyr, Taylor 18n.16

D'Arms, Justin 33, 63–4
d'Holbach, Paul-Henri Thiry 13n.14
Darwall, Stephen 40, 133, 140n.3
Davidson, Donald 18–19
Deery, Oisín 18n.16
DeCaro, Mario 18–19
De Leersnyder, Jozefien 6
Deigh, John 80–1, 171
Demetriou, Kristin 18n.16
Dennett, Daniel C. 11n.10, 18n.16, 24n.22, 29–31, 70, 79–80, 97–8
Descartes, René 153–7
Dewey, John 149, 169
Doggett, Tyler 60, 62n.9, 65, 66n.12
Doris, John 30–1, 30n.2, 62n.7, 63–4, 64n.11, 97

## 200 INDEX OF AUTHORS

Douglass, Frederick 74–5
Duggan, Austin 12–13, 27–8, 42–3, 49

Ekstrom, Laura W. 18–19
Epictetus 151–2
Ellis, Fiona 124–6

Fara, Michael 144n.6
Farrell, Daniel M. 85–9, 96, 102
Feinberg, Joel 12–13
Ferzan, Kimberly Kessler 54–5, 59–61, 65, 67, 81n.6
Fischer, John Martin 11, 15, 18n.16, 27, 39, 61–3, 70, 127
Flint, Thomas 149
Focquaert, Farah 13n.14, 88
Forth, Adelle 62n.7
Foucault, Michel 114
Frank, Robert H. 4n.4, 5n.6
Frankfurt, Harry G. 9–10, 10n.9, 126
Franklin, Christopher 18–19, 19n.17
Fricker, Miranda 36n.8, 111
Frowe, Helen 57–60, 65–6, 69

Garrard, Eve 90–1, 104
Gill, Michael 83
Ginet, Carl 15, 15n.15, 21–3, 24n.22, 128
Glick, David 18n.16
Goetz, Stewart 21–3
Goldberg, Julie H. 3n.3, 42–3, 105–6
Goodman, Charles 5, 80–1
Goodwin, Doris Kearns 73–4
Gordon–Solmon, Kerah 67n.14
Gosseries, Axel 90n.12
Graham, Peter 143–4
Grau, Christopher 124–6
Greene, Joshua 13n.14, 63–4, 83
Greenspan, Patricia 33–4
Griffith, Meghan 19n.17
Griffiths, Paul 32n.5, 71–2
Griswold, Charles 103

Haas, Daniel 18n.16
Haji, Ishtiyaque 18n.16, 19, 24n.22, 44–5, 57n.2, 58–9, 127, 144–6
Hampton, Jean 2n.1, 106n.3, 111–12
Hanser, Matthew 44–5, 58–9
Hare, Robert D. 62, 64n.11
Harris, Sam 13n.14
Hartman, Robert J. 19n.18

Hasker, William 149
Hegel, G. W. F. 168–9
Hemenway, David 4n.4
Hick, John 158–9, 163–4
Hieronymi, Pamela 39–40, 44–5, 106, 108, 111
Hobbes, Thomas 15
Hodgson, David 99–102
Hohfeld, Wesley N. 57–8
Honderich, Ted 33, 104
Howard–Snyder, Frances 141–2
Huddleston, Andrew 75–6
Hume, David 15, 19, 22, 170–1
Husak, Douglas 81n.6

Inwood, Brad 151–2
Israel, Jonathan 168–9

Jackson, Elizabeth 150, 166–7
Jackson, Frank C. 35
Jacobson, Daniel 33, 63–4
James, William 10
Jefferson, Anneli 36n.7, 36n.8
Jeppsson, Sofia 14, 18n.16
Jollimore, Troy 124–6

Kamm, Frances 65–6
Kamtekar, Rachana 80n.5, 81
Kane, Robert 15n.15, 18–19, 19n.18, 124, 129–30
Kant, Immanuel 19n.17, 30–1, 81n.6, 90n.12, 95, 141n.4, 142, 149–50, 170–1
Kapitan, Tomis 24n.22, 25
Kearns, Stephen 18n.16
Kelly, Erin 85
Kershnar, Stephen 81n.6
Khoury, Andrew 18n.16
Kierkegaard, Søren 130
Kiehl, Kent 62n.7
Kilner, Peter 55–7, 61, 71–3
King, Matthew 18n.16
Kittle, Simon 9n.8, 151n.2
Kleiman, Mark 94
Kolodny, Niko 124–6
Kraut, Robert 125–6

Latham, Noa 9–11, 11n.11, 15n.15, 19, 29n.1
Lazar, Seth 55, 67, 69–70
Lazarus, Richard 32–3

## INDEX OF AUTHORS 201

Leiter, Brian 13n.14
Lemos, John 99–102
Lenman, James 29, 70
Lerner, Jennifer S. 3n.3, 42–3, 105–6
Levy, Neil 13n.14, 24n.22, 31, 98–9
Lewis, David K. 22, 128, 143–4, 160–2
Litvak, Paul M. 3n.3, 42–3, 105–6
Lowe, E. Jonathan 19n.17
Lucretius 18–19
Lycan, William G. 17–18, 18n.16

Mackie, John L. 160n.6
Machiavelli 18–19
Macnamara, Coleen 36n.7, 36n.8, 45, 140n.3
Mahon, James 35
Maibom, Heidi 64n.11
Manley, David 144n.5
Mann, William E. 166–7
Manne, Kate 4n.5, 76
Marcus Aurelius 152–3
Markovits, Julia 44–5, 58–9
Martin, Adrienne M. 150–1, 166–7
Mason, Elinor 36n.8, 37n.9
Matheson, Benjamin 18n.16
McCann, Hugh 21–3
McCormick, Miriam 150
McGeer, Victoria 30n.2, 36n.7, 36n.8, 102n.15, 150–1.
McKenna, Michael 2, 11, 12n.12, 18n.16, 29, 29n.1, 31, 36–7, 36n.8, 39, 47n.13, 50–1, 58–9, 61–3, 70, 84, 104, 106, 127, 133–4, 144n.6
McMahan, Jeff 66–7
McNaughton, David 90–1, 104
Mele, Alfred 15n.15, 18n.16, 19, 19n.19, 128, 143–4
Menninger, Karl 88–9
Milam, Per-Erik 13n.14, 108–9, 111–14, 120–1, 138–9
Miller, Dale E. 30n.2
Milona, Michael 150
Milton, John 123–4, 128–9
Mokros, Andreas 64n.11
Moore, Michael 59n.6, 81n.6
Montague, Philip 84n.9
Morris, Herbert 82n.7
Morris, Stephen 13n.14
Morse, Stephen J. 81–2, 81n.6
Murphy, Dominic 62n.7, 63–4, 64n.11
Murphy, Jeffrie E. 2n.1, 103, 106n.3, 111–12

Nadelhoffer, Thomas 13n.14, 42–3, 99–100
Nagel, Thomas 59–60
Nahmias, Eddy 18n.16, 23
Nelkin, Dana K. 6, 11–13, 18n.16, 24n.22, 27, 40, 44–5, 51–2, 58–9, 61, 63–4, 70, 85, 91, 104, 112–13, 118–19, 127, 140–8
Nichols, Shaun 13n.14, 63–4, 83–4, 132–3
Nietzsche, Friedrich 13n.14, 75–7
Norcross, Alasdair 147
Nowell-Smith, Patrick 14
Nozick, Robert 59–60, 65–6, 125–6
Nussbaum, Martha C. 32–3, 32n.4, 43–4, 47–8, 80–1, 104, 114–17, 131, 170–1

O'Connor, Timothy 19, 19n.17, 21n.20
Otsuka, Michael 59–60, 64–5

Palmer, David 21–2, 22n.21
Parfit, Derek 58, 88n.10
Parker, Theodore 172–3
Parr, Tom 90n.12
Persson, Karl 18n.16
Perry, John 143–4
Pettit, Philip 24n.22, 36n.7, 36n.8, 84n.9, 150
Pinker, Steven 173n.10
Plantinga, Alvin 153, 159, 159n.5
Plato 81
Priestley, Joseph 13n.14
Prinz, Jesse 63–4, 83

Quinn, Warren 85
Quong, Jonathan 54–67, 59n.4, 59n.5, 66n.12, 69n.15

Radzik, Linda 103
Raine, Adrian 78–9, 88
Ravizza, Mark 62–3, 127
Rawls, John 29–31, 170–1
Reginster, Bernard 76–7
Reid, Thomas 19n.17
Renzo, Massimo 58n.3
Roberts, Robert C. 33–4, 113, 117–18
Rosch, Eleanor 36–7, 37n.9
Rosen, Gideon 13n.14
Rowe, William L. 157n.4
Russell, Paul 15, 148

Śāntideva 7–8, 81
Sapolsky, Robert M. 13n.14

## 202  INDEX OF AUTHORS

Sartorio, Carolina  9, 10n.9, 11, 18n.16, 39, 61, 70, 92n.13, 127
Scanlon, T. M.  12–14, 27, 83–4, 111
Schlick, Moritz  14
Schoeman, Ferdinand  88
Schopenhauer, Arthur  13n.14
Schwitzgebel, Eric  39–40
Searle, John  24n.22
Sekatskaya, Maria  18n.16
Seneca, Lucius Annaeus  152
Setiya, Kieran  124–6
Shabo, Seth  2, 130–9
Shakespeare, William  126
Shaw, Elizabeth  13n.14
Sher, George  27, 134–7
Shoemaker, David  14, 27, 40–7, 50, 55, 62n.8, 63–4, 105, 137
Singer, Peter  83
Sinnott-Armstrong, Walter  64n.11, 99–100
Slattery, 'Trick  13n.14
Slote, Michael  13n.14, 128, 143–4
Smart, J. J. C.  14
Smilansky, Saul  13n.14, 98–100
Smith, Angela  14, 27–8, 39–40, 44–5, 80, 106
Solnick, Sara J.  4n.4
Solomon, Robert  32–3
Sommers, Tamler  13n.14, 131
Speak, Daniel  19n.17
Spinoza  8–9, 13n.14, 167–9
Sripada, Chandra  18n.16
Stemplowska, Zofia  88n.10
Stockdale, Katie  170–1
Strawson, Galen  13n.13, 13n.14, 31
Strawson, Peter F.  1–3, 2n.1, 27, 30n.2, 40, 43, 103, 105, 128, 130–41, 140n.3
Stump, Eleonore  158–9, 164–5
Swinburne, Richard  19n.17, 112, 120–1, 149, 158–63, 165–6

Tadros, Victor  42, 57–8, 60, 65–7, 81, 82n.8, 86–7, 88n.10, 90n.12, 91–6
Talbert, Matthew  39–40, 80, 106

Taylor, Charles  169n.9
Taylor, Richard  15n.15, 19n.17
Telech, Daniel  12n.12, 38, 140
Ten, Chin Liew  84n.9
Tetlock, Philip E.  3n.3, 42–3, 105–6
Thomson, Judith Jarvis  58–60, 65, 67–70
Tierney, Hannah  18n.16
Todd, Patrick  18n.16
Tognazzini, Neal  18n.16, 27
Twambley, Paul  118–19

Usher, Marius  18n.16

van Inwagen, Peter  9, 19, 24–5, 24n.22, 128
Vargas, Manuel  29–31, 30n.2, 36n.7, 36n.8, 70, 79–80, 97
Velleman, J. David  124–6
Vicens, Leigh  9n.8, 151n.2
Vihvelin, Kadri  10–11, 18n.16
Vilhauer, Benjamin  13n.14, 29, 52, 70, 81–2
Vranas, Peter  141–2

Walker, Margaret Urban  140n.3
Wallace, R. Jay  2, 27–8, 32–3, 61, 103, 139–41, 34n6
Waller, Bruce  13n.14, 24n.22, 31, 49
Warfield, Ted  24n.22
Warmke, Brandon  104, 118–22
Wasserman, Ryan  144n.5
Watkins, Eric  141n.4
Watson, Gary  2, 14, 27, 61, 63–4, 70, 140n.3
Wedgewood, Ralph  143–4
Wegner, Daniel  13n.13, 13n.14
Wheatley, J. M. O.  150–1
White, Heath  9n.8, 151n.2
Whittle, Ann  143–4, 144n.5
Widerker, David  9–10, 24n.22
Williams, Bernard  148
Wolf, Susan  61, 111, 127, 162–3, 162n.8
Wonderly, Monique  125–6
Wykstra, Stephen J.  157–8

# Index of Topics

*Note*: Bold type indicates definitions and core characterizations

For the benefit of digital users, indexed terms that span two pages (e.g., 52–53) may, on occasion, appear on only one of those pages.

accountability **14**, 40–7, **46**, 63–4, 70, 105–7
anger 1–9, 30–48, 52–3, 56–7, 71–7, 104–7, 109–10, 113, 117–20, 137–8, 151
answerability **14**, 63–4, 71

basic desert **11–12, 28–9**, passim
blame 11–12, 27–53, passim
   as moral protest **44–8**
Buddhism 5–8, 27, 79n.4, 149

compassion 3, 5–7, 9, 108, 115–16, 123, **170–1**
compatibilism **10–13**, 14–18, 39, 81–2, 85, 127, 143–6

defensive harm 54–102
defensive killing 54–102
   robust liability to **60**, 69–70
deliberation 23–6, 169–70
desert, basic **11–12, 28–9**, passim
determinism 1–26, passim
determinism, theological 9, 149–71
deterrence theories of punishment 84–96
   special 84–6, 89
   general 89–96
disappearing agent argument (against event–causal libertarianism) **19–20**

forgiveness 103–22
forward–looking moral responsibility **36–9**, passim
free will **7–14**, passim
free will skepticism **7–23**, passim

Gandhi, Mahatma 7
God 123–4, 128–9, 141, 149–71
guilt 1, 12–13, 27–8, 33–4, **48–53**

hard determinism **10–11**
hope 25–6, 88–9, 116–17, **149–51**, 157–9, 166–73

incapacitation 84–6, 89
incompatibilism **10–13**, passim
indignation 2–3, 12–14, 28, 30–7, 40–1, 46, 76, 103–6, 128, 130–41

King, Martin Luther 7, 47–8, 172

liability to defensive killing 54–70
   robust **60–70**
libertarianism 7–18, 21–4, **10–13**
   event–causal **18–19**, 20
   agent–causal **18–19**, 20–1
   non–causal 18–19, **21–2**, 23
love 114–16, 123–48, **124–6**, 154–7, 163–4, 167–9, 171

manipulation argument (against compatibilism) **15–18**, 92–3
measured aggression **71–7**
monitoring 93–4, 98–9
moral formation 6–7, 27–8, 36–9, 48, 51–3, 71, 80, 107, 109–10, 118, 138
moral protest 6–7, 12n.12, 27–53, **39–40**, 73–4, 80–1, 103–22, 131–3, 136–8, 147–8, **170–1**
moral responsibility *passim*; *see* desert, basic; desert, non–basic; forward–looking moral responsibility; accountability; answerability

positional goods 4–5
praise 11–12, 28–9, **38**, 123–4, 128–9, 140
problem of evil 149, 157–67

## 204 INDEX OF TOPICS

Prodigal Son, parable 114–17
providence 149–73
public health model (for treatment of criminals) **89–91**
punishment 11–12, 28–9, 49–50, 78–96

quarantine model (for treatment of criminals) **88–9**, 97–9

reactive attitudes **2–3**, 12–14, 28, 30–7, 40–1, 43, 46, 73–7, 103–6, 109–11, 117–22, 128, 130–41
reconciliation 3–7, 10, 36–8, 48, 52, 71, 80–1, 107, 116–19, 123, 132–3
regret 37–8, **48–53**
rehabilitation (of criminals) 88–9, 98–9
reintegration (of criminals) 88–9, 98–9

relative status 4–5
religion 5–6, 149–73
resentment 3, 12–14, 28, **2**, 30–7, 40–1, 43, 46, 73–7, 103–6, 109–11, 117–22, 128, 130–41
ressentiment 75–7
retribution 1–7, 78–84
retributive theories of criminal punishment **78**, 83–4
Roosevelt, Theodore 73–4

self-blame **48–53**
self-defense 54–102

use objection (to deterrence theories of criminal punishment) **91**, 97–8
Utkuhiksalingmiut 6